WEST V...................... LIBRARY

WEST VAN MEMORIAL LIBRARY

14405682

MacNeill
038147.
7/93
19.95

CONCEIVED IN WAR, BORN IN PEACE

Canada's Deep Sea Merchant Marine

D0048790

S. C. Heal

65 VN
GC

Cordillera Publishing Company

Vancouver, B.C.

Withdrawn from Collection

Copyright ©1992 S.C. Heal

ISBN- 1-895590-01-9

Cover artwork by Wendy C. Mars

Typesetting by J & P Gunderson

Printed by Friesen Printers
      P.O. Box 720, Altona, Manitoba, Canada ROG OBO

Published by Cordillera Publishing Company
      8415 Granville Street,
      Box 46,
      Vancouver, B.C. Canada V6P 4Z9

All rights reserved. No part of this publication may be reproduced or transmitted in any form or by any means, electronic or mechanical, including photocopy, recording, or in any information storage and retrieval system, without the prior written permission of the author.

TABLE OF CONTENTS

Introduction   5

1. Merchant Shipbuilding in Canada during the First World War   10

2. The Canadian Government Merchant Marine: The CGMM   21

3. John Coughlin: Vancouver Shipbuilder and Shipowner   36

4. Forbes Corporation of Montreal: the SYLIA VICTORIA   47

5. Overloading and Underfuelling   50

6. Merchant Shipbuilding during the Second World War   58

7. Twice Torpedoed: the FORT CAMOSUN   94

8. A Narrowly Averted Disaster: The GREENHILL PARK   97

9. Tragedy at St. Pierre et Miquelon: The loss of the FORT BOISE   103

10. The special role of a Halifax Shipping Agency: I.H. Mathers & Son Ltd.   105

11. The Fleet Train   110

12. A Brief Prosperity: Canadian Postwar Shipowners (East Coast)   121

13. A Brief Prosperity: Canadian Postwar Shipowners (West Coast)   146

14. A West Coast Family Tree: Western Canada Steamship Co. Ltd.   159

15. What of the Canadian Shipyards?   180

16. Fednav Limited: The Story of a Canadian Enterprise   202

17. Will Canada ever again be a Major Deepsea Shipping Country?   211

Appendix I - List of Canadian Museums with Marine Collections, and
                Ship Research Organizations.   221

Bibliography   222

Photo Acknowledgements   223

General Index   224

By the same author:

FULL LINE, FULL AWAY: A Towboat Master's Story
(in conjunction with J.E. Wilson)
THE MAPLE LEAF AFLOAT (Vol 1) West Coast Maritime Memories

Introduction

Originally projected to be the second volume in the author's "Maple Leaf Afloat" series, it became obvious that as this deals extensively with Canada's very special war shipping effort in both world wars, and gives attention to the postwar aftermath the subject deserved equally special treatment, and a special title. Both wartime shipbuilding programs also gave life to a number of private shipping companies which emerged after each war in order to take advantage of the opportunities created to acquire Canadian-built wartime emergency ships, after they had been offered as part of the government disposal process. Added to this was the attraction of making money with these ships, so long as the high postwar freight rates pertained at a sufficient level to make Canadian flag operation remunerative.

By any measure Canada's industrial contribution to both wars was stupendous. In 1914 there was very little heavy industry, and most of what there was, was associated with the railways and such civil works as the building of bridges, and the structural steel for new high-rise buildings in rapidly expanding cities, as the railways moved west. Steel shipbuilding except on the Great Lakes, and to some extent as a logical part of the ship repair industry on both coasts, was almost but not entirely unknown, the nation having been founded on wooden shipbuilding, for which its east coast shipbuilders in particular were famous. Such steel ships as Canada possessed were for the most part, either lakes grain and ore vessels, and ships owned by the Canadian Pacific, Grand Trunk and Canadian Northern railways in a variety of trans-oceanic and coastal services. In fact Canadian Pacific was the country's largest, and with the exception of Canadian Northern, the only owner of large ocean-going ships, but it was to Britain that these companies turned for their newly-built ships, as well as most of their management and operating personnel.

When the First World War commenced, Canada as a source of new ships was not considered as even an outside possibility. It was not until losses by U-boat and surface raider attacks caused such depredations amongst British merchant shipping that the U.K. mounted an unprecedented wartime ship replacement program. This program was underway by 1917, but with ever mounting war losses the U.K. shipyards could not turn out enough ships, naval work taking precedence. As a result contracts were placed in the U.S. Japan and Hong Kong, but it was from Canada that the heaviest contribution came.

Altogether 43 steel ships were built for British account, while a further five vessels of one or other of the same classes, ordered for Norwegian or Japanese account were requisitioned. To these can be added 46 additional wooden vessels actually completed while others were cancelled before commencement.Five further vessels were built, three for private Canadian owners account and two more for Swedish owners.

To the foregoing 94 vessels can be added a further 67 steel vessels built for Canadian government account. These were vested in what was organised as the Canadian Government Merchant Marine (CGMM) and operated competitively on world trade routes into the nineteen thirties. The three vessels mentioned in the previous paragraph made up the Coughlan fleet, and this ownership, and Forbes Corporation, owners of one of the ships which was built as a part of the British program were the other two ownerships which were born as the result of the first world war shipbuilding program. Canadian Pacific and Canada Steamship Lines also operated on foreign trade routes but beyond noting that fact, neither have a place in this book as neither they or their ships were products of the war programs of either war.

When Canada found itself at war again in 1939, the peril of the U-boat was fully recognised by Britain from the beginning. Convoy operations started almost immediately, and all British owners found themselves quickly under complete government control. The Ministry of War Transport remembering the lessons of the first war, not only took over all the prerogatives of private owners, which cut out the potential for speculating in high freight rates, but also immediately commenced plans for instituting a wartime shipbuilding program incorporating designs of simplicity and economy in order to facilitate the most efficient war effort.

Second-hand ships mainly of the "Hog Island" type and similar first world war ships were acquired from the U.S. reserve fleet and a program for the construction of sixty standard ships, the "Ocean" class, was instituted in U.S. yards for British account. The "Oceans" were of British design, and were the forerunners of the Canadian-built classes, based on the North Sands design, all of which carried names beginning with "Fort" or ending with "Park". The American-built Oceans were indistinguishable from the Canadian ships except in matters of structural detail. The 10,000 ton ship became the standard for the war, being greatly augmented by the huge fleet of Liberty-type ships built in the U.S. The Canadian ships and "Oceans" had a traditional split profile, the Liberties took on a different appearance with their single box-type superstructure slightly aft of amidships. Otherwise the hull design and machinery installations of both the American and Canadian-built ships of all these classes were virtually identical. When war commenced in 1939, 2000 people were employed in ten shipyards capable of handling large scale steel shipbuilding across the country. By 1942 some 80 building berths were in operation of which 46 were engaged in merchant ship building. By 1943 the total number of people employed in the yards was 85,000 of which an estimated 57,000 were engaged in merchant shipbuilding.

Indeed it was a tremendous effort for a country which ranked as a minor industrial power when war broke out, and altogether it produced 456 merchant ships in several classes, with a deadweight of close to four million tons. Of this total 176 ships, not including some of the coasters, were built or acquired for Canadian-flag operation and were managed by the crown corporation, Park Steamship Company Ltd. Following the return to peace, Park divested itself of its ships mostly to Canadian owners, and it is this group, again not including some of the coasters, which concerns the chapters dealing with Canadian postwar ownerships, which were established with the close of the second war.

This book is arranged so that the first five chapters deal with the First World War program including the Canadian Government Merchant Marine. Chapters six to 15 relate to the second world war ships, while chapter 15 is an historical overview of the actual yards which contributed to the war effort in both war. The final chapter offers some thoughts on Canada's future as a shipowning and shipbuilding nation, without the author claiming to be the possessor of unique knowledge in this regard. As appropriate, relevent fleet lists accompany each chapter and while the "Ocean" class of sixty ships were built in the U.S. I have dealt with them in chapter six as a matter of record and also, because they were the direct forerunner, and virtually exact sisters of the Canadian "Fort" and "Park" ships.

Like many wartime ships built in the U.S. and Britain, these ships had a considerable versatility and a long life in service, so for this reason the Admiralty maintenance ships and those merchant ships specially fitted out to serve in the fleet train are dealt with in a separate chapter.

It is true that this may give some readers an impression of being somewhat "chopped up", but the general vessel index at the end of the book covers all vessels involved, including the vessel names of the first private owners following post-war disposal, where they are known to have gone into a fleet legally described as Canadian, and also any ships connected with individual stories.

In writing this book the author acknowledges the assistance of the Vancouver Maritime Museum's extensive facilities as well as access to its photo collection. Also special thanks to the Maritime Museum of the Atlantic at Halifax, Nova Scotia, British Columbia Archives and Records Service in Victoria, North Vancouver Museum & Archives, and the Prince Rupert City & Regional Archives. Any other sources are acknowledged in the photo acknowledgements list at the end of the book. Also I acknowledge the great value of the only books previously written specifically on both war shipbuilding programs. Included in the bibliography, these are *British Standard Ships of World War 1* which includes a Canadian section and *The Oceans, Forts and Parks,* both by W.H. Mitchell and L.A. Sawyer. These excellent books, published in Britain have long been out of print but are recommended as a basis for both research and informative reading.

Two matters remain for comment which I personally find very perplexing. I have read a number of books dealing with the Canadian war effort all written by eminent Canadian historians, who give exhaustive treatment to many aspects including the industrial effort involved in building warships, tanks, planes and a whole variety of munitions and military hardware. Likewise the contribution of the three arms of the services receive much detailed attention as they richly deserve. But seldom if at all, is any but the lightest mention made of our merchant shipbuilding effort and the fine ships which it produced, and in some instances lost to enemy action.

One could easily gain the impression that the Canadian shipbuilding industry, and the contribution of merchant seamen, officers and management personnel to the operation of many of the ships it produced, are non-events, worthy of no significant remembrance and generally unrewarded in any way. I can hardly think that it is another manifestation of our national psyche, by which we more often than not tend to downgrade the achievements of fellow Canadians and many matters we should regard and remember as being proudly Canadian.

The pattern contrasts sharply with the public tribute and remembrance accorded seamen and shipbuilders in countries such as Britain and the U.S.A. The evidence confirms that there are many Canadians still alive at this late date, who worked in the Canadian shipyards, and others who sailed in our ships through treacherous war zones, braving the perils of the U-boats, mines and aerial attack, at great risk to life and limb.

My second comment is that while this book is offered as a factual record, nothing is ever complete in terms of maritime research. There will always be new facets of history which show up, and to be able to add a human face adds much additional interest. I have incorporated as much anecdotal material as I can find to this date, but know that there is far more out there, undiscovered and untold, laying fallow as it were, in old cabinets, trunks, photo albums, often tucked away in basement or attic. Unfortunately people die and with them their personal stories. Appeals through enquiries via the press are surprisingly unproductive, perhaps because the parties involved are already dead, or simply do not get around to doing today what they find it more convenient to put off "until tomorrow" and for many, tomorrow never comes!

Also over the years much valuable material has ended in the ash-can particularly from company records and archives. This includes everything from corporate minute and ship's log books, ship voyage accounts, personnel records, photographs, plans and a great variety of other interesting material, which once lost is lost forever. In an appendix I have listed names and addresses of maritime museums, or organizations possessing major collections. This includes the unique World Ship Society, the international research and ship-lovers group with branches in Canada. I suggest that when a member of the public or a corporation has material of interest they should contact one of these organizations to be assured that their material will find a use with others. The National Archives in Ottawa does possess the largest collection of such material, but accessing it is neither easy or convenient for most.

On the subject of factual record I would also like to note that as a subject for historical research this entire field of merchant shipbuilding in Canada needs and deserves a lot of attention as an important part of our history. My original plan was that this book, supported by a grant from the Canada Council which was never approved following proper application with strong sponsorship, was originally intended as being the ultimate authoritative record while there were people who played a part, and were still alive who could be contacted. To round up all the information from many sources would have been a painstaking, time-consuming and expensive exercise and this author's resources at that time did not stretch to that objective without help. This book does however fill the broad program that I originally had in mind.

So far as I am aware this is the first book written and published in Canada dealing with this subject. I am proud and happy to present it in the hope that it will fill a real gap on the bookshelves of ship enthusiasts everywhere where shipping history respects and remembers the achievements of those who passed before us fifty years ago, and the earlier generation of the first world war, now approaching three quarters of a century back, of whom few can still be alive.

S.C. Heal
Vancouver B.C. December 1992

USING THIS BOOK TO BEST EFFECT

Space, time and the economics of book publishing have had an influence on this book. For that reason much detailed information about precise tonnages, actual year of build, and subsequent history of each vessel through to final loss or scrapping has been eliminated. The first program lasted from 1918 through to 1920, while the second program was in being from 1941 to 1946. So with the exception of Western Canada's three post-war acquisitions and Fednav's post-war fleet all vessels were built in the periods just mentioned, and generally follow the tonnages of the individual class or type to which the vessel belongs.

The First World War program for both British and Canadian account is set out in chapters 1 and 2. Chapters 3, 4, 10, 14 and 16 take a more detailed look at the affairs of individual shipping companies of interest, which in some instances take them beyond the immediate postwar aftermath. Chapters 1 through to 4 contain individual listings of ships in each program or fleet. Chapter 6 is perhaps the most important in the book as it lists all the wartime vessels built as part of the second war program.

The key is the extensive general index at the end of the book. Vessels are indexed in their original commissioning names and the name upon acquisition by the fleet listed Canadian owner. In a few instances there might have been a brief interlude under another short-lived Canadian ownership, and wherever possible this has been noted. In the chapters dealing with the wartime programs when each type of vessel is listed, the first name upon disposal to a private owner is noted, followed by a (C) for a Canadian privately owned ship. For example the original commissioning name was say RUPERT PARK. Upon disposal she became LAKE OKANAGAN (C), which means that she is indexed under both names, and will show up as being a member of the fleet of Western Canada Steamship Co. Ltd.

With this method it is possible to keep each group of ships on display in appropriate chapters and fleet lists to illustrate the importance of each class, the actual ownerships, and the comparisons of the outputs of the various yards in both world wars.

In a larger more comprehensive work it would have been possible to give greater attention to the two classes of coasters, and have followed each ship through its entire career.

The asterisk (*) before certain vessel names indicates a war loss.

Chapter One

Merchant Shipbuilding in Canada during the First World War

When the first explorers came to Canada they found impressive forests of huge softwood trees growing down to the water's edge. These forests were a challenging barrier, only being bisected by numerous rivers which became the main highways of commerce for the early settlers.

In a day and age when the sailing ship ruled, masts and spars were always a prime consideration in the outfitting of any vessel, and many softwood trees ended up for this purpose, either when the vessel touched Canadian shores or by being carried to naval dockyards and shipyards in the British Isles. Early boat and shipbuilding grew with the arrival of settlers from France and Britain, and with an influx of United Empire Loyalists from the newly independent United States of America.

Vessels built in Nova Scotia, New Brunswick and in the lower reaches of the St. Lawrence found a ready market throughout much of the nineteenth century. They were particularly salable in the U.K. where they were sailed over with a full cargo of lumber, and auctioned at such ports as Liverpool and Glasgow, giving many a British shipowner his first start as a shipowner. Maritimes-built trading and fishing schooners became famous and many remained in operation when the second world war broke out.

In British Columbia early construction of oared fishing craft for the burgeoning salmon fishing industry gave many an early boatbuilder his initial impetus, and gradually this grew into the building of sailing schooners and a relatively large on-going industry building powered fishing vessels, tugs and scows, which persisted until the 1960's when fibreglass, steel and aluminum largely took over.

By the middle of the first world war British losses from the depredations of the German U-boat campaign had became so serious that several programs were initiated to cope with the emergency. Britain moved in a number of directions more or less simultaneously. Its own shipyards turned over as much as possible to the construction of standard ships which incorporated an increasing percentage of prefabicated parts, so that the shipyard became more of an assembly plant for parts fabricated elsewhere, and less of a conventional shipbuilder. The first of these standard ships, named WAR SHAMROCK, came out of the giant Harland & Wolff, Belfast shipyard in August 1917 and from thereon a great flow of similar ships followed.

Britain's Imperial Munitions Board, which functioned essentially as a purchasing agency for the government, placed contracts for new ships in Japan, Hong Kong and China. The biggest group of contracts went to American yards, but almost all were acquired by the U.S. government upon that country's entry into the war.

By 1916 Canada remained the one source of shipbuilding potential whose possibilities had been largely untapped. The pool of experienced steel shipbuilding personnel in the country was very small and had to be augmented by skilled management, down to foreman level which was brought in from the U.K. The Imperial Munitions Board ordered 42 steel vessels, and acquired the building contracts for five additional vessels, building for foreign owners, all of which were the lead vessels in certain of the standard designs.

Based on deadweight tonnage eight different classes of ships were built. The two largest sizes were an 8,800 tdw design built exclusively, by J. Coughlan & Sons, Vancouver (whose history is recounted in more detail in chapter 3) and a 7,200 tdw ship built by Canadian Vickers Ltd. of Montreal. The remaining six classes ranged from a 4,600 tdw down to a 1,800 tdw size all of which are included in the lists at the end of this chapter.

The other part of the program was filled by 48 wood-built steamers of 3,330 tons deadweight size. Available pictures depict an ungainly looking vessel, with two hatches forward sharing a long forward well-deck, the superstructure well aft of centre and a third hatch aft. From the aft end of number two hatch the rest of the vessel featured a raised quarterdeck which did nothing for the vessel's appearance. Built of unseasoned softwood most had a very short life with every one except WAR YUKON either scrapped, or lost by fire or marine perils by 1925. In the case of WAR YUKON she must have led a charmed life as her hull managed to last as a barge until 1937.

Machinery was a problem with some units coming from Manchester, England and at least four American manufacturers. Seven manufacturers were located in Ontario, Quebec and Nova Scotia, while one, Wallace Shipbuilding & Drydock built engine units in North Vancouver.

After the war all vessels were quickly disposed of by the British Government to a variety of British and foreign owners. The one exception which passed to a Canadian owner was the WAR CAVALRY, built by Coughlan's, which was briefly owned by Forbes Corporation of Montreal until 1922, when she passed to the Greek flag. Aside from marine losses in the intervening period the larger number of vessels lasted to give service during the second world war, and of those that came through, a number lasted until the late fifties and into the sixties before succumbing to the scrappers torch.

Two lists follow which set out the various vessels by class, using the deadweight tonnage as the method of labelling, with the steel vessels being followed by those built of wood. While the classes approximate to the five groups making up the CGMM list in the next chapter, there is sufficient variation in equivents to indicate that the original British plans were either amended or gave way to a wholly new design.

Mention should be made of the wooden schooners built on the West coast under the terms of the B.C. Shipping Act. This was a program initiated by the B.C. government of the day to develop a fleet beyond the control of either London or Ottawa in order to meet the needs of the local economy. I have chosen to deal with them outside of the scope of this book but have included a few photos in the chapter to indicate the activity which occurred in British Columbia before the programs covered by this book were initiated.

To cross locate in the individual builders lists in chapter 15, please refer to the general index at the end of the book.Measurements given are deadweight tonnage, length between perpendiculars, x beam, x moulded depth.

8,800 tdw type
410ft x 54ft x 29ft. Two decks, powered by turbine, designed speed 11.5 knot

Alaska	War Camp	War Cavalry
War Charger	War Chariot	War Chief
War Column	War Company	War Convoy
War Noble		

7,200 tdw type
381ft x 49ft x 30ft 1in. Single deck T 3cyl, 11 knots

Porsanger	Samnanger	War Duchess
War Earl	War Faith	War Joy

4,600 tdw type
300ft x 45ft x 27ft. Single deck T 3cyl, 10 knots

War Dog	War Power	War Storm

4,300 tdw type
251ft x 44ft x 28ft 3in. Single deck T 3cyl, 10 knots

War Fish

3,500 tdw type
251ft x 43ft 5in x 20ft 2in. Single deck T 3cyl, 10 knots

Tento	Asp	War Algoma
War Badger	War Dance	War Fiend
War Fury	War Halton	War Hamilton
War Hatbor	War Horus	War Hydra
War Isis	War Karma	War Leveret
War Magic	War Osiris	War Racoon
War Temiskaming	War Taurus	War Vixen
War Wallaby	War Weasel	War Wombat

2.900 tdw type
251ft x 43ft 5in x 19ft. Single deck T 3cyl, 10 knots

War Witch	War Wizard

2,400 tdw type
248ft x 35ft x 20ft, Single deck and well deck

War Bee,

800 tdw type
220ft x 35ft x 20ft. single deck

War Wasp

Variations in size between one yard and another for similar ships have created what amounts to sub-classes. Some of these variations appear to have arisen because of particular circumstances, such as length and size of building ways. Most of the ships below the 4,600 tdw type were built at yards on the Great Lakes so this again would have accounted for sizes capable of travelling through the locks on the Welland Canal in order to reach the sea.

The Wooden Ships
250ft (bp) x 43ft 6in x 25ft 6in. Single deck T 3cyl, 10 knots, 2,300 grt, 3,330 tdw
The construction of this fleet of 46 sister ships involved shipyards on both coasts, all of whom are listed as to individual yard output in chapter 15. Reading alphabetically across:-

War Atlin	War Babine	War Camchin
War Cariboo	War Casco	War Cayuse
War Chilcat	War Comox	War Edensaw
War Erie	War Ewen	War Fundy
War Gaspe	War Haida	War Halifax
War Huron	War Kitimat	War Masset
War Matane	War Mingan	War Mohawk
War Moncton	War Nanoose	War Niagara
War Nicola	War Nipigon	War Nootka
War Ontario	War Ottawa	War Puget
War Quebec	War Radnor	War Selkirk
War Seneca	War Sioux	War Skeena
War Songhee	War Sorel	War Stikine
War Sumas	War Suquash	War Tanoo
War Tatla	War Toronto	War Tyee
War Yukon		

MABLE BROWN
The first of several schooners built with assistance under the B.C. Shipping Act of 1916, for Canada West Navigation Co. Ltd.

LAUREL WHALEN
Another in the fleet of Canada West Navigation Company. Smart looking vessels they were already out of date when they were built, and were too slow, too unreliable and only suitable for carrying lumber.

JESSIE NORCROSS
All the vessels in the fleet were named after the wives of the directors of Canada West Navigation Company. The directors themselves were all prominent members of the business community.

THE LYALL SHIPYARD
In this composite photo the workcrew at W. Lyall Shipbuilding Company at North Vancouver pose before five wooden hulls at various stages of construction.

WAR BABINE
Evidently judging by the flags and the spectators this was launching day at the Foundation
Company, Victoria shipyard. The fore welldeck and the long raised quarterdeck can be clearly
discerned in this design.

WAR DOG
Reposes on the launching ways at Wallace Shipyards. May 17, 1917 was her launch date and on
her stern her name and port of registry of Liverpool can be made out. The frame structure under
which the ship lays has long since been removed.

WAR DOG
Launching day for this first of three steamers built at Wallace Shipyards in 1917. Built for the British government she was one of the 4,600 tdw type.

PRINCE RUPERT DRY DOCK COMPANY
Yard view of the Prince Rupert shipyard. Three stack vessel is the Grand Trunk coastal passenger
steamer PRINCE RUPERT, while the CANADIAN SCOTTISH lays alongside at the fitting out
berth. In the foreground a sister ship is in frame on the launching ways.

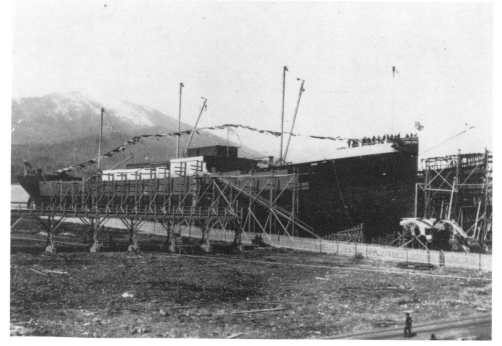

CANADIAN SCOTTISH
Ready for launch at Prince Rupert. Note a sister ship on the adjoining ways.

CANADIAN SCOTTISH
The ship was completed in 1921. The famous steam tug LORNE has the ship's bow line following launch, while a fish packer type vessel assists at the stern.

WAR CAVALRY
Built for British account at the Coughlan shipyard in False Creek. Judging by the style of lighters in the foreground she appears to be in a European port.

CANADIAN VOLUNTEER
With a shipyard crew in charge, the vessel gets under way for trials from the Wallace shipyard in North Vancouver. Tall signal mast between the bridge and funnel was a typical wartime appendage.

WAR STORM
The third of the three steel ships built at Wallace Shipyards for British account. Smoke issues from the funnel and she looks as though she is about ready for delivery.

Chapter Two

The Canadian Government Merchant Marine: The CGMM

The Canadian Government Merchant Marine, the CGMM as it was popularly known was born out of the First World War, when as recounted in the previous chapter, Canada found that it had a role as a builder of large steamships, as a part of its contribution to the war effort.

The Canadian nation also found itself as the owner of what was proudly proclaimed as the biggest railway system in North America. This came about as the result of heavy overbuilding of railways, all of which were designed by their promoters to share in the success of the Canadian Pacific Railway. In succession the Intercolonial railway, the Grand Trunk and its subsidiary the Grand Trunk Pacific, and the Canadian Northern were all rolled into the Canadian National, as each of its components went through bankruptcy procedures. Few people were elated by this development because with the formation of Canadian National an enormous debt was assumed which in effect was guaranteed by the Canadian taxpayer. Railways were the lifeblood of the country and no matter whatever else happened, the idea of abandoning this rail system was unthinkable, in light of national need.

The thrust behind the idea of acquiring a large fleet of war-built steamers was sound enough in theory, in the sense that the Canadian economy was geared to its ability to deliver its export products to foreign markets. The country had been heavily dependent on British and other foreign shipping over most of its history, with few exceptions, one being its commerce carried overseas in Maritimes-built and owned sailing ships. With wartime shipping controls Canada's requirements had become subject to the overall needs of the allied war effort. In building and controlling its own ships it was felt that this dependence could be greatly reduced, and that when normal peacetime conditions returned, Canadian ships could compete on world shipping routes.

With a national railway system and now a major shipping fleet, the belief of the then Minister of Marine & Fisheries, Hon. J.M. Ballantyne was that the nation now possessed a system which would rival its private competitor the Canadian Pacific, and what the Canadian Pacific did well, the new Canadian National and its shipping associate the CGMM should be able to do just as well or even better.

The list at the end of this chapter shows a total of 67 steamers in five classes. All were built in Canadian yards from wartime designs. Many were coal burners, and some of the larger ships oil burners. Essentially they were tramp style ships, which as peacetime conditions returned along with a higher degree of competitiveness, were less able to compete against modern foreign ships, which could offer greater speed, more efficient cargo handling ability, and a far higher ratio of reliability. At one point there were discussions about a joint service on Transpacific routes with the major Liverpool firm of Alfred Holt & Company who operated the powerful Blue Funnel Line, but when comparison was made between the ships of the two lines it was like comparing oil to water. Another project was to co-operate with the venerable British India Line in running a joint service from eastern Canadian ports as far as Calcutta, but likewise this had a short life for probably much the same reasons.

For any joint service to operate successfully the ships of the participating lines must be a reasonably compatible match in terms of speed, size and efficiency, which was far from the case in this example as Holt's steamers were larger, faster by as much as three knots, and while they carried larger crews the manning costs on average were considerably lower as they relied heavily on Oriental crews as did British India with East Indian lascars.

The CGMM was operated under Canadian National management and functioned with some degree of success during the nineteen twenties. Transpacific services were operated from Vancouver and Prince Rupert to the Orient, Australia and New Zealand. A North Atlantic service was provided to British and European ports, in addition to an inter-coastal service between Canadian east and west coast ports via Panama. The services to the Orient were pursued with particular vigour, even to the extent of maintaining trade offices in conjunction with Canadian National in Shanghai, Hong Kong, Melbourne and Sydney.

One of the properties taken over with the assets of the Grand Trunk Pacific was a dry dock at Prince Rupert, well known as the Prince Rupert Dry Dock Company, which actually built four of the 8,800 tdw freighters owned by the CGMM. This was a process repeated in the second world war when the same dock turned out a number of the 10,000 tdw "Fort" and "Park" ships. Like its parent, Prince Rupert D.D. struggled to keep itself afloat through the depression, and when CGMM went out of business ownership reverted to Canadian National. There are further comments on this undertaking in chapters six and 15.

The Wall Street crash of 1929, heralded the worst trade depression in history and over the years immediately following huge fleets of ships around the world went to the scrapyards, or were laid up to await better conditions. By 1934 there were signs of a significant pick-up, and during the balance of the thirties, major newbuilding programs were undertaken in Britain, Japan, Europe and the U.S. all of which would make the Canadian ships even more obsolete. As the world economy recovered there was a lack of a corresponding recovery in the affairs of the CGMM, and the Canadian Government of the day had other priorities, and was neither in the mood or capable of bailing its shipping line out.

By 1936, the Canadian Government Merchant Marine was at an end. Among the last vessels disposed of were six ships purchased by the newly established Greek-Argentine shipping tycoon Aristotle Onassis, who at $20,000 a vessel, paid about scrap value for them. This was truly a case of one company's misfortune being the making of another, for Onassis went on to become one of the world's leading shipowners in the quarter century which followed. The Canadian ships did not make him into a millionaire but they certainly gave him a good start.

Canadian National Steamships (West Indies) Ltd was organized out of the CGMM, and made a specialty out of running a service from Canadian east coast ports to the West Indies. This company employed a fleet made up of some of the smaller CGMM freighters and attractive passenger cargo ships of the "Lady" Class, some of which became war casualties. After the war the service was restarted with the acquisition of several of the 4,700 tdw class of ships built during the war for the Park Steamship Company, and the construction of a larger, much improved class of ship during the late 1940's all of which are listed hereunder.

Ships built for CGMM broke down into five basic groups. I have been unable to classify them by deadweight tonnage as with the British ships described in the previous chapter. I have therefore labelled them as type "A" through to "E". These initials are strictly my own and do not relate to any official description of which I am aware. Again the length between perpendiculars, beam, and moulded depth are set out along with the gross registered tonnage. The ships were not necessarily identical to the British ships but allowing for some latitude in measurement variations, the types from the two different program can be matched approximately and this in turn will give an indication of deadweight tonnage.

All vessels carried the prefix "Canadian" as part of their name. To avoid constant repetition, the symbol "C/" has been used in substitution for "Canadian".

"A" type
400ft x 52ft x 28ft 5in, gross registered tonnage on average about 5460. Deadweight believed to have been 8,800 tons.

C/ Armourer	C/ Britisher	C/ Challenger
C/ Commander	C/ Composer	C/ Conqueror
C/ Constructor	C/ Cruiser	C/ Explorer
C/ Exporter	C/ Freighter	C/ Harvester
C/ Highlander	C/ Importer	C/ Inventor
C/ Leader	C/ Mariner	C/ Miller
C/ Pioneer	C/ Planter	C/ Prospector
C/ Ranger	C/ Reaper	C/ Scottish
C/ Seigneur	C/ Skirmisher	C/ Spinner
C/ Thrasher	C/ Transporter	C/ Traveller
C/ Victor	C/ Winner	

"B" type
331ft x 46ft 7" x 23ft 2in draught. 3384 grt on average. These vessels were rather longer and have more beam and draught than the 4,600 tdw size in the British program. Estimated deadweight about 5,600 tons.

C/ Aviator	C/ Fisher	C/ Forester
C/ Hunter	C/ Raider	C/ Rancher
C/ Settler	C/ Trapper	

"C" type
320ft x 44ft 2in x 22ft 9in. 3180 grt on average. Estimated deadweight about 4,300 tons.

C/ Carrier	C/ Navigator	C/ Otter
C/ Runner	C/ Squatter	C/ Trooper
C/ Volunteer	C/ Voyager	

"D" type

270ft x 38ft x 17ft 5in. 1766 grt. Estimated deadweight about 2,600 tons. This small group were all built by Nova Scotia Steel & Coal Company at New Glasgow. They were relatively longer and narrow and of shallow draught compared to any of the other designs, for which there is no explanation at this point in time.

C/ Miner	C/ Sapper	C/ Sealer

"E" type

251ft x 43ft 6in x 23ft 6in. 2409 grt. Estimated deadweight about 4,000 tons.

C/ Adventurer	C/ Articifer	C/ Beaver
C/ Coaster	C/ Engineer	C/ Farmer
C/ Gunner	C/ Logger	C/ Observer
C/ Pathfinder	C/ Recruit	C/ Rover
C/ Sailor	C/ Signaller	C/ Sower
C/ Trader	C/ Warrior	

According to the above the fleet totalled 68 vessels all told, although some were disposed of quite quickly hence a lower figure of about 65 from other sources. The names are interesting at least to the extent that they reflected the mood of the times in the immediate postwar aftermath, with their generous use of military names and those which reflected pre-occupation with developing the country.

Following reorganization as Canadian National Steamships Ltd. in 1936 the fleet names became:

Canadian National Steamships (West Indies) Ltd.

Lady Drake	Lady Nelson	Lady Rodney
Cathcart	Cavelier	Chomedy
ex C/ Hunter	ex C/ Aviator	ex C/ Freighter
Colborne	Connector	Cornwallis
ex C/ Skirmisher	ex C/ Sapper	ex C/ Transporter

Canadian National Steamship Co. Ltd.

Prince David	Prince George	Prince Robert
Prince Rupert		

CANADIAN CONQUEROR.

CANADIAN EXPORTER.

CANADIAN FREIGHTER.

CANADIAN HIGHLANDER.

CANADIAN IMPORTER.

CANADIAN MILLER.

CANADIAN PIONEER.

CANADIAN PLANTER.

CANADIAN PROSPECTOR.

CANADIAN RANGER.

CANADIAN SEIGNEUR.

CANADIAN TRANSPORTER.

CANADIAN VICTOR.

CANADIAN WINNER
This and all the preceding vessels illustrated in this chapter are the author's type "A" designation.

CANADIAN AVIATOR
An example of the author's type
"B" designation.

CANADIAN RUNNER
Author's type "C" designation.

CANADIAN VOLUNTEER
Type "C".

CANADIAN FARMER.

CANADIAN OBSERVER
Type "E".

CANADIAN ROVER
Type "E".

CATHCART
Originally CANADIAN HUNTER looks very smart in her livery on the West Indian service of
Canadian National Steamships (West Indies) Ltd.

CANADIAN CONSTRUCTOR
A good-looking post-war unit of Canadian National Steamships, built by Burrard Dry Dock
Company in 1946.

Chapter Three

John Coughlan:
Vancouver Shipbuilder and Shipowner

This story is about a small Vancouver-based shipping company which functioned in international trade with a modest degree of success from 1920 to 1936. Before describing its 16-year history a little background on its antecedents should be of interest.

J. Coughlan & Sons were owners and operators of a bridge building and structural steel fabrication yard on the south bank of False Creek, a minor inlet bisecting downtown Vancouver and its financial district from the Grandview slopes to the south, which look across the city's core towards the north shore of Burrard Inlet and the mountains beyond. False Creek was for many years the cradle of much of the city's heavy industry with sawmills, foundries, gas works, railway yards, and many other industries. It was here in this industrial belt that Coughlan's located their plant, so that when the first world war shipbuilding program developed they were in a good position to start shipbuilding.

From the records, it was one of the most prolific of all Canadian shipyards in that period, until its demise was ensured by a disastrous fire in 1920 and a lack of independent orders.

History was to repeat itself during the second world war, as an entirely new yard, West Coast Shipbuilders Ltd. rose on the site of the old Coughlan yard. West Coast built 54 "Fort" and "Park" freighters, and navy auxiliaries for the Royal Navy, all based on the standard 10,000 tdw hull. Like Coughlan the West Coast yard enjoyed some post-war prosperity building large barges after it was reconstituted as Allied Builders Ltd. and moved to a new yard location in North Vancouver, where it continues in business to this day. The original site of both the Coughlan, and West Coast yards is today occupied by an extensive condominium development, and I wonder how many of its present day residents know of this piece of important local history upon whose site their homes now stand.

J. Coughlan & Sons was a private company, and so far as can now be determined it was owned or at least controlled by John Coughlin and his family. The name Coughlan is clearly Irish in origin, but little can be ascertained now about the family roots, except that they seem to be have been part of the early industrialization of Vancouver, erecting the framework of a number of then prominent downtown buildings, and a variety of bridgeworks for the railways. The recently removed Kitsilano swing bridge was a monument to their industrial activities and no doubt a number of older buildings in downtown Vancouver still retain a Coughlan steel frame.

In 1917 a plan to build steel cargo ships in Canada for the account of the Imperial Munitions Board was initiated, as outlined in Chapter One. I.M.B. was an agency of the British government which placed shipbuilding contracts at ten shipyards, eight of them in Eastern Canada and two on the west coast, namely Coughlan and Wallace Shipyards & Drydock Company in North Vancouver.

The program consisted of 42 ships in eight size classes, the largest of which was an 8,800 tdw class of United States Shipping Board design which only Coughlan's built. With eleven such ships to their credit almost a quarter of the vessels, with a higher percentage of total deadweight tonnage, made Coughlan's the largest Canadian shipbuilder in the I.M.B. program. Wallace's role was relatively more minor, but in the second world war they outstripped all other Canadian yards in merchant shipbuilding as well as conversion of navy auxiliaries, and U.S.-built pocket aircraft carriers.

No steel ship had been built by Coughlan prior to the Imperial Munitions Board orders. They were not unusual in this regard as this was the position with the majority of Canadian yards which turned to wartime steel shipbuilding. Generally it is a Canadian characteristic to adopt the course of modesty, but considering how small the industrial establishment of the country was at the outbreak of both wars, Canadian output of new ships was really quite phenomenal, helped as it was by the import of key British shipbuilding managers from major British yards. Coughlan's hired several such skilled personnel, and in a manner of speaking became instant shipbuilders with a reputation for building first class vessels many of which enjoyed a long life until years after the second world war.

As noted in the previous chapter, the British program was extended by an even larger fleet for Canadian government account, with generally the same or similar ship types being incorporated into it. The Canadian ships all carried the prefix "Canadian" as part of a standard naming procedure and were placed under the management and ownership of the Canadian Government Merchant Marine, which in practice functioned as the shipping arm of the Canadian National Railways, the state owned competitor to the private sector Canadian Pacific Railway, as described in more detail in chapter 2.

In the case of the "Canadian" 8,800 tonners, Coughlan's did not have a monopoly, as other yards joined them in building this design. These were Prince Rupert Dry Dock Company, Prince Rupert, Harbour Marine Ltd. of Victoria and Canadian Vickers Ltd. Montreal.

In the immediate postwar flush of building for private and foreign owners, which followed the war and created a brief climate of prosperity, Coughlan's built two ships of this class for the Swedish Brostrom group. One the INDUS was designated to their owners Far Eastern service, and the second, the BRAHEHOLM, was employed in their service to the Gulf of Mexico.

Coughlan's built three vessels for their own account. The first was the MARGARET COUGHLAN named for John Coughlan's wife. She had a shorter history within the fleet, her registered owner being a single vessel subsidiary company, Canadian Western Steamships Ltd. In 1923 she was transferred to another Vancouver based company, the Atlantic S.S. Company but managed following transfer by Ocean Carriers Inc. of New York. For information on this period I am indebted to the memoirs of the late Captain Trevor W. Bridges, to which I have access.

Captain Bridges relates how he left Canadian Pacific's North Pacific passenger service, with some relief as he found after joining that company that his job was more or less a dead-end situation. He was hired by Coughlan as the chief officer of the newly-built CITY OF VANCOUVER, and took her out of the False Creek yard on her maiden voyage which involved proceeding to Bellingham, Washington to load a full export cargo of lumber. Captain James Boyd who had previously had the MARGARET COUGHLAN was her master, but Bridges was not to remain chief officer for long as he was soon appointed master of the MARGARET COUGHLAN and thus achieved his first command.

His account gives considerable detail of her voyages which unlike the other two sister-ships were mainly to Europe, and then from 1923 she became largely based on Montreal. In 1923 the bondholders of the Canadian Western company who were secured by a mortgage on the ship, foreclosed through a Cleveland, Ohio bank. It is not known who the bondholders were except that they appeared to have been American. It was at this point that the new registered owner became the Atlantic S.S. Company of Vancouver, remaining under the Canadian flag. To what extent Coughlan's might have had any ongoing interest in the vessel is not known; all that Bridges says is that nothing changed except for the source of his salary cheque, and the orders he received, which now came from New York.

In any event the MARGARET COUGHLAN was disposed of by the Atlantic S.S. Company in 1926, becoming the CHILCOP owned by Chile S.S. Co. Inc. of New York. This ownership appears to have been the shipping subsidiary of a large mining concern, Chile Copper Corporation. In 1936 she was sold to T.K. King of Cheefoo, China, later becoming the KYOKUSEI MARU owned by Asahi Shoji K.K. of Tokyo. She became a Japanese war loss, having been torpedoed by the USS BLUEFIN in position 17.00N, 116.17E, November 8, 1943. This would have placed her in a position in the South China Sea, roughly midway between Manila and Hong Kong.

The second and third ships were the CITY OF VANCOUVER and CITY OF VICTORIA respectively. They were also completed in 1920, and the steel was assembled for a fourth sister ship, but apparently she was cancelled which is not surprising given the state of world shipping which was now in slump after a short-lived boom. Captain Bridges makes another comment, which cannot now be corroborated, in stating that having met Mr. John Coughlan he was inclined to believe that some persuasion was brought to bear on the Coughlan concern to go into the ship-owning business.

He seemed positive that the persuasion came from an unnamed "silken-tongued Welshman" as he described the party, formerly with either Blue Funnel or Furness Withy, both prominent British concerns well known in Vancouver shipping circles. He believed that Coughlan did not fully understand the nature of the shipping business, but already being the owner of a shipyard he had visions of turning Vancouver into the Liverpool of the Pacific! Shipping was not for neophytes, and Coughlan may have been driven to some extent by the old adage "that fools step in, where angels fear to tread" The fact that Coughlan's, no doubt in spite of early difficulties, managed to stay in business unsubsidized in any way through the depression of the early thirties, not retiring until 1936, speaks well of their resilience and quality of management, where many others far more experienced went under.

The entry in Lloyds register dealing with both ships shows that the VICTORIA had a length between perpendiculars of 411'5", a breadth of 54'1" and a moulded depth of 27'5". The VANCOUVER was evidently one foot shorter, with the gross tonnage of both ships being 5,698 and 5,697 respectively. The MARGARET COUGHLAN had the same dimensions exactly as the VICTORIA but with a g.r.t. of 5,704. As noted designed deadweight was 8,800 tons. Triple expansion reciprocating machinery of 520 NHP giving a speed of 10 knots was supplied by Fairfields, Glasgow in the case of the VANCOUVER and by J. Dickinson & Sons of Sunderland for the VICTORIA.

This contrasted with the ships for British and Canadian government account which were powered by turbines giving a designed speed of 11.5 knots, although I doubt that many ever operated at this speed as fuel consumption to gain the extra 1.5 knots would have involved a sizeable increase over the commonly accepted ten knots for tramp type-vessels. The three Coughlin ships were however capable of burning oil or coal.

The CITY OF VANCOUVER was registered as being owned by the Vancouver S.S. Co. Ltd. and the CITY OF VICTORIA by British Canadian Steamships Ltd. The managing company for both vessels was Ocean Shipping Co. Ltd. The actual shareholders in Ocean Shipping and the two owning companies cannot be established but it seems safe to say that all three were controlled by the Coughlan family, and collectively were popularly known as the "Johnny Coughlan Line." There is no evidence of any connection between Ocean Shipping of Vancouver, and Ocean Carriers of New York, the similarity of names being probably coincidental.

Manned by white officers and an all-Chinese deck and engineroom crew it seems that from the beginning both vessels were committed largely to the British Columbia export lumber trade, being mostly engaged in the carriage of sawn lumber and logs to Northern Chinese and Japanese markets. Frequent ports of call were Shanghai, Tsingtao, Dairen, Port Arthur, Taku Bar and Muroran, the most usual route being through Hakodate Straits after a call at Muroran on Hokkaido Island. There is some record of the ships making periodic voyages to the U.K. where typical lumber cargoes were discharged at Garston near Liverpool, and at other North European ports.

As a specialist lumber carrier, Ocean Shipping Company must have enjoyed an unusually strong niche in the lumber freight market. It started operations at the height of the post-first world war shipping recession, piloted its way through the tricky shipping markets of the 1920's followed by the world-wide depression of the thirties. Canada as a major exporter of raw materials and primary products was badly hit and few areas in the country were more badly hurt than Vancouver, whose lumber industry fought for life itself in those perilous years.

Ocean Shipping advertised in the local marine press and appears to have had close working connections with the Robert Dollar interests of San Francisco and their export lumber mill at Dollarton, as well as the associated Melville Dollar interests in the form of Canadian-American Shipping Company. It is a good question as to how they survived against the competition of modern Scandinavian diesel lumber carriers, and the new British "economy" diesel tramps built by yards such as William Doxford at Sunderland. It seems unfortunate that Coughlan could not find conditions sufficiently conducive to have enabled them also to undertake a modernization program, but clearly the economics of Canadian flag shipping were mounting against them.

MARGARET COUGHLAN
The first vessel in the fleet.

MARGARET COUGHLAN
At Montreal.

MARGARET COUGHLAN.

CITY OF VICTORIA
Entering Vancouver Harbour.

What seems more probably is that they hung on through the depression in the hopes of an improvement in freight rates and shipping values, and indeed 1936-7 saw a fairly strong recovery after the depression years. With the loss of the CITY OF VICTORIA in 1936, opportunity was obviously taken to sell the CITY OF VANCOUVER and retire from the business, about which more later.

The two ships struggled through many severe North Pacific storms, and loss of deck cargo was a frequent occurence, sometimes with structural damage, injury and loss of life. Captain James E. Wilson in his book, "Full Line, Full Away" which he wrote in conjunction with this author tells something of two of the last voyages of the CITY OF VANCOUVER which he joined as a 16-year old cadet in 1934.

In the first instance the ship lost most of her forward deck load which carried away the starboard rails. The fore topmast collapsed bringing down the radio aerial. Fortunately a distress call from the ship was picked up by the EMPRESS OF ASIA before the aerial came down. With her forward deck load largely cleared, thus lightening the vessel for'ard, the ship was now badly down by the stern which might have resulted in pooping or swamping. To improve her trim and recover her seakeeping ability the master ordered the after deck cargo to be jettisoned, but in the process three Chinese seamen lost their lives. With the aerial gone the ship could send out no further messages. Meanwhile the EMPRESS OF ASIA found herself steaming through floating lumber and logs, and the immediate concern of all was that the CITY OF VANCOUVER had foundered because of the lack of radio messages, and now all this jettisoned material. Happily they did rendezvous with the CITY OF VANCOUVER and stood by her until the weather moderated, and it was safe for her to proceed.

The other incident occurred on the second of Cadet Wilson's two voyages in this ship while returning to British Columbia with a cargo of soya bean oil in barrels, and general produce. A giant wave snatched the chief officer from the bridge wing from which he disappeared and was thought to be lost overboard. With one officer short Wilson was sent forward with the Chinese bosun, and three Chinese seamen to resecure a small leaking hatch on the foc's'le. In the event that the captain thought that an approaching sea would endanger them, he undertook to give warning by a blast on the ship's siren. As so often happens when the all-engulfing wave they feared developed there was almost no warning. Wilson saw the bow going under and shouted to everyone to hang on, but all five were swept off the foc's'le. Wilson and the bosun landed in the portside scuppers and both sustained injuries, Wilson receiving a broken arm and dislocated shoulder. One Chinese seaman smashed into the cargo winches between number one and two hatches, and was instantly killed, and a second quite badly hurt. The third man appears to have got off lightly with a shaking and a soaking.

The CITY OF VANCOUVER survived this battering, but the CITY OF VICTORIA was less lucky because in 1936 she stranded in Hakodate Straits and became a total loss. There was no loss of life, and as passengers two of John Coughlan's young granddaughters were on board. Some said that it was a deliberate attempt at wrecking, while others blamed the Japanese authorities for not posting a change in shore lights in "Notices to Mariners". In any event this seems to have been the signal for the Coughlan interests to withdraw from shipping as previously noted.

The CITY OF VANCOUVER was sold in 1936 to V.K. Song of Tsingtao, China who renamed her VEN-KOH. It would be interesting to know how this Chinese owner survived, as the Sino-Japanese war had been under way since 1934, and North China subjugated. Song evidently did survive as there was a note in the "Vancouver Sun" newspaper of July 1939 stating that the VEN-KOH had arrived at Seattle to pick up a cargo of flour for Dairen, Manchuria while under charter to the Japanese Yamashita Shipping Company.

In the 1942-43 Lloyds Register the VEN-KOH, now minus the hyphen in her name became VENKOH, was shown as being owned by Skibs A/S Thule, a company managed by T.B. Torgersen of Oslo, but by 1947-48 she had disappeared from that issue of Lloyds Register. As there is no evidence of a renaming or transfer of ownership it seems reasonable to assume that the ship had finally reached a shipbreaking yard or been lost at sea.

Interestingly enough another Coughlan-built sister ship also found its way into the fleet of V.K. Song and then followed VEN-KOH to Torgersen and the Norwegian flag. This ship was the CANADIAN PROSPECTOR which was disposed of by the CGMM in 1934 becoming PROSPECTOR. On passing to Song she became the MITWO and finally SHENG HWA when she showed up in the 1946-7 Lloyds Register under Torgersen ownership. One can speculate a little on unrecorded shipping connections, but it does seem possible that there might have been a prior connection between Coughlan's and V.K. Song. Perhaps the latter also functioned as ship's agent at Tsingtao for Coughlan ships. Also this connection might have lead further to Torgersen who seems to have had some sort of business arrangement with Song. Torgersen appears to have been one of that small number of Norwegian owners with a special affinity for the Far Eastern and China coastal trades, when conditions for European and British firms were a lot more favourable then they became with the rise of communism in China.

An aspect of Coughlan's shipowning activities worth noting is that so far as I can determine the first world war shipping effort only spawned two truly private sector shipowners, these being Coughlan and the Forbes Corporation of Montreal, who briefly owned the SYLVIA VICTORIA, ex WAR CAVALRY, which had also been built at the Coughlan yard.

The record following the second war with Park Steamships Ltd. was rather dissimilar. The reigning government had no illusions about starting a crown-owned shipping company to compete in the private sector. Government enterprises most commonly have had a dismal record, and the Mackenzie King government showed considerable wisdom in the matter. Park was to get out of the business as soon as it could find buyers for its ships, and quite a few private owners came forward to take advantage of incentives available. Many such were not Canadian-owned even if the corporate entity was a Canadian corporation. All but five had gone by the mid-sixties, and of those only four survive to this day. The survivors are of course Saguenay Terminals, the shipping arm of Alcan Limited, Canadian Transport, the shipping subsidiary of McMillan Bloedel, and Seaboard Shipping, the shipping subsidiary of Seaboard Lumber Sales. The fourth is Fednav Limited, the only one which is still an actual shipowner, the other three relying on chartered foreign.

There is a postscript to all this. When the second world war arrived, the shipbuilding program which was initiated in 1941 created an enormous expansion in the

CITY OF VICTORIA
Outward bound for North China with a full cargo of lumber products.

CITY OF VICTORIA
Makes a jaunty entrance through Lions Gate, Vancouver harbour.

CITY OF VANCOUVER
Partly laden with the aft well deck already covered, enters Vancouver to top off her cargo.

CITY OF VANCOUVER
Working cargo.

industrial capacity of the country. Coughlan's perhaps remembering their success in the first war, saw the opportunity of getting back into shipbuilding, but of course their original yard was occupied by West Coast Shipbuilders. They made application to lease or acquire land at Kitsilano fronting on to English Bay, close to where the existing museum complex is today, but the city council of the day turned them down and rightly so. Considering the present day beauty of this spot and its popularity as a major park area in Vancouver, one wonders at this stage if Coughlan's were really serious about their proposal, as there were excellent sites available which could have been developed in North Vancouver and even in the Fraser River delta.

I have heard it suggested that Mr. Coughlan did not like the then prevailing railway connections to North Vancouver, but historically the north bank of Burrard Inlet has been the major shipbuilding centre for Greater Vancouver since the beginning of the century. The Lyall shipyard of the first world war should not be overlooked, but Burrard Dry Dock and their associated North Van Ship Repairs Ltd. between them far exceeded the capacity of any other city in terms of wartime shipbuilding. Allied Builders and Vancouver Shipyards flourish today as post-war developments, while Mckenzie Marine Ways and defunct Belaire Shipyards have both made sizeable contributions to local coastal shipbuilding

Chapter Four

The Forbes Corporation of Montreal: The SYLVIA VICTORIA

So far as this book is concerned, the identity of the people behind the Forbes Corporation, shipowners of Montreal, is in itself almost a mystery of the sea.

The company evidently came into being to purchase the Coughlan-built steamer WAR CAVALRY from the British government for whom she had been built. Coughlan's suffered a major fire and the CAVALRY is believed to have been one of the ships whose completion was delayed. Her completion date was May 1919, and the probability was that she was sold to Forbes before being actually delivered to the British government who were heavily into the business of disposing of their already large fleet of war-built shipping.

As built the WAR CAVALRY was a standard 8,800 ton class of ship, which was the only size and design built by Coughlan either for the British or Canadian governments, or for their own account, as discussed in the three previous chapters. She was fitted with two steam turbines built by Halliday Machinery Company of Spokane, Washington. Her three Scotch boilers were built by Coughlin at the False Creek yard, but as with her sisters the turbines proved unsatisfactory and were replaced by a new T-3cyl reciprocating engine giving 10 knots. When built with turbines her designed speed was 11.5 knots but it is doubtful if these ships ever came up to this speed in practice.

From a local Vancouver point-of-view Forbes evidently engaged Captain John Park of Victoria as master. Scottish-born Park was well-known and highly thought of as a ship's master. He had joined Union Steamships of British Columbia in 1910 from a career in sail taking command a few years later. What persuaded him to return to deepsea tramping after the war is not known, but one suspects that there might have been a personal connection between Park and Forbes.

In choosing to rename the WAR CAVALRY as the SYLVIA VICTORIA there may also have been a local connection in that Park lived in Victoria. Such material as exists indicated that the ship was engaged in voyages to Europe. The accompanying photo of the SYLVIA VICTORIA shows her laying at a coaling dock at a French port. Visible in the original print, ahead of the ship are typical European 4-wheeled coal wagons, while up on the hill behind can be seen a large factory sign in the French language.

In 1922 the ship was sold to Greek owners and became the ALANTICOS which was the point also when she was re-engined, probably for account of the new owners who had no doubt purchased her as a bargain. In 1932 she became MOUNT PENTILIKON owned by well-known Greek owners Rethymnis & Kulukundis but was quickly resold by them to Japanese owners as the KINSHU MARU and then without apparent further change of ownership as the KINSYU MARU.This would be explainable because of adjustments in English translation of Japanese written characters.

SYLVIA VICTORIA
Lays alongside soon after her change of name from WAR CAVALRY.

SYLVIA VICTORIA
Coaling at a French port.

Her end came on June 17, 1944 when the submarine USS HAKE, sank the ship by torpedo in position 06.17N 126.17E, which was off Cape San Agustin on the south-east side of the island of Mindanao in the Philippines.

Chapter 5

Overloading and Underfuelling

In the coal-burning era it was by no means unknown for a ship to run out of fuel short of her destination. Most coal burning steamers filled their cross bunker to the brim when loading coal fuel. This bunker was located just ahead of the boiler room and was meant to sustain the ship through whatever leg of the voyage was involved until reaching the next location where bunkers could be replenished.

Calculating the quantity of bunker coal required was an exercise in fine-tuning. Excess bunkers over and above a reasonable margin for contingencies meant that the available freight-earning deadweight cargo capacity was reduced by the amount of the excess. Cargo earned money for the ship; excess bunkers diminished the returns that the owner could expect from the voyage, as they represented non-paying deadweight.

A wrong calculation on the part of the responsible engineer could be expensive in other ways. If the ship ran out of fuel before reaching her destination she might, if she was fortunate enough to be carrying combustible cargo such as lumber, have to break into consignee's cargo to feed the furnaces. If she did not have such cargo, perhaps for example be carrying iron ore, the only resort would be to await a tow, a costly procedure at best, but also while awaiting arrival of the tug, often a danger to the ship if the weather was poor.

Maritime law has for long recognised the legal principle of "general average". The Marine Insurance Act of 1906, which was British legislation adopted verbatim as a Canadian statute, set out the guiding definition of general average, which is almost exactly repeated in the York-Antwerp Rules of 1974. The York-Antwerp rules are an international convention widely accepted as being the instrument for settling losses occurring under general average. York-Antwerp sets out the governing rule A:-

> "There is a general average act when, and only when, any extraordinary sacrifice or expenditure is intentionally and reasonably made or incurred for the common safety for the purpose of preserving from peril the property involved in a common maritime venture."

General average might be described as a pooling of risk in a maritime venture. A cargo-laden vessel is termed a venture, to which a number of parties contribute jointly. There is the owner of the ship, the party who benefits from freight earnings, who may be the shipowner or a charterer, and the owners of the cargo, who may be a single entity, or in the case of a mixed cargo, a multiplicity of owners.

If a ship runs aground for example, and cargo is voluntarily jettisoned in order to lighten the vessel and thus save her and the remaining cargo from further loss, this action is known as a general average sacrifice. Clearly the owner of the jettisoned cargo has sustained a loss but once the ship's master has declared a general average all parties to the joint venture will contribute pro-rata on the independent value of the ship, the freight earnings, and all the cargo including that sacrificed by jettisoning.

The cargo thus lost by general average sacrifice and the amounts contributed by the other interests which have been saved is termed a general average contribution. Drawing up a general average adjustment is invariably a long and sometimes costly matter which is customarily settled by an expert called an average adjuster. Essentially average adjustment requires meticulous identification and calculation of every factor involved in drawing up the statement.

Marine insurance is heavily involved. Provided that the interests that make up the joint venture are insured, the underwriters eventually end up by reimbursing the insured party for their general average contribution to the original sacrifice.

Instances of faulty stowage, inadequate securing of deck cargo, overloading and underfuelling are all matters which reflect on the managers, and the responsible officers in the ship. Ill-considered decisions in these matters can in the event of loss or accident open up the potential for legal liability.

A good example of an actual incident concerns the vessel CANADIAN BEAVER, one of the smaller units of the CGMM fleet detailed in chapter two. This steamer was assigned to an intercoastal service from Eastern Canada to Vancouver and B.C. ports, with calls in the West Indies and at selected ports in Central America. In this instance dating back to 1933, the ship loaded fertilizer at Vancouver, for Puerto Rico and lumber for Hamilton, Ontario. The fertilizer was stowed below deck and the lumber was carried as deck cargo. As the ship had very little bunker coal on board after completing cargo loading, she left Vancouver for Union Bay on Vancouver Island to replenish her bunkers. She already had a noticeable list to port clearly due to miscalculations in stowing cargo, plus possibly the fact that whatever residue of coal remained might have been on the port-hand side of the ship.

Upon arrival at Union Bay it was decided to commence the loading of coal into the starboard side of the bunkers to bring the ship to an even keel. This loading was overdone so that when enough coal had been taken aboard to overcome inertia, and bring the ship back to an even keel, the ship suddenly went over to a list on her starboard side. She was now leaning against the dock, which is what saved her from rolling over onto her starboard beam.

The ship evidently left Union Bay having taken in her bunkers, and sailed for Panama. She must have been very tender to have reacted in the manner which she did and in view of events as she approached Panama it is equally questionable as to whether she had adequate bunkers in the first place. In any event a spell of bad weather used up her available coal and the captain decided that the ship would have to resort to burning lumber from the deck cargo. The timbers were a mix from 14" x 14" down to 2" x 4" up to 30 feet in length. There were few tools on board other than carpenter's hand tools, sledge hammers and wedges but the entire crew set to, cutting the material into about five foot lengths capable of being handled into the furnaces.

The ship took about seven days to reach Balboa during which time about 40,000 board feet of consignee's lumber deck cargo was cut up and fed to the furnaces. To illustrate how precarious the ship's condition now was, in order to send a radio message steam had to be used to power the electric generator. When this was done the generator would use up most available steam so that the ship would be brought almost to a standstill until steam pressure had been regained.

CANADIAN BEAVER
Another of the author's "C" type designation, which ran out of bunkers before reaching Balboa.

CITY OF VANCOUVER
The list to starboard is mostly caused by camera distortion, but note the deckload above number two hatch.

CITY OF VANCOUVER
Another view showing the deckload and its supporting stanchions trying to splay out. Notice how little the freeboard was, by comparing with the man working on the log boom at extreme right of the photo.

CITY OF VANCOUVER
The ship evidently left fully laden but without correction of the condition pointed out in the two previous pictures. The conclusion today would be that the load was unsafe.

On arrival at Balboa where undoubtedly CANADIAN BEAVER would have replenished her bunkers, the first act of the master would have been to proceed ashore in order to swear out a "protest' setting out the circumstances of the occurrence which would lead to a general average being declared. It is always the master's first duty, rather than the owners, to initiate the process as part of ship's business, as he is in charge of the ship and would be the first to know of actual events while under his command.

On the face of it this appears to be a general average sacrifice of deck cargo to save the ship and the remaining cargo, but given the circumstances there also appears to be a case of negligence on the part of the ship in that inadequate bunkers were loaded at Union Bay. Admittedly when a ship is fighting her way through bad weather there is every likelihood that there will be heavier consumption of fuel, but ordinary prudence indicates that the chief engineer should be able to calculate bunker needs with an adequate margin of safety. After all bad weather is a circumstance likely to arise on any voyage.

What probably happened in this case was that the general average would firstly have been fully adjusted. As underwriters paid out they acquired the rights of the original property owners who had been compensated under the terms of their insurance policy, by a process known in insurance as subrogation. If underwriters believed, as appears possible in this case, that there was a case of negligence to be answered by the owners, they would no doubt have pursued their right to recover damages as an offset to their losses paid out on the general average.

When I read this account, rendered at a meeting of the Kerrisdale Historical Society and reported in the "Vancouver Courier" of January 23, 1985, my first reaction was why would a prudent master not load bunkers first and then deal with cargo? There would have been no need to gamble on fuel and with her bunkers already in place she would have been a much more stable ship for the reception of the cargo.

If there was an answer it might be found in the ship's management insisting on saving every penny particularly at a time when ships operated on very narrow margins and more often at a loss. CGMM as her owners, were already deeply in the red and 1933 was just about as bad a year as had ever been experienced by the international shipping industry.

The CANADIAN BEAVER probably had to clear customs and health examination at Vancouver as her first port of entry if she did not do it at Victoria. Had she cleared at Victoria she could have sailed directly for Union Bay, bunkered and then made for Vancouver for cargo. By completing loading first and then bunkering she could sail on her outward trip directly from Union Bay which saved a second call at Vancouver.

Had the ship been lost it sounds as though there would have been much criticism of the master and the chief engineer at the very least. If a general average was declared which is virtually a certainty, it is likely that no record of it is available today. This means that it is only possible to make assumptions at this late date, but it does seem likely that cargo underwriters would have sought a recovery against the ship for negligence in the loss of cargo, as the chain of events saw faulty cargo stowage creating a situation where the ship could not be fully bunkered thus creating the condition of unseaworthiness, which led to the crisis

WHEN A GREYBEARD COMES ABOARD
**CANADIAN AVIATOR off the Philipines in relatively fine sunny weather. The ship is rolling in
heavy swells as a mass of water comes aboard.**

causing deliberate destruction of cargo.

It is not implied that the CANADIAN BEAVER was leaking or in poor physical condition, but any circumstance of faulty loading, improper stowage, and inadequate fuel can render a vessel legally unseaworthy.

Another case concerns the Canadian steamer CITY OF VANCOUVER of the J. Coughlan Line (see Chapter 3) which sailed from Port Alberni in 1934 with a full cargo of sawn lumber and logs for the Orient. The ship had a distinct list with her plimsoll line being perhaps a foot below water on one side while on the opposite side her plimsoll line was out of the water by a similar measurement. Her draught marks at bow and stern indicated that the vessel was loaded to her safe maximum capacity. She was not overloaded but she was poorly trimmed, a condition which was not uncommon in loading lumber cargoes. Usually the second mate was in charge of the stowage plan and supervising loading but in this case if an inclinometer was in use its reading was evidently regarded as being inconsequential.

A foot sounds like a nominal enough measurement but when one considers that these ships only had a freeboard of about eight feet at the lowest point of the well-deck, when fully laden, it really becomes quite an important consideration

Technically the ship was unseaworthy when she departed, and at a point past mid-Pacific she ran into severe weather conditions which carried away her forward deck cargo and did severe damage to the ship. She was now down badly by the stern and to improve the trim of the vessel the captain decided to jettison a large part of the aft deck cargo to save the ship. The loss of forward well-deck cargo arose from a peril of the sea, and that part of the loss would be treated as a particular average or partial loss and would have been covered by the lumber cargo insurance policies. Likewise the physical damage to the ship occasioned by the bad weather would be treated as a particular average against the ship. The act of jettisoning after well-deck cargo to improve trim and restore seaworthiness, was a perfect case of a general average sacrifice. The fact that the ship had a list and loss of freeboard on one side might have contributed to her predicament even though the proximate cause of her accident was the consequence of extreme and disabling weather conditions.

As it turned out she also had to burn deck lumber cargo as she became very low on bunker coal. Burning the lumber would have also been treated as a general average sacrifice but this was not a case of having left port with inadequate fuel. She simply had to burn a lot more due to the extreme weather conditions.

In 1934 the British tanker LA CRESCENTA left Long Beach with a full cargo of California crude for Japan. The master was aware that she was overloaded beyond her marks when she was due to depart. In fact there was communication between him and his London managers, who demanded that he ignore the overload and carry on with his voyage. The master also wrote to his wife before he left Long Beach expressing his misgivings. The LA CRESCENTA sailed and was last heard of north-west of Hawaii, and then she disappeared without trace, thus becoming another mystery of the sea.

The enquiry into her loss was held in London and the evidence of the master's notice to his owners as to overloading, and his letter to his wife provided damning confirmation of the manager's lack of concern for the safety of their ship and crew. As a result they came in for a lot of severe criticism at the enquiry. The extra 200 tons of oil she carried might have made a difference between a profit or loss on the voyage as shipping rates were still in the depression doldrums.

The ship was otherwise well-found and was only eleven years old at the time of her loss. Technically she was unseaworthy as she had exceeded her safe loading draft although it is doubtful that this would have contributed materially to her loss, as with small almost indestructible tank tops, and no hatches to be stove in as with a dry-cargo freighter, the ingress of heavy seas was unlikely to swamp the ship. For a fairly large tanker to disappear she must have been overwhelmed by extreme natural conditions and perhaps broke in two, with the vital radio installation in the accomodation island amidships going under before a distress signal could be sent out. Fully laden she would have inevitably sunk with the two halves forming a "V" which ensured the drowning of the 'midships accomodation right at the outset.

Some would argue with justification that the master did not properly exercise his prerogative, which is that it is his duty to do whatever he considers expedient to preserve the safety of his ship, cargo and crew, with or without reference to the owners. Being a tanker she was easily capable of self-discharge and at this late date it seems a matter of common sense that the ship should have simply pumped her excess oil back into the shore tanks. However in the midst of a severe depression with thousands of ship crew members "on the beach", a master might be forgiven for being tempted to take a risk which seemed perhaps small at the time, by placing personal employment considerations ahead.

Economy can be carried too far, the three cases cited all carry with them elements of carelessness and possibly the false economics dictated by the depression conditions that ruled at the time. However many ships have been lost before and since through similar circumstances. Of course what the public usually reads or sees on television are only the dramatic circumstances. What I hope this brief chapter will convey is something of the technicalities and legalities of ship losses and how they are handled behind the scenes.

I have chosen to use as my examples, three cases all of which occurred in the Pacific, involving two Canadian ships which are mentioned elsewhere in this book. The third vessel, the tanker LA CRESCENTA is a true mystery of the sea, wide open to speculative theory as to her fate. Whether overloading actually contributed to her fate is impossible to establish, but when such an act occurs it must always be a matter of concern to an enquiry, in evaluating every possibility when seeking to establish cause.

Chapter Six

Merchant Shipbuilding in Canada during the Second World War

When war came in 1939, Canadian shipyards such as they were, depended almost entirely upon repair and maintenance work. At the termination of the first world war shipbuilding program which was substantially over by 1921, building quickly reverted to mostly small wooden vessels such as fishboats, tugs and barges, many of which were built in small specialist yards often in more remote communities where they had little impact on the wellbeing of the steel shipbuilders such as Canadian Vickers, Burrard, Davie, Marine Industries and Yarrows, who depended entirely on repair and maintenance work of Canadian coastal and government vessels. Foreign ships were mostly confined to emergency repairs.

In terms of shiprepairs, foreign owners tended to reserve their deferable repairs and maintenance until they could work their ships back to the home country or at least to a cheaper foreign location. For this reason huge ship repair industries developed around the British ports, Rotterdam, Antwerp, Hamburg, and in the Orient, where in many instances the work was undertaken for a great range of foreign clients. Of course the outbreak of war vastly altered the entire pattern of both shipbuilding and repair business. German yards were out of the picture, and as each country fell, the continental yards in France, the Scandinavian countries, Holland, and Belgium quickly followed suit, as did shipyards in Italy and Japan and the Orient generally as those two countries came into the war.

With the fall of France in 1940 the task of the German submarine arm of the Kriegsmarine became that much easier. French ports on the English Channel and the Bay of Biscay became available. Britain stood alone against a mounting onslaught of increasingly efficient U-boats plus long range Focker-Wulfe Condor bombers and light surface forces such as the E-boats. Merchant ships were a priority but even more urgent was the need for the British shipbuilders to construct massive fleets of anti-submarine vessels, such as destroyers, sloops, frigates and corvettes. At the same time cruisers, battleships and aircraft carriers were also under way. Britain's shipbuilding resources, while massive, were strained to the absolute limit, with the shipyards crammed with new building, repair and conversion contracts of all types.

I remember as a youth and later in the navy being in shipyard ports. The clatter of rivetting hammers, the light from flame cutters and metal grinders went on day and night, while the railways worked around the clock between air raids to keep the materials of shipbuilding on the move without letup. Often one would see ships only barely afloat, half sunk, sometimes a half ship, or another with its bows blown off by torpedo or as the result of hitting a mine, waiting for shipyard attention. Following the blitz of the Liverpool docks one could go to a point in Bromborough on the opposite side of the river and see burned-out hulks, or as on one occasion, the stern half of a munitions ship laying on the mud awaiting a new bow half.

One such I remember was the Newcastle tramp MERTON. Her stern section from the bridge aft had been salvaged after a dock explosion. She was evidently awaiting a new bow back to and including number two hold. Eventually this was built somewhere at a British yard and towed into the Mersey so that the ship could be joined together again. I saw her in the fifties when she visited Vancouver to pick up a cargo of grain and so far as I know she gave many good years of further service.

The facilities available in Hong Kong and Singapore became more valuable than ever and just as happened in 1917, Britain turned to the two large shipyards in Hong Kong for new war-built ships. Pearl Harbour put a stop to that activity and indeed a few partly built "Empire" ships fell into Japanese hands. Outside of the United States, the only allied countries with any available shipbuilding capacity were India, Australia and Canada.

India possessed two small yards at Bombay and Vizagapatam on the east coast. Mazagon Dockyard at Bombay was mainly engaged in work for the small Indian Navy, while Hindustan Shipyard at Vizagapatam very slowly worked its way into building average size steamships for its parent company, Scindia Steam Navigation Company of Bombay, but except for repair work the Indian shipbuilding industry had no potential for providing ships for the allied war effort.

Australia was even further behind Canada in terms of its capacity for building steel ships. Its main shipyards had never built anything approaching the size of an average freighter but by 1942 the Commonwealth government was giving attention to building a steam freighter which like the *North Sands* class was based on British plans of the SCOTTISH MONARCH and looking remarkably similar, although at a deadweight tonnage of 8,500 tons, to the 10,000 tonners built in Canada they were a little smaller. Eventually some 60 ships were ordered but only ten were built under this program, all carrying the readily identifiable prefix "River" followed by Darling, Murray or less familiar names such as River Murrumbidgee.

An interesting footnote is that the Allies tried to persuade the Australians to build Liberty Ships. This was not pursued as the existing Australian yards could not handle a larger size ship.

All such ships were owned by the Commonwealth of Australia and gave good service for the balance of a normal ship life, around the Australian coast and in South East Asia and Southern Pacific waters.

For the British, the obvious first source to tap was the United States with a large number of first world war-built ships in its reserve fleet, laid-up around the country. Most of these ships came into operation originally after 1918. Some had been in reserve for many years, some had been more recently laid-up because of the effects of the U.S. Neutrality Act, while others had been added as the result of new ships in its replacement program, coming into service from 1937 on. The United States Maritime Commission had instituted this program with the realization that most of its ships built in the 1918-20 period where coming to the end of their economic life, even though they were far from worn out otherwise. Most of the American ships in the laid-up fleet were in two main size groups; those which had a carrying capacity of about 9,000 deadweight tons and a smaller size mostly built in Great Lakes yards with a carrying capacity of roughly 4,000 t.d.w.

Ninety-six such ships were transferred to British flag operation which temporarily

OCEAN VERITY
In peacetime guise as the CLAN KEITH. The American-built "Oceans" had a plain funnel
without the distinctive "lid" on top of the funnel which was a feature of all but a few of their
Canadian built sisters. The ship has just transited the Manchester Ship Canal hence her signal
mast being hinged down to allow passage under bridges. The "Oceans" numbered nine all told in
the Clan Line fleet.

FORT A LA CORNE
New out of the North Van Ship Repairs yard in August 1942. This vessel was lost by submarine
torpedo off Algiers in March 1943.

HULL No. 121 - FORT GROUARD
Almost ready for launching at North Van Ship Repairs. As the ERNEST G. PATHY this vessel became a unit in the Federal Commerce (Fednav) fleet, whose story is told in chapter 16.

FORT CARLTON.

FORT AKLAVIK
This ship was next in line to the author's ship in the landings at Morib, as part of the recovery
of Malaya from the Japanese.

ROSEDALE PARK.

FORT CHESTERFIELD
Entering Birkenhead docks as the HAWK.

FORT LA CLOCHE
Newly arrived and at anchor in Singapore Roads following the recovery of Malaya.

gave some respite from the losses inflicted by the German U-boats. Fortunately the USMC replacement program in 1937 saw a rekindling and expansion of American shipbuilding skills, so that as expansion was called for there was always a big enough pool of skilled management and supervisors to call upon instead of importing them from Britain as Canada had to do. Also the U.S. builders had developed a lot of experience with welding techniques so that as it turned out it became a lot easier to train unskilled labour, including many women, as welders rather than rivetters and other traditional trades.

Rivetting tended to be more labour intensive, was somewhat slower and produced a rather heavier hull, as the weight alone of the rivets and plate overlaps was greater than the amount of welding material which became a permanent fixture in the ship. Welding had the advantage that it produced a smoother external skin thus reducing surface resistance and promoting a more economical ratio of propulsive power to deadweight. This was because plates could be welded edge to edge without overlaps at the butts or the seams. However welding techniques at the time also tended to produce a hull more likely to crack and even cause a ship to break in two. Sometimes this was caused by inferior steel but a more likely cause was to be found in the quality of welding, perhaps caused by inadequate fusion when welding in low temperatures.

In 1941 the British government sent a purchasing commission to the U.S. and Canada. Existing U.S. yards were fully occupied with the fifty ship per year USMC replacement program in addition to naval work, so that any new program for British account had to be implemented by new yards especially laid out for the purpose. The British met with a syndicate comprising Henry J. Kaiser and Todd Shipyards Corporation. Todd was one of the largest U.S. builders with a first class reputation and a long history of involvement in the shipbuilding and repair industry. Kaiser knew little about shipbuilding but was well known as a "mover and shaker", who as an industrialist had the reputation of achieving big results with major projects. He was an organizing genius and with these qualities he was able to achieve some incredible results.

A contract to build sixty tramp freighters for the British government was negotiated. This was a normal commercial transaction with the ships being paid for in cash as they progressed and were completed. Two yards were laid out, each to build thirty ships. The first yard was located at Richmond, California in the name of Todd California S.B. Corporation, later becoming Permanente Metal Corporation Shipyard No. 1. This yard was laid out on conventional lines with a series of launching ways, but with the addition of a large prefabrication and assembly platform at the head of each set of ways, where large sections were assembled and slid into place on the ways. It put its first ship, the OCEAN VANGUARD into commission in October 1941. By July 1942 it had completed its program of thirty ships, six months ahead of contract date.

The second yard was located in Portland, Maine, being operated in the name of Todd-Bath Iron Shipbuilding Corporation. It took rather longer to get under way as the developers of the yard created seven steel graving docks in which the hulls were erected. The first ship was completed in March 1942 and the final vessel completed in November of the same year one month ahead of contract time. Upon completion of these contracts both yards moved into Liberty ship construction.

Both contracts were negotiated in January 1941, but with the coming of Pearl Harbour in December of that year, the U.S. quickly turned to the Liberty ship and expansion of its other shipbuilding programs. The Liberty of course had exactly the same hull design as the *Ocean* class and the Canadian ships described below, so that the yards were able to move into the Liberty program with little alteration to their operations.

Because the *Oceans* were really part of the same program as what commenced in Canada at the same time, and being sisterships of the *North Sands* vessels, I have listed for the record all the vessels built in this U.S. program in one of the appropriate tables at the end of this chapter.

The same British purchasing commission then visited Canada after setting up the contracts for the *Ocean* ships. Contracts for a virtually identical ship were let for 20 such vessels, the first of the *North Sands* design to distinguish them from the *Oceans*. North Sands was the name of the J. L. Thompson & Sons Ltd. shipyard of Sunderland from which of all ships in the program originated. The prototype was the EMPIRE LIBERTY built at the Thompson yard, while the first ship out of the Bath, Maine yard was the OCEAN LIBERTY. Of the 20 contracts, later increased to 26, eight went to Burrard Dry Dock Company in North Vancouver and the balance where split between Davie and Canadian Vickers at Montreal.

The American-built *Oceans* and the *North Sands* group were all coalburners, that decision being based on the fact that Britain had abundant supplies of good quality steam coal available, thus obviating the need to import fuel oil. Three Scotch boilers provided steam for triple expansion steam reciprocating engines of a time-tested design by North Eastern Marine Engineering Company of Britain. This machinery was regarded as being out of date in the U.S. and likely it was, but it had the advantage of being relatively cheap and easy to build and was adopted for the U.S. Liberties which were to pour out in their thousands. In fact the Americans were quite critical of the "outdated" *North Sands* design and its antique machinery, but it was a workhorse and just what the Allies needed being adaptable for many other purposes. In both the U.S. and Canada, the Liberties and the *North Sands* type and its variants, were fitted out as tankers, naval auxiliaries and even hospital ships in the American case.

The important point to remember is that with all the other demands on U.S. and Canadian industry there was still sufficient engine-building capacity in both countries to keep up with the demand. No ships were ever delayed awaiting an engine unit and when American engine builders fell behind, Canadian machinery was substituted, being later returned, so that some U.S. ships had Canadian machinery and vice-versa with some of the Canadian ships. The engine units were identical in any event so that the supply of interchangable parts and repairs never caused a problem.

The sixty U.S. *Oceans* followed American practice in that they were all welded, the original Thompson design being adapted to permit this. The Canadian ships followed the British design more or less without any important alteration, the Canadian experience at that time with welding being more limited.

In fact the biggest result of welding was that the butt ends of the shell plates were welded giving a smooth run along each layer of plating. The plates were still rivetted along the seams and to the frames so that an extremely strong hull resulted.

FORT ASSINIBOINE
Became the Canadian LAURENTIAN LAKE following disposal.

FORT TREMBLANT
Victoria-built for the USMC. She was one of the few disposed of by the Americans to foreign
owners becoming the BEATUS, owned in Cardiff by W. H. Seager & Co.

A TRIO AT WEST COAST SHIPBUILDERS, VANCOUVER YARD.
Left to right: MONTEBELLO PARK, WINONA PARK, FORT DUQUESNE.

FORT CUMBERLAND
Enters Vancouver Harbour as Lyle Shipping's CAPE FRANKLIN. Registered in Glasgow.

FORT FROBISHER.

FORT GRANT
Arriving at Capetown with a South African tug on her port side.

FORT LA TOUR.

FORT McLOUGHLIN.

Welding was used in the superstructure but the end result was that only about ten per cent of the content of the Canadian ships depended on welding, the balance being rivetted. One advantage was that no warbuilt Canadian ship, according to available records ever suffered from a structural failure, when in operation, which tended to support the opinion often offered at the time that rivetting was superior to welding in terms of strength.

As the war progressed the style and pattern of ownership also changed. None of these ship were sold to Britain. In fact ownership was vested in a crown corporation called Wartime Shipping Ltd. who in turn bareboat chartered the ships to the British Ministry of War Transport. Individual British shipping companies then took the ships off the Ministry of War Transport under management agreements.

The exceptions were the 90 ships of the *North Sands* type which were built for account of the United States Maritime Commission under the terms of the Hyde Park Declaration of April 20, 1941. Under this agreement between Canada and the U.S. the ships, which all carried the "Fort" prefix, were to be bareboat chartered to the British under Lease-Lend in the same way as the vessels vested in Wartime Shipping Ltd. Of the 90 a total of 22 were lost from war causes. After the war the survivors were returned to the USMC for lay-up in the reserve fleet, with a few being sold to foreign owners but the majority going to the scrappers in the late fifties and early sixties.

The remaining balance of 66 *North Sands* ships also carried the "Fort" prefix, and a further 47 the "Park" suffix. As with the other "Forts" they went to British bareboat charter, while the "Park" ships were operated on behalf of the Canadian government by Park Steamships Ltd. a crown corporation based in Montreal.

As the war progressed two adaptations of the *North Sands* were developed. These were the *Victory* not to be confused with the quite dissimilar American Victory ships, and the *Canadian*. The first of the two types had two watertube boilers and relied on oil fuel. The *Canadian* which followed, was designed to be more versatile in that it could fire its boilers on coal or oil, being fitted with both fuel oil tanks and coal bunkers. The *Victories* were used exclusively for the Royal Navy repair and maintenance ships detailed in chapter 11.

The Fleet Train supply ships covered in the same chapter were also *Victories* except for the three *Canadian* type built by United Shipyards at Montreal. A further 12 *Victories* were completed as tankers, which seemed to make sense as they were oilburners in any event. What seems more puzzling is why one of the coalburning *North Sands* type was also converted to a tanker to make a total of 13 all told. Of the three sub-types the *Victory* appears to have been the most highly regarded hence its choice as a Navy ship as well as for most of the other adaptations.

The accompanying table gives a breakdown of the actual number of each class of vessel along with war and marine losses up to the time that the vessels were disposed of from government ownership. Obviously the most numerically important are the *North Sands* type and its two improved versions the *Victory* and *Canadian*, plus the 42 ships making up the three sub-groups of the *Scandinavian* type. Descriptions of each of the yards involved in both the first and second world war is set out in chapter 15, I have listed the output of each yard, which it will be noted often includes several classes. This does not mean that these lists encompass the entire output of each yard, because many of the major yards also engaged in the building of warships.

As an example, take Burrard Dry Dock's extensive conversion programs, with the adaptation of American pocket aircraft carriers to Royal Navy standards, and the rebuilding of existing cargo liners into amenities ships as described in chapter 11.Also Yarrow's output of merchant ships was very small, but on the other side of the ledger they became prolific builders of naval vessels.

I should also comment on the war losses in these ships. The largest and first group were the North Sands/"Forts" built for either Canadian or American account for bareboat charter to the British. In total 155 such ships were built with the first delivery, the FORT ST JAMES coming into commission on Jan 29, 1942 and the last the FORT BRUNSWICK on December 20, 1943. These two years were extremely intensive in terms of submarine warfare so it was inevitable that this was the group most affected. The table will also demonstrate the very low level of losses in all the remaining groups because they followed on after mid-1943 and therefore had less exposure. One ship, the Scandinavian type AVONDALE PARK had the distinction of being the very last British vessel to be lost by enemy action. Even though she was owned by Park Steamship and registered in Canada, she was still legally a British ship as were all Commonwealth vessels. With the change in relationships within the Commonwealth that position no longer applies today, so that Canadian ship registration requirements now leave off the referance to nationality.

There is some disparity between the final net numbers of vessels for post-war disposal and figures quoted by the late Hon. J.V. Clyne in his book *Jack of all Trades: Memories of a Busy Life.* This disparity may have arisen because some vessels had already been disposed of prior to Mr. Clyne's appointment in 1947 described below.

Clyne was a well-known and highly respected marine lawyer practicing in Vancouver, who subsequently became a prominent judge and later after leaving the bench, became a leading businessman, retiring eventually as chairman of McMillan, Bloedel Ltd. Among his many appointments, and prior to going on to the B.C. bench, he served in the capacity of chairman of the Canadian Maritime Commission, a body which supervised the disposal of government-owned tonnage. This was made up of ships previously noted as being on bareboat charter to Britain, plus one on loan to Australia and the ships owned in the name of the Park Steamship Company, all of which latter group had always operated under the Canadian flag. Clyne's description of his dealings with the highest levels of government in presenting his recommendations is probably the best hands-on account of what went on at cabinet level leading to the formulation of a policy, which thus determined the future of these ships,

Mr. Clyne's appointment as chairman of the Canadian Maritime Commission was a reflection of the high esteem in which he was held. He took up his position as a servant of the then Liberal government, lead by W.L. McKenzie King who had been Canada's prime minister through the war. The prime minister seemed to have a knack for choosing strong capable men for the various positions in his cabinet. Such names as Louis St. Laurant and C.D. Howe will always have their names prominently in Canadian history. The Minister of Transport at the time was Lionel

Chevrier and it was he who approached Clyne to head the Commission.

There were many misconceptions in the public mind regarding the permanent maintenance of a government sponsored merchant marine. There was the euphoria of victory and talk about the strength of the Canadian economy coupled with much patriotic comment about the "second half of the twentieth century belonging to Canada". In the minds of some, Canada was a force in the world capable of surmounting any obstacle, and the country's merchant marine should therefore be developed as an instrument of national policy.

The world wanted our products of the forest, grain and and minerals, so why should we not insist in delivering in our own ships? Alas the world's shipping markets did not follow patriotic lines being more interested in efficient movement of cargoes at the most competitive rates. At the other end of the scale there were many who remembered the quite recent demise of the Canadian Government Merchant Marine which finally folded in 1936, having accumulated a net capital loss to the Canadian taxpayer of $82 million, plus the additional loss of interest on capital. CGMM failed precisely because of the workings of the market place in depressed trading conditions.

To these considerations could be added some highly important and practical aspects of shipping economics. Canadian manning and overall operating costs were already far higher than any country except the U.S. being further exacerbated by the attitude of militant, largely Communist dominated Canadian Maritime unions who seemed to have only one objective, namely to stir up strife on each and every occasion for short term gain. The smallest infraction might result in a shipboard strike leading to costly delays, and a mounting reputation for Canadian managed ships of unreliability.

A factor which was also recognised was that a healthy modern merchant fleet depended on continuous renewal with new up-to-date ships. Coupled with the advantage of favourable terms of sale, this gave rise to the requirement in the original sale to a Canadian owner, that upon disposal off the Canadian register, within a given time-frame, (usually ten years being the deemed economic life under the Canadian flag), the owner covenanted to place the proceeds of gain on resale into a special escrow fund so that these funds could be used to build or purchase new more modern replacement tonnage.

The requirement was far sounder than any notion that the government should repeat the mistakes of the first world war and become an ongoing shipowner. As explained elsewhere in this book, the economics of international shipping intervened so that most of the escrow funds were sold at a discount and the capital thus released went into domestic coastal shipping.

Creation of huge war-built fleets helped serve the purpose of defeating the enemy, but when it was all over it left a major surplus of shipping of the tramp types, which would never have come into being except for wartime conditions. The Americans learned this to their cost after launching a huge shipbuilding campaign in 1917 when they were left with an aging uneconomic fleet, which by the mid-nineteen thirties required the commencement of a planned replacement program in order to catch up.

After 1918, the British and other European maritime nations concentrated on fostering a healthy ongoing shipping and shipbuilding industry, so that the process of renewal was continuous as also was the rate of technical progress particularly in the widespread adoption of the diesel engine. The effects of the world-wide trade recession of the thirties dislocated much of this progress, but when war broke out, to a greater or lesser extent, all the European maritime countries, as well as Japan, possessed a high proportion of modern efficient vessels with an average age vastly less than the average for American shipping.

As explained in chapter 16 operating subsidies are an unsupportable proposition in most economies, unless it can be shown that inflowing benefits are even greater. The American experience was that the government did in fact provide operating subsidies to cargo and passenger lines on given trade routes where it was deemed to be of overall strategic importance to the interests of the United States. Shipbuilding subsidies being a single once-only proposition in the life of a new ship are supportable, and in my opinion a disservice has been done to the Canadian economy by abandoning them after a very successful period commencing in the fifties which enabled renewal and expansion of the important Canadian coastal fleet. There is a case for maintaining them perhaps on a more restricted basis to ensure the viability of a core shipbuilding industry.

Clyne mentions that he sought and received valuable input from Admiral Emory S. Land, his opposite number at the United States Maritime Commission, which convinced him that the provision of operating subsidies would simply be unacceptable. There was a lobby in Ottawa who wanted to maintain a Canadian merchant marine at any cost. When C.D. Howe, Minister in charge of postwar reconstruction, had sold some ships in the immediate postwar wake to Greek owners, and before Clyne took over, Howe had already come in for much criticism even up to cabinet level, but as Clyne subsequently affirmed by his actions, Howe's move was the right one.

In any event, Clyne framed proposals he was able to present to cabinet. They included one that all vessels should be disposed of to private operators as soon as their charters expired. Some charters were to private operators, such as Western Canada Steamships which had commenced business with one chartered *North Sands* vessel, but as soon as the superior oil burners became available, the company purchased this type. In fact overall the West coast companies acquired *Victory* and *Canadian* types in preference to the *North Sands* ships which went mostly to Eastern Canadian-based Greeks or foreign buyers.

Superiority or inferiority between one type and another is a relative term. As noted earlier the *North Sands* vessels were coalburners because of the huge quantities of cheap coal available in Britain, and ships voyaging to North America including the B.C. coast could obtain good bunker coal supplies.However some British first-class liner companies stayed with coal until quite late after the war, for particular reasons of their own.

One example was T & J Brocklebank, a company based in Liverpool and controlled by Cunard. Brocklebank ran a liner service to India and could obtain cheap bunkers there also. Although Indian coal was very dirty and did not have the thermal qualities of best Welsh steam coal, it was evidently satisfactory for those used to utilizing it, and this included many of the regular traders to and around India. Brocklebank acquired the very first North Sands hull to be built in Eastern Canada.

FORT STURGEON.

FORT CONNOLLY.

FORT ST. FRANCOIS.

CLEARWATER PARK
One of the Victory Tankers seen as the NORSE MOUNTAIN.

OTTAWA PANDORA
One of the China "B" type coasters. Seen as HAI YU at the commencement of her
delivery trip to China.

OTTAWA PAGE
Seen as SKEENA PRINCE in Northland Navigation service. Compare her B.C. coast masts and
derricks with the original cargo gear typified by OTTAWA PANDORA above.

This was the FORT VILLE MARIE which they ran as the MAKALLA until 1963 when she was scrapped in Belgium.

Incidentally the average cost for the first batch of Burrard-built *North Sands* ships was $1.85 million, which compared with the American built *Oceans* at $1.6 million per vessel.

The 13 tankers built from *Victory* and one *North Sands* type, evidently filled a wartime and immediate post-war need as tankers, but by 1954 the majority had been converted to dry cargo ships under various owners and then served out a normal ship life.

Among the lesser classes down to coaster size, the *Scandinavian* type were ideal for such as the North Atlantic timber trade to the U.K. and Northern Europe and for service to and from the West Indies. Being handysized they were also more versatile in going in and out of small ports, such as those around the Gulf of St, Lawrence, the Baltic and on the run to Murmansk.

The Canadian-designed 3,600 ton size tankers were few in number with all six going to Canadian east coast owners. They were versatile enough to go into the Great Lakes and make the occasional voyage to Venezuela for Maracaibo oil.

Of the two coaster classes, designated the "B" type of 1,250 tons deadweight and the "C" type of 300 tdw, all came into service after the end of the war, in fact 1946-7. Built in eastern Canadian yards, on the Great lakes and in the Maritimes, most of the smaller "C" type were taken up initially by Canadian owners. The only one to find its way to the west coast was the OTTAWA MAYFERRY which became the CAPILANO in the Union Steamships of B.C. fleet and later Northland Navigation's HAIDA PRINCE.

The "B" type, popularly known as China coasters were originally built for Pacific and Far Eastern service, all being constructed in four west coast yards. Clarke Steamships of Montreal acquired two which gave long service as NORTH COASTER and NORTH PIONEER. Two passed into the fleet of Union Steamships of B.C. as the CASSIAR and CHILKOOT, and one, the YUKON PRINCESS, served for a time in the Canadian Pacific west coast coastal fleet. The rest went to Far Eastern buyers, most of whom were Chinese. Of these the greater number passed into the fleet of the China Merchants Steam Navigation Company, formerly of Shanghai and later of Taipeh, Taiwan. My understanding is that they were virtually given to the Chinese for a nominal payment only, as a gift from the Canadian government to the Chinese government.

In the following fleet lists, each type is briefly described followed by a list of the ships pertaining to its own class. Ships built in Canada under these programs followed much more rigid specifications than the ships built in the first war. Such variations in size as did occur were very minor and have not been recorded here other than taking the same size for all ships of a given class. In instances where the vessel became part of a Canadian postwar ownership its new name is followed by a (C). War losses are indicated with an (*). Reference to the general index at the end of the book will provide a means of picking up the vessel again in her postwar fleet listing in chapters 12 and 13, when she passed into a Canadian fleet.

A comment on names is also appropriate. many of the Park Steamship vessels originally had "Fort" names allocated to them,while a few "Parks" became "Forts".

The reason for this is not clear fifty years later, but it may have been caused by manning problems. In other words an allocated Park vessel could not put a qualified crew together so rather that hold the vessel up perhaps she was reallocated to the British under a Fort name. Qualified Canadian crews were hard to find with such enormous expansion under way, and the British certainly had similar problems particularly in the supply of officers.

Certain names recurred on multiple occasions. FORT St. IGNACE, FORT SIMCOE and FORT CHIMO were used twice but no vessel went to sea under those names. FORT MIAMI was used three times but likewise never went to sea. MOHAWK PARK was also used three times but at least two of the ships had brief spells under the name. Why this confusion over names should have occurred is very hard to imagine as it is easy to find potential names of both Forts and Parks which were never used, but the above and one or two others appeared to fill a special role as "caretaker" names until a better one was found. When a name was settled the yard received a fancy scroll naming the Fort or Park with a brief history and geographical description. Some of these scrolls have been preserved in mint condition in the files of shipyards which have become archival material, but whether or not a similar scroll was mounted in the ship I have never found out.

Details and fleet lists follow for each group or type of vessels:

The OCEAN type
441ft 6in overall length x 57ft beam. All welded ships. Coal fuel. Vessels in alphabetical order from each yard. 7174 g.r.t. and about 10,500 d.w.t.

Built by Todd Bath Iron S.B. Corporation, Bath, Maine

Ocean Angel	Alcyone Angel
Ocean Athlete	Govert Flink
*Ocean Courage	
Ocean Courier	Clan MacBean
*Ocean Crusader	
Ocean Faith	Avisvale
Ocean Fame	Firby
*Ocean Freedom	
Ocean Gallant	Bennevis
Ocean Glory	Clan MacBeth
Ocean Gypsy	Clan MacBride
*Ocean Honour	
Ocean Hope	Bialystok
*Ocean Hunter	
*Ocean Justice	
Ocean Merchant	Jan Lievens
Ocean Messenger	Clan MacBrayne
*Ocean Might	
Ocean Pilgrim	Pikepool
*Ocean Peace	
Ocean Pride	Oakby
Ocean Rider	Nicholas K
*Ocean Seaman	

Ocean Stranger	Alcyone Fortune
Ocean Strength	Broompark
Ocean Trader	Merchant Royal
Ocean Traveller	Cape Corso
Ocean Wanderer	Ruysdael
Ocean Wayfarer	Clan MacQuarrie

Built by Todd California S.B. Corporation, later known as Permanente Metals Corporation Shipyard No. 1, Richmond, Cal. Same dimensions and fuel as above:

*Ocean Vagabond	
Ocean Vagrant	Atlantic Vagrant
Ocean Valentine	Benlomond
Ocean Valley	Malmesbury
Ocean Valour	Heronspool
*Ocean Vanity	
*Ocean Vanguard	
Ocean Vanquisher	Nereo
Ocean Vengeance	Ingleby
*Ocean Venture	
*Ocean Venus	
Ocean Verity	Clan Keith
Ocean Vesper	Clan MacQueen
Ocean Vestal	Farningham
Ocean Veteran	Belgian Veteran
Ocean Viceroy	Clan Kenneth
Ocean Victory	Jan Steen
Ocean Vigil	Ramsey
Ocean Vigour	Ramillies
Ocean Viking	Alceo
*Ocean Vintage	
Ocean Virtue	Andrea C.
Ocean Viscount	Clan Kennedy
Ocean Vision	Avismere
Ocean Vista	St. Edmund
*Ocean Voice	
Ocean Volga	Sithonia
Ocean Volunteer	Alcyone Union
*Ocean Voyager	
Ocean Vulcan	Cape Nelson

A high proportion of these vessels were acquired by first class British concerns such as Clan Line, Ben Line, Lyle Shipping and Ropner. By way of contrast relatively few of the Canadian-owned ships were sold directly to British owners, the probable reason being that it was easier for the shipping companies concerned to deal directly with London, rather than with Ottawa on ships which were basically the same.

The NORTH SANDS type built for account of the United States Maritime Commission

441ft 6in x 57ft. Some were a little shorter by up to three feet, from certain yards even though the length between perpendiculars never differed by more than six inches. The variation had no significant effect on gross tonnage and was probably the result of setting up the stem post at a slightly different angle. Coal fuel. Vessels named alphabetically across. 7130 g.r.t., over 10,000 d.w.t.

Fort Abitibi	Fort Acton
*Fort a la Corne	Fort Alexandria
Fort Ann	Fort Augustus
*Fort Babine	*Fort Battle River
Fort Bourbon	Fort Brule
*Fort Buckingham	Fort Camosun
Fort Cataraqui	*Fort Cedar Lake
Fort Chambly	Fort Charnisay
*Fort Chilcotin	Fort Chipewyan
Fort Churchill	*Fort Concord
Fort Confidence	Fort Drew
Fort Douglas	Fort Ellice
Fort Fairford	Fort Finlay
*Fort Fitzgerald	Fort Fork
*Fort Franklin	Fort Fraser
Fort Frederick	Fort Frobisher
Fort Gaspereau	Fort George
Fort Gibraltar	*Fort Good Hope
Fort Grahame	*Fort Halkett
*Fort Howe	Fort Hudson's Hope
Fort Jasper	*Fort Jemseg
Fort Kootenay	*Fort Lac la Ronge
Fort Lajoie	*Fort la Maune
*Fort la Montee	Fort la Reine
Fort la Trait	Fort Lawrence
Fort Liard	Fort Livingston
Fort Longeueil	Fort Louisbourg
Fort Maurepas	*Fort McLeod
Fort McLoughlin	Fort McMurray
Fort Meductic	Fort Mumford
Fort Nipigon	Fort Norman
Fort Nashwaak	Fort Paskoyac
*Fort Pelly	Fort Pembina
Fort Pine	Fort Pitt
Fort Poplar	*Fort Qu'appelle
Fort Rae	*Fort Rampart
Fort Reliance	Fort Remy
Fort Rupert	Fort Senneville
Fort Simpson	Fort Slave
Fort Souris	Fort Stager
Fort Steele	Fort Stikine
Fort St. Francois	Fort Tadoussac

Fort Thompson	Fort Tremblant
Fort Vermillion	Fort Walsh
Fort Wedderburne	*Fort Yale

Of the ships returned to the USMC the bulk were held in the Reserve fleet and eventually were scrapped in the late fifties through to the early sixties. A few were sold by the USMC to foreign owners mostly in Greece and Italy but no effort has been made to record names upon disposal.

NORTH SANDS type built for the Canadian government and bareboat chartered to the British government.

Measurement and other details as above with the previous block of vessels. List placed in alphabetical order, followed by name on disposal and a * for war losses and (C) where disposed of to a Canadian owner. Post war Canadian ownerships are covered in chapters 12 and 13.

Fort Aklavik	Irene Dal
Fort Albany	La Fleche (C)
Fort Ash	Royston Grange (C)
Fort Assiniboine	Laurentian Lake (C)
*Fort Athabaska	
Fort Beausejoir	Theogennitor
Fort Bedford	Othrys
Fort Bell	North Cambria
Fort Brandon	Laurentian Hill (C)
Fort Brunswick	Mulberry Hill (C)
Fort Buffalo	Radnor
Fort Cadotte	Fry Hill (C)
Fort Capot River	Haligonian Duke (C)
Fort Caribou	Falcon
Fort Carillon	Mount Royal (C)
Fort Carlton	Sorel (C)
Fort Chesterfield	Hawk
Fort Connolly	Marina Hill (C)
Fort Coulange	Andover Hill (C)
Fort Covington	Bedford Earl (C)
*Fort Crevier	
Fort Cumberland	Cape Franklin
Fort Dauphin	Warkworth
Fort Dease Lake	Ivor Jenny (C)
Fort Enterprise	Tavistock
Fort Erie	Maidenhead (C)
Fort Esperance	Nimaris (C)
Fort Fidler	Alcoutim
Fort Frontenac	Laurentian Valley (C)
Fort Glenlyon	Glenlyon (C)
Fort Glenora	George K.
Fort Gloucester	Bedford Prince (C)
Fort Grant	Commodore Grant (C)
Fort Grouard	Sea Crest (C)

Fort Henley	Pine Hill (C)
Fort la Cloche	Akti Hill (C)
Fort la Prairie	Elm Hill (C)
Fort la Tour	Assimina K (C)
Fort Lennox	Cariboo County (C)
*Fort Maissoneuve	
Fort Mattagami	Haligonian Princess (C)
Fort McPherson	Labrador (C)
Fort Michipicoten	Oak Hill (C)
Fort Mingan	Haligonian King (C)
*Fort Missanabie	
Fort Moose	Haligonian Prince (C)
Fort Musquarro	West Hill (C)
Fort Nakasley	Argodon (C)
*Fort Norfolk	
Fort Nottingham	Alendi Hill (C)
Fort Pic	Haligonian Baron (C)
Fort Richelieu	Beech Hill (C)
Fort Romaine	L'Alouette (C)
Fort Rouille	Ivor Rita (C)
Fort St. James	Temple Bar
Fort St. Joseph	Mavis Hill (C)
Fort St. Paul	Tarsian (C)
Fort St. Regis	Yale County (C)
Fort Sturgeon	East Hill (C)
Fort Ticonderoga	Ivor Isobel (C)
Fort Turtle	Arundel Hill (C)
Fort Vercheres	Maple Hill (C)
Fort Ville Marie	Makalla
Fort Wellington	Haligonian Queen (C)
Fort Wrigley	Pantrooper (C)

NORTH SANDS type built for Canadian government and managed by Park S.S. Company

Alder Park	Arthur Cross (C)
Algonquin Park	John Star (C)
Banff Park	Oakhurst (C)
Belwoods Park	Brookhurst (C)
Chippewa Park	Argobec (C)
Dentonia Park	Cedar Hill (C)
Elk Island Park	Louisburg (C)
Elm Park	Tricape (C)
Gatineau Park	Alkis (C)
Glacier Park	Wabana (C)
Green Gables Park	Papachristidis Vassilios (C)
High Park	Woldingham Hill (C)
Hillcrest Park	Bembridge Hill (C)
*Jasper Park	
Kawartha Park	Haverton Hill (C)

Kildonan Park	Inverness County (C)
Kootenay Park r/n Fort Nisqually	Kingsmount (C)
Lafontaine Park	Peterstar (C)
La Salle Park	Triland (C)
Laurentide Park	Winter Hill (C)
Mohawk Park r/n Fort Spokane	La Orilla
Mount Douglas Park	(marine loss 8.19.46)
Mount Orford Park	Orford (C)
Mount Revelstoke Park	Laurentian Forest (C)
Mount Robson Park (1)	Midhurst (C)
Nemiskam Park	Darton (C)
*Point Pleasant Park	
Port Royal Park	Fernhurst (C)
Prince Albert Park	Champlain (C)
Rideau Park	Amersham Hill (C)
Riverdale Park	Tridale (C)
Riverview Park	Shelburne County (C)
Rocky Mountains Park	Wynchwood Hill (C)
Rondeau Park	Sycamore Hill (C)
Rosedale Park	Poplar Hill (C)
Runnymede Park	Lake Michigan (C)
Sibley Park	Kenilworth (C)
Stanley Park	Haligonian Duchess (C)
Tweedsmuir Park	Bedford Queen (C)
Westmount Park	Nordicstar (C)
Whiteshell Park	Fir Hill (C)
Withrow Park	Kingsbridge (C)
Yamaska Park	Yamaska (C)
Yoho Park r/n Fort Highfield (1)	Darfield (C)

VICTORY type built for Canadian government and bareboat chartered to the British government
Measurements as with the NORTH SANDS type.

Fort Aspin	Triport (C)
Fort Astoria	Yarmouth County (C)
*Fort Bellingham	
Fort Biloxi	Maria G
Fort Boise	(marine loss 8.23.46)
Fort Brisebois	Pictou County (C)
Fort Clatsop	Montclair (C)
Fort Columbia	Sunrell (C)
Fort Crevecoeur	Trimont (C)
Fort Dearborn	Manx Navigator (C)
Fort Hall	Argofax (C)
Fort Island	Mont Rolland (C)
Fort Kaskaskia	Hants County (C)
Fort Kullyspell	Westminster County (C)
Fort la Baye	Digby County (C)
Fort la Have	Angusglen (C)

Fort Machault	L'Emerillon (C)
Fort Marin	Argojohn (C)
Fort Massac	(marine loss 2.1.46)
Fort Orleans	Mont Sorrel (C)
Fort Panmure	Sunvalley (C)
Fort Perrot	Rockside (C)
Fort Prudhomme	Cumberland County (C)
Fort Sakisdac	Marchcape (C)
Fort Saleesh	Argomont (C)
Fort St. Antoine	Manx Fisher (C)
Fort St. Croix	Argovic (C)
*Fort St. Nicholas	
Fort Venango	Colchester County (C)
Fort Wallace	Vancouver County (C)
Fort Yukon	Nanaimo County (C)

VICTORY type

Built for the Canadian Government and operated by the Park S.S. Company. All were transferred to Canadian owners except for GREEN HILL PARK sold foreign as a constructive total loss.

Measurements as with the NORTH SANDS type

Aspen Park	Lake Athabaska (C)
Atwater Park	Lake Atlin (C)
Beaton Park	Lake Babine (C)
Bowness Park	Manx Marine (C)
Bridgeland Park	Cambray (C)
Buffalo Park	Fort Charlotte (C)
Connaught Park	Seaboard Ranger (C)
Cornish Park	Fort Beauharnois (C)
Coronation Park	Seaboard Star (C)
Crystal Park	Chandler (C)
Dominion Park	Waihemo (C)
Dorval Park	Lake Canim (C)
Dunlop Park	Lake Chilco (C)
Dundurn Park	Marchdale (C)
Earlscourt Park	Lake Chilliwack (C)
Goldstream Park	Cottrell (C)
Green Hill Park	Phaeax II
Hastings Park	Lake Kamloops (C)
Kitsilano Park	Lake Kootenay (C)
Kootenay Park (3)	Seaboard Pioneer (C)
Leaside Park	Lake Lillooet (C)
Louisbourg Park	Harmac Chemainus (C)
Mewata Park	Harmac Crofton (C)
Mission Park	Ottawa Valley (C)
Mohawk Park (2)	Manx Sailor (C)
Mount Robson Park (2)	Lake Manitou (C)
Parkdale Park	Waikawa (C)
Queens Park	Seaboard Queen (C)

Queensborough Park	Fort Duquesne (C)
Richmond Park	Lake Nipigon (C)
Salt Lake Park	Wairuna (C)
Seacliff Park	Harmac Westminster (C)
Sapperton Park	Harmac Alberni (C)
Strathcona Park	Cabano (C)
Sunnyside Park	Waitomo (C)
Tecumseh Park	Argovan (C)
Temagami Park	Lake Pennask (C)
Tipperary Park	Lake Shawnigan (C)
Tobiatic Park	Seaboard Trader (C)
Tuxedo Park	Angusdale (C)
Wascana Park	Cargill (C)
Westbank Park	(marine loss 10.7.45)
Westend Park	Triberg (C)
Weston Park	Lake Sicamous (C)
Westview Park	Seaboard Enterprise (C)
Whiterock Park	Tantara (C)
Windermere Park	Lake Sumas (C)
Winnipegosis Park	Bayside (C)
Yoho Park (2)	Lake Winnipeg (C)

VICTORY type tankers
Built for the Canadian government and operated by Park S.S. Company. List includes one North Sands type, the POINT PELEE PARK which is listed below for convenience.
Measurement as with the NORTH SANDS type

Arlington Beach Park	Ageroen
Brentwood Bay Park	Norse King
Clearwater Park	Norse Mountain
Cypress Hills Park	Halcyon II
Moose Mountain Park	Benoil
Mount Bruce Park	Port Jerome
Mount Maxwell Park	Mount Maxwell
Mount Royal Park	Adna
Silver Star Park	Santa Cecilia
Wildewood Park	Irvingdale (C)
Willowdale Park	Georgia
Point Pelee Park	Ranella

CANADIAN type
Built for the Canadian government and operated by Park S.S. Company
Measurements as with the NORTH SANDS type.

Albert Park	Harmac Victoria (C)
Alexandra Park	Mont Sorrel (C)
Champlain Park	Vinland (C)
Cromwell Park	Harmac Vancouver (C)
Eastwood Park	Sunavis (C)

Elgin Park	Royal Prince (C)
Fairmount Park	Montreal City (C)
Frontenac Park	Victoria County (C)
Garden Park	Lake Cowichan (C)
Gaspesian Park	Mont Gaspe (C)
Grafton Park	Sunray (C)
Hampstead Park	Cheticamp (C)
Highland Park	Sunjewel (C)
Lakeside Park	Lakeside (C)
Lakeview Park	Halifax County (C)
Montebello Park	Walton (C)
Noranda Park	Oceanside (C)
Outremont Park	Brazilian Prince (C)
Portland Park	Marchport (C)
Princeton Park	Lake Minnewanka (C)
Rupert Park	Lake Okanagan (C)
Selkirk Park	Tahsis (C)
Seven Oaks Park	Seaside (C)
Simcoe Park	Sunmont (C)
Sunalta Park	Mont Alta (C)
Waverley Park	Dingwall (C)
Wellington Park	Sunwhit (C)
Winona Park	Lake Tatla (C)

4,700 tdw, SCANDINAVIAN type.

Built for the Canadian government and operated by Park S.S. Co. Ltd. Built in three groups to a common measurement, the original design, the "Revised" and the "Dominion". The Revised incorporated differing derrick and accomodation arrangements, while the "Dominion was fitted with a 'tween deck which made them more suitable for liner berth service. One ship only, launched as the HECTOR PARK, was bareboat chartered to the British government being named CAMP DEBERT and for convenience is included in the list below-

Measurements 315.5' length bp, 328" length overall, beam 46.5'
3cyl engines, coal fuel

ORIGINAL Design

Ainslie Park	Henri Mahout
*Avondale Park	
Beresford Park	Federal Ambassador (C)
Bloomfield Park	Sundale (C)
Camp Debert	Capitaine Do Huu VI
Cataraqui Park	Pigneau de Behaine
Chignecto Park	Alexandra de Rhodes
Confederation Park	Gialong
Crescent Park	Julia
Dartmouth Park	Captain Polemis
Dufferin Park	Dufferin Bell (C)
Fawkner Park	Kooralya

Kelowna Park	La Petit Hermine (C)
Kensington Park	Yersin
Lansdowne Park	Federal Trader (C)
Liscomb Park	Saint Malo
Manitou Park	Albert Calmette
Mayfair Park	Siderurgica Quatro
Montmorency Park	August Pavie
Oakmount Park	Oakmount
Rockcliffe Park	Brigus
Rockwood Park	La Grande Hermine (C)
*Taber Park	
Taronga Park	Federal Ranger (C)
Victoria Park	Tatuk (C)
Wentworth Park	Sundial (C)
Woodland Park	Huynh Khuong An

REVISED design

Argyle Park	Liverpool Packet (C)
Ashby Park	Siderurgica Tres
Baldwin Park	Chi Chung
Evangeline Park	Federal Mariner (C)
Hamilton Park	D'Arcy McGee
Mulgrave Park	Dun Yu
Rockland Park	Lin Kuo
Shakespeare Park	Sunprince (C)
Sunset Park	Siderurgica Cinco
Willow Park	Docteur Roux

DOMINION design

Bell Park	Federal Pioneer (C)
Cartier Park	Canadian Victor (C)
Lorne Park	Canadian Leader (C)
Maissoneuve Park	Canadian Highlander (C)
Sutherland Park	Canadian Conqueror (C)
Westdale Park	Canadian Observer (C)

3.600 tdw tanker

Eglinton Park	John Irwin (C)
Millican Park	Firbranch (C)
Nipiwan Park	Irvinglake (C)
Norwood Park	Elmbranch (C)
Otterburn Park	Sprucebranch (C)
Springbank Park	Poplarbranch (C)

"B" Type China coaster
For Canadian operation in Far Eastern coastal service

Measurements 214' bp 224' oa x 37' beam, T3cyl engine, oil fuel

Ottawa Page	Blue Peter II
Ottawa Pageant	Cebu
Ottawa Paget	Hai Shui
Ottawa Painter	Hai Tsin
Ottawa Palette	Hai Yun
Ottawa Palmer	Hai Hu
Ottawa Panda	North Pioneer (C)
Ottawa Pandora	Hai Yu
Ottawa Pangis	Luzon
Ottawa Parade	Hai Hang
Ottawa Parapet	Island Connector (C)
Ottawa Parian	Chilkoot (C)
Ottawa Pasqua	Hai Nan
Ottawa Patience	Panay
Ottawa Patrol	North Coaster (C)

"C" Type coasterFor Canadian operation in general coastal service.
Measurements 114.5' bp, 151' oa, x 27' beam, T3cyl engine, oil fuel.

Ottawa Maybank	Marinier
Ottawa Maybeech	Mary Sweeney
Ottawa Maybird	Tai Hang III
Ottawa Maybrook	Wolfe Islander
Ottawa Maycliff	Marleen
Ottawa Maycloud	Blue Cloud
Ottawa Maycove	Tai Hany IV
Ottawa Maycrest	Inagua Crest
Ottawa Mayfall	Mayfall
Ottawa Mayferry	City of Belleville
Ottawa Mayglen	Mayglen
Ottawa Mayhaven	Mayhaven
Ottawa Mayhill	C.P. Edwards
Ottawa Maymere	Maymere
Ottawa Mayrock	Keltic
Ottawa Mayspring	Maysprin
Ottawa Maystar	Maystar
Ottawa Maythorn	Maythorne
Ottawa Maytor	Hibiscus
Ottawa Mayview	Patricia Sweeney

Table of vessels built at all Canadian yards by class in Second World War Program:

Type	Number built
North Sands Forts	155
North Sands Parks	44
North Sands Park SS tanker	1
Victory Forts	32
Victory Parks	49
Victory R.N. ships	21
Victory Fleet Supply	9
Victory Tankers	12
Canadian Forts	0
Canadian Parks	28
Canadian Fleet Supply	3
Scandinavian original design	26
Scandinavian Revised	10
Scandinavian Dominion	6
3600 ton tankers	6
Coasters "B" type	15
Coasters "C" type	20
Conversion	1

List of War and Marine losses when vessels still owned by an agency of the Canadian Government or the United States Maritime Commission (USMC).

Avondale Park	WL	-May 7, 1945. Submarine torpedo, 1 mile S.E. of May Island, Firth of Forth, Scotland.
Fort a la Corne	WL	-Mch. 30, 1943. Sunk by submarine torpedo, 36.52N 01.47E. NW of Algiers,North Africa.
Fort Athabaska	WL	-Dec. 2, 1944. Blew up and on fire after explosion during air attack. Bari, Italy.
Fort Babine	WL	-Sep. 13, 1943. Bombed and sunk 41.31N, 14.39 W. SW of Cape Finisterre, N.W. Spain.
Fort Battle River	WL	-Mch. 6, 1943 Sunk by submarine torpedo, 36.33N 10.22W. West of Gibraltar.
Fort Bellingham	WL	-Jan. 25, 1944. Sunk by submarine torpedo 73.25N, 25.10E. Off NorthCape, Norway.
Fort Boise	ML	-Aug. 23, 1946. Aground. On Grand Shoal east of St. Pierre and Miquelon.
Fort Buckingham	WL	-Jan. 20, 1944. Sunk by submarine torpedo. Approx 08.50N, 66.25E. Near Maldive Islands, Indian Ocean.
Fort Cedar Lake	WL	-Mch. 17, 1943. Sunk by submarine torpedo. 52.14N, 32.15 W. Mid-Atlantic.
Fort Chilcotin	WL	-July 24, 1943. Sunk by submarine torpedo. 15.03S, 32.35W. SE of Bahia, Brazil.
Fort Concord	WL	-May 12, 1943. Sunk by submarine torpedo. 46.05N 25.20W. North of the Azores.
Fort Confidence	ML	-July 16, 1943. On fire and beached. Algiers, North Africa
Fort Crevier	ML	-Apr. 14, 1944. Severely damaged in FORT STIKINE explosion. Used as a hulk, scrapped 1948.
Fort Fitzgerald	WL	-Oct. 4, 1943. Sunk by aircraft torpedo. 36.42N 01.17E. West of Algiers.
Fort Franklin	WL	-July 16, 1943. Sunk by submarine torpedo. 22,36S, 51.22E. Off Reunion, Indian Ocean.
Fort Good Hope	WL	-June 11, 1942. Sunk by submarine torpedo. 10.19N, 80.16W. Off PanamaCanal zone, western Caribbean.
Fort Halkett	WL	-Aug. 6, 1943. Sunk by submarine torpedo. 09.30S, 26.50W. SE of Pernambuco.
Fort Howe	WL	-Sep. 30, 1943. Sunk by submarine torpedo. 37.19, 06.40E. Off Bona, North Africa.
Fort Jemseg	WL	-Sep. 23, 1943. Sunk by submarine torpedo. 53.18N, 40.24W. Off Cape Farewell. South tip of Greenland.

Fort la Maune	WL	-Jan. 25, 1944. Sunk by submarine torpedo. 13.04N,56.03E. North east of Socotra, Gulf of Aden.
Fort la Montee	ML	-Aug 4, 1943. On fire, forepart blew up, stern sunk by gunfire. Algiers.
Fort la Reine	WL	-Aug 17, 1942. Sunk by submarine torpedo. 18.30N, 75.20W. NE of Jamaica
Fort Lac la Ronge	WL	-Aug.3, 1944. 49.22N, 00.21W. Damaged by torpedo, towed into Appledore, N. Devon, England. Condemned and scrapped 1948.
Fort Longueuil	WL	-Sep.19, 1943. Sunk by submarine torpedo, 10S 68E. SE of Chagos Islands, Central Indian Ocean.
Fort Maissoneuve	WL	-Dec.15, 1943. Sunk by mine. Scheldt estuary.
Fort Massac	ML	-February 1, 1946. 51.53N 1.32E. Collision with THORNABY. Off Sunk Lightship. East coast of England.
Fort McLeod	WL	-Mch 3, 1944. Sunk by submarine torpedo and gunfire. 02.01N 77.06E. East of Maldive Islands.
Fort Missanabie	WL	-May 19, 1944. Sunk by submarine torpedo 38.20N 16.28E. Of Calabria, Italy.
Fort Mumford	WL	-Mch. 20, 1943. Approx 10n 71E. Sunk by submarine torpedo. Off Laccadive Islands, Arabian Sea.
Fort Norfolk	WL	-June 24, 1944. Mined and sunk off Normandy.
Fort Pelly	WL	-July 20, 1943. Bombed and sunk off Augusta, Sicily.
Fort Qu'appelle	WL	-May 17, 1942. Sunk by submarine torpedo. 39.50N 63.30W. South of Halifax.
Fort Rampart	WL	-Apr.17, 1943. Sunk by submarine torpedo. 47.22N 21.58W. SW of Cape Clear, eastern Atlantic.
Fort Stikine	ML	-April 14, 1944. On fire, exploded at Bombay. Remains scrapped.
Fort St. Nicholas	WL	-Feb. 15, 1944. Sunk by submarine torpedo 40.34N, 14.37E. Gulf of Salerno, Italy.
Fort Yale	WL	-Aug 8, 1944. Damaged by mine 49.26N, 00.33W. Aug 23, 1944 torpedoed while in tow 50.23N 00.55W. English Channel.
Green Hill Park	ML	-Mch. 6, 1945. On fire and explosions, beached at Vancouver, B.C. Salved but disposed of as a constructive total loss.
Jasper Park	WL	-July 6, 1943. Sunk by submarine torpedo. 32.52S, 42.15E. SE of Durban, South Africa.
Mount Douglas Park	ML	-Aug. 19, 1946. ashore 14.48N, 93.43E. On Preparis Shoal, Andaman Islands, Bay of Bengal.

Ocean Courage	WL	-Jan. 15, 1943. Sunk by submarine torpedo. West coast of Africa.
Ocean Crusader	WL	-Nov. 26, 1942. Presumed sunk by submarine attack. About 50,30N, 45.30W. North Atlantic.
Ocean Honour	WL	-Mch. 13, 1943. Sunk by aircraft bombs at Murmansk, N. Russia.
Ocean Hunter	WL	-Sep. 16, 1942. Sunk by submarine torpedo and gunfire, 12.48N, 50.50E. Indian Ocean.
Ocean Justice	WL	-Nov. 6, 1942. Sunk by submarine torpedo, 10.06N, 60.00W. West Indies.
Ocean Might	WL	-Sep. 2, 1942. Sunk by submarine torpedo, 00.57N, 04.11W. West coast of Africa.
Ocean Peace	WL	-July 12, 1943. Sunk by aircraft bombs mid-Mediterranean.
Ocean Seaman	WL	-Mch 15, 1943. Sunk by submarine torpedo, 36.55N, 01.59E. Western Mediterranean.
Ocean Vagabond	WL	-Jan. 1, 1943. Sunk by submarine torpedo, 50.17N, 20.11W. Mid-Atlantic.
Ocean Vanguard	WL	-Sep. 13, 1942. Sunk by submarine torpedo 10.43N, 60.11W. West Indies.
Ocean Venture	WL	-Feb. 8, 1942. Sunk by submarine torpedo, 37.05N, 74.46W. East coast U.S.
Ocean Venus	WL	-May 3, 1942. Sunk by submarine torpedo, 28,23N, 80.21W. Gulf of Mexico.
Ocean Viking	WL	-Oct. 11, 1943. Mined off Taranto. Condemned, sunk as blockship at Bari. After war salved by Italians, re-commissioned as merchant ship ALCEO.
Ocean Vintage	WL	-Oct. 22, 1942. Sunk by submarine torpedo, 21.37N, 60.06E. Indian Ocean.
Ocean Voice	WL	-Sep. 9, 1942. Damaged by submarine torpedo. 71.23N, 11.03W. Sunk by Royal Navy off Greenland.
Ocean Voyager	WL	-Mch. 20, 1943. Sank after bombing previous day at Tripoli, North Africa.
Point Pleasant Park	WL	-Feb. 23, 1945. Sunk by torpedo and gunfire 29.42S, 09.58E. N.W. of Capetown.
Taber Park	WL	-March 1945. Submarine torpedo, 52.22N, 01.53E. S.E. of Yarmouth, England.
Westbank Park	ML	-Oct. 7, 1945. Ashore at Magdalena Bay, Lower California, W. coast of Mexico.

Note:

FORT MUMFORD, OCEAN CRUSADER.

Positions listed at time of sinking presumed to be uncertain as evidence as to actual sinking of the vessels not available until German and Japanese records examined after the war.

FORT CONFIDENCE, FORT CREVIER, FORT LA MONTEE, FORT STIKINE

British war records list the above as marine losses. All were lost in warlike circumstances although evidently not the subject of a specific warlike act.

Chapter Seven

Twice Torpedoed: The FORT CAMOSUN

The FORT CAMOSUN had the unusual distinction among Canadian war-built ships of being twice torpedoed and living in both instances to sail again. In fact by any standard such an event was quite unique among merchant ships of any nationality, and there is nothing in the annals of wartime merchant shipping that I have ever seen, to quite equal this record. The two instances were roughly one and a half years apart. The second attack, which took place roughly eighteen months after the first on December 3, 1943, was in the Indian Ocean off the East African coast, and beyond mentioning it for the record it is not central to this story.

The FORT CAMOSUN was the first of eight "North Sands" type freighters built at Victoria Machinery Depot, Victoria, B.C. Completed on June 2, 1942, the ship loaded a typical B.C. cargo of lumber, plywood, zinc and lead. She departed on June 19 bound for the U.K., rounded Cape Flattery and was running in very calm weather down the Washington Coast when she was spotted by the Japanese submarine I-25 under the command of Commander Tagami of the Imperial Japanese navy. It was now in the early hours of June 20, when a torpedo from the Japanese submarine struck the ship roughly below the bridge, opening up No. 2 and No. 3 holds to the sea.

An immediate radio message from the FORT CAMOSUN gave the ship's position (47.22N, 125.30W) and confirmed that she had been hit and was sinking. The radio message was received by the Commanding Officer Pacific Coast Command and the corvettes HMCS QUESNEL, (Lt. J.A. Gow, commanding officer) returning from convoy duty, and EDMUNDSTON (Lt. R.D. Barrett, commanding officer) on anti-submarine patrol off southwest Vancouver Island, were instructed to go to the sinking ship's assistance.

As the corvettes sailed at top speed to the south, the submarine was shelling the ship presumably to save its limited supply of torpedoes. By this time the crew of the FORT CAMOSUN were safely in the boats with the ship laying dead in the water. One shell hit her on the starboard side amidships likely flooding the engine room.

HMCS QUESNEL reached the still floating and stricken vessel by 0800 hours. I-25 was picked up on QUESNEL's asdic and a depth-charge attack was commenced. HMCS EDMUNDSTON which was following, stopped to pick up the 31-man crew of the FORT CAMOSUN. EDMUNDSTON then proceeded to take the FORT CAMOSUN in tow, which by now was almost down to her main deck. She had no power and was not capable of being steered by even her emergency steering. Two hours later EDMUNDSTON had to slip the towline as the tow was making no progress. Lt. Barrett then put a party on board the CAMOSUN to jettison the deck cargo of lumber and to start pumping the holds, but the portable pumps placed on board were ineffective.

Next on the scene was the powerful Vancouver tug DAUNTLESS, while HMC corvette VANCOUVER (Lt. P.F.M. De Freitas) along with the U.S. armed yacht V994 arrived to assist with the anti-submarine duties.

The tow undertaken by the DAUNTLESS had to be abandoned at midnight of the 20th as the waterlogged ship yawed so badly as to be unmanagable. At 0230 the following morning the American tugs USS TATNUCK and HENRY FOSS of Tacoma, together with the salvage tug SALVAGE QUEEN from Victoria all arrived. Even with four tugs it remained a very difficult tow with the ship slowly settling further in the water. They managed to get her round Cape Flattery and took her into Neah Bay, on the Washington side of the Straits of Juan de Fuca, with the four tugs secured alongside steering the vessel under the direction of an officer from the QUESNEL.

She was then anchored in seven fathoms of water with part of her hull resting on the bottom, her foredeck awash and stern barely above water. SALVAGE QUEEN and HMCS EDMUNDSTON continued to stand by while HMCS QUESNEL returned the CAMOSUN's crew to Victoria.

When divers from HMCS NENAMOOK went down it was quickly ascertained that the plywood forming the bigger part of her cargo had been responsible for keeping the ship afloat. By June 24 the CAMOSUN was ready for towing to Esquimalt drydock this time with the help of the former first world war salvage tug CANADIAN NATIONAL No. 2 to assist. Being down by the bow as the accompanying photos depict she remaining difficult to steer as she yawed badly. EDMUNDSTON secured alongside to steer thus enabling the tugs to make about four knots up the Strait of Juan de Fuca and on the 25th the ship was safely moored in Esquimalt harbour.

While this drama was going on the same Japanese submarine shelled the lighthouse at Estevan Point without injury or effect to anyone on shore, but the two events did bring home to the Canadian public that the war was not as far away as it perhaps appeared.

Examination of the photos show that efforts were made to lighten ship. Part of the deck cargo can be seen to have been jettisoned, and all derricks or cargo booms had also been removed, including the huge standing net booms on either side of the two masts, which were a feature of these ships.

The FORT CAMOSUN was one of the group of 90 Canadian ships of the "North Sands" type, which were purchased from Canada by the U.S.A. under the terms of the Hyde Park Convention of April 1941, for bare-boat charter and flag operation by Britain. All were delivered between February 1942 and March 1943, and placed under the management of individual British shipping companies. War losses took 22 and of the remainder all had been returned to the U.S. Maritime Commission by 1948. A few were resold by the USMC to foreign owners but the majority ended up as scrap.

In 1947 she was returned to the United States Maritime Commission as her legal owners, and remained in lay-up until being disposed of for scrap in 1960.

FORT CAMOSUN
Beached at Neah Bay, Washington. SALVAGE QUEEN alongside. Much of her deck cargo and deadweight items like her derricks and the four big standing booms have been jettisoned in an effort to lighten ship.

FORT CAMOSUN
In tow following torpedoing.

Chapter Eight

A Narrowly Averted Disaster: The GREENHILL PARK

Few single events have etched themselves so deeply into the Canadian memory as the great Halifax explosion of 1917, when the munition-laden French steamer MONT BLANC blew up in the harbour entrance, following a fatal collision with the Norwegian S.S. IMO. The author's father was a crewman aboard the Cunard managed troopship JUSTITIA which arrived in Halifax the day after the explosion, and the memory of total devastation and raging fires everywhere remained a vivid recollection for the rest of his life.

During the second World War, Canadian-built steamers, created some sort of record in that no less than five were total, or constructive total losses in dockside explosions while working wartime cargoes of munitions. This in no way implies that there was some deficiency in the Canadian-built ships which had a bearing on these explosions. They were in truth all victims of wartime circumstances as with many other ships.

The first of these events was the loss of the FORT LA MONTEE which caught fire on August 4, 1943, at Algiers. The forepart of the ship blew up with tremendous force, damaging much of the neighbouring shipping in the harbour, while the floating stern section was eventually towed outside the harbour and sunk by gunfire. In the explosion a British escort vessel of some sort reputedly went up with her, although I have not been able to find a suitable reference in the British warship loss records.

The second such event took place at Bari, Italy, on December 2, 1943 when an American munitions ship took a direct hit from raiding enemy aircraft and blew up with tremendous force. The FORT ATHABASKA caught fire presumably from burning debris and exploded becoming a total loss. One other Canadian ship, the FORT LAJOIE was severely damaged in the same event but was saved, repaired and sailed again. Both these ships were built at Burrard Dry Dock Company, North Vancouver yard.

The next occurance was far closer to the scale of damage done in 1917 at Halifax. On this occasion the FORT STIKINE caught fire in the Alexandra Dock at Bombay on April 14, 1944. With a full cargo of high explosives and other munitions, plus considerable baled cotton the ship was a floating bomb. Efforts to put the fire out proved to be ineffective and the ship blew up with a most devasting explosion which destroyed a large section of Bombay, killed or injured thousands, and either destroyed, or severely damaged the other ten ships with which she shared the dock, including another Canadian-built sister ship, the FORT CREVIER, which was laying a full 1200 feet, or almost three ship lengths away from the STIKINE. At the time of the explosion the FORT STIKINE had 124 bars of gold on board worth over a million dollars, all of which disappeared as it was showered over the neighbouring area. The FORT STIKINE was just so much scrap metal, while the FORT CRE-

VIER was so severely damaged that she never sailed again, ending her days as a storage hulk at Bombay being broken up a few years later. The FORT CREVIER was built at United Shipyards Ltd. Montreal, while the FORT LA MONTEE came from North Van Ship Repairs Ltd (the former Pacific Dry Dock Company) at North Vancouver, and FORT STIKINE was built by Prince Rupert Dry Dock Company at Prince Rupert, B.C. shipyards.

Probably very few today remember how closely Vancouver came to sharing a similar fate on March 6, 1945, when the Canadian-built and operated steamer GREEN HILL PARK suffered four successive explosions, while loading lumber and explosives at Pier B at the foot of Burrard Street.

The GREEN HILL PARK was launched at Burrard Dry Dock Company, South Yard, which today is the site of the modern Vanterm Container Terminal. Following launch she was towed over to the North Vancouver yard for completion during January 1944, after which she left on wartime voyaging. She was of the Canadian Victory type, of 10,000 deadweight tonnage and an overall length of 441 feet. Launched as FORT SIMCOE she was transferred to the Canadian Crown Corporation, Park Steamship Company, while still in process of fitting out.

After 14 months of voyaging she had returned to her birth-place, Vancouver, in time for that fateful day in March, 1945. What caused a fire to break out has never been fully established, but the first evidence of a major problem was an explosion in No. 3 hold, located between the bridge structure and the boiler and engine rooms, which was followed by a further three powerful explosions.

The ship quickly became a blazing inferno with flames shooting high in the air, while with each new explosion lumber,and other debris rained down on the dock, and surrounding area and water. Every available ambulance in the city was called out but 6 longshoremen and 2 crewmen died and a further 19 were injured in the blasts. The death toll and lists of injured could have been far greater but for the fact that the explosions took place during the lunch hour. Had the four separate explosions been compressed into one concentrated explosion it is obvious that events could have been closer to the Halifax and Bombay catastrophies in intensity.

Every building for blocks around shook with the explosions, and many hundreds of windows as far away as Georgia Street were shattered while flying glass injured a number of people including some standing at their office buildings, such as in the Marine Building. Press reports of the day mention glass losses valued at $40,000, a piddling sum today but a large amount then.

Nearby vessels, including a sister ship the BOWNESS PARK, moored astern of the GREEN HILL PARK, were moved away as quickly as possible.

The harbour fireboat, the J.H. CARLISLE poured water into the ship, in fact an estimated 9 million gallons over three days and three nights, during which period the ship was cautiously towed out of the harbour, and beached at Siwash Rock in English Bay. The entire bridge structure collapsed into number three hold, with number two, being burned out entirely and number one hold severely damaged. The after part of the ship was evidently spared serious damage but the lifeboats on either side were destroyed by fire. Throughout the funnel managed to remain defiantly standing.

On March 12 the ship was pulled clear of the beach and towed around to

Ballentyne Pier, where she lay until August 20th, by which time she had been determined a constructive total loss. This means that the insurance underwriters paid out her full insurable value on the basis that she would cost more to repair than she was actually worth.

Official enquiries in both the FORT STIKINE and GREEN HILL PARK disasters indicated that while the probable cause of the fires could only be inferred as being the result of illegal cigarette smoking or similar carelessness, faulty stowage under wartime conditions of high explosives with other cargo was the cause of the explosions. A lot of short cuts were taken often under the authority of people who had little real experience of shipboard conditions. In an effort to speed cargo movements sometimes unwise decisions were made and probably the case of the FORT STIKINE was one of the worst examples. Through their positions of authority, port captains or others charged with getting the cargo through, could override the traditional authority of a ships captain and officers so it was here, particularly when a port was under the supervison of the military, that some of the problems arose.

In any event the GREEN HILL PARK was probably saved from dismantling as scrap by the war's end, as foreign shipowners scoured the world looking for anything that looked like a bargain in ships, even those which were severely damaged but otherwise repairable.

On August 20, 1945 she was returned to her builders, Burrard Dry Dock Company for reconstruction, having been purchased by Greek owners. She became firstly the PHAEAX 11 and was then sold again in 1956 to other Greeks, when she became the LAGOS MICHIGAN.

By the early 1960's scrappings of war-built ships were going on around the world on a large scale, as most of them were uneconomical to maintain in class and operate in competition against the new post-war ships. It was during this period that the GREEN HILL PARK came to her end in a shipbreaker's yard. Today only one of the war-built Canadian freighters still survives, this ship being HMCS CAPE BRETON which is laid up in reserve at Esquimalt, and is now in her forty-fifth year. She never sailed as a merchant ship having been completed as a naval auxiliary for the British Navy as HMS FLAMBOROUGH HEAD, but her hull and machinery and overall basic design was just like the GREEN HILL PARK and the FORT STIKINE and their sisters.

What a pity that this one remaining survivor of a memorable Canadian shipbuilding achievement cannot be preserved. However one artifact from these ships is to be found at Porpoise Bay, Sechelt, B.C. where one of the extra long standing net booms which were a feature of their wartime appearance is still at last report, rigged for log handling at the old B.C. Fir sawmill site. All record of its origin has long since disappeared, but quite a few of the "Park" ships were converted back to peace time service at Vancouver. Who knows, this boom quite possibly might have even come off the GREEN HILL PARK when she was stripped for rebuilding 45 years ago, and to this writer at least this seems like a relic which could be usefully preserved at say the Vancouver Maritime Museum, as a small memorial to all those fine 10,000 ton ships which were built in no less than seven B.C. Shipyards, and four more in Quebec. It is a sad commentary on Canadian shipbuilding, but of the wartime yards only five survive of the original twelve which built the North Sands type.

JUSTICIA ex STATENDAM
Was one of the first ships to reach the port of Halifax with the author's father on board following the disastrous explosion.

GREEN HILL PARK
Fireboat J. H. CARLYLE pours water into the shattered hull as the ship is eased out into Vancouver Harbour. Note the shell plating ripped open like a sardine can.

GREEN HILL PARK
The vessel is beached at Siwash Rock on the seaward side of Stanley Park. The bridge structure
has collapsed into number three hold, while the ship's ribs can be seen outlined under the
jet of water.

GREEN HILL PARK
Another view of the burning ship up against the shore of Stanley Park.

GREEN HILL PARK
Safely lifted out of the water at Burrard's floating dock. Reconstruction under way for her new Greek owners.

Chapter Nine

Tragedy at St. Pierre et Miquelon: The FORT BOISE

The brand new steamer FORT BOISE was eased out of her builder's berth in False Creek, Vancouver on September 17, 1943. Launched during the summer of that year, she was hull No. 127 at West Coast Shipbuilders Ltd. and had been built as one of the "Victory" version of the original "North Sands" type. She would have spent a few days on trials, but at last now being turned over by the builders, it is almost a certainty that she would have entered Vancouver harbour, loaded there with perhaps zinc and lead ingots topped off with lumber, plywood and possibly paper or pulp for her maiden voyage to the U.K.

This is pure speculation of course as few records can be accessed today covering those wartime voyages, many of which were never completed for this was still the height of the U-boat war and some of FORT BOISE's sisters never reached their first overseas destinations, being lost on their maiden voyages.

About five weeks short of her third completion date anniversary, she ran aground on the rocks off the French Island of St. Pierre. This was August 23, 1946, by which time the war had ended and the large fleet of the Canadian war-built vessels were busily engaged once again in peacetime voyaging.

Like all the "Fort" ships, excepting the 90 built for account of the U.S.M.C. under a form of lease-lend, she was owned by the Government of Canada, but bare-boat chartered to the British Ministry of War Transport, who in turn placed her out to the management of a British shipping company.

She had left Botwood, Newfoundland with a cargo of zinc concentrates according to available reports destined for a Northern French port, when she ran onto Grand Shoal, a rock strewn hazard lying to the east of St. Pierre. In doing so she drove in, past the surf pounding on to the Lost Children Shoal, a mournful name which requires little imagination as to how the shoal got its name.At the time visibility was very poor but it appears that the course she was on cut too finely towards the French islands, while a short distance to the south she would have avoided this hazard.

Farley Mowat in his book *Grey Seas Under*, which described the circumstances of the wreck, and the role of the famous salvage tug FOUNDATION FRANKLIN, owned by Foundation Maritime, with all the highly charged drama, which is Mr. Mowat's specialty. Beyond mentioning that she was inbound for the gulf the available records add little to the fact that the actual amount of concentrate loaded at Botwood was about 5000 tons. Nor does Lloyd's Confidential Index add anything, so one is left to the conclusion that the ship was on a coasting leg of the voyage to top off with additional cargo from a Gulf port such as Cornerbrook.

The first intimation of the casualty reached Foundation Maritime's office in Halifax via a radio messaage from a shipping agent at St. Pierre, who added that the weather was good and that the FORT BOISE had not sustained serious damage.

All this hinted at good salvage prospects. The FRANKLIN was in the process of having her annual inspection and refit, but Captain Woollcombe the general manager was able to convince the steamship inspectors from the Department of Transport to issue a temporary permit, thus enabling bunkers, stores and salvage gear to all be loaded for quick departure during the course of the same day that the casualty occurred, i.e. August 23. Under Captain Brushett the FRANKLIN ploughed out to sea and by the 25th reached the stricken steamer.

Laying at anchor a half mile outside the shoals, the FRANKLIN'S salvage foreman Tom Nolan made his way by dory to take a first look at the wreck. What he found was a dismaying sight, with the ship firmly impaled among a sea of rocks from her bridge forward. Edging in through the reefs and sunken rocks Brushett was able to put a salvage crew aboard with five powerful salvage pumps and work commenced immediately to pump out the two forward holds, while clamshell buckets using the ship's gear did their best to keep up with the torrent of slimy concentrate in an effort to lighten the ship and make her fit for pulling off.

While this was going on the FRANKLIN laid out two sets of ground tackle 2000 feet to seaward. Captain Brushett knew that the weather was the big risk. It could either assist or intervene at the wrong time and he calculated that they needed another 48 hours of uninterrupted fine weather to finish the job. As so often happens on salvage jobs the fates were not kind. The weather worsened. The tug TRAVERSE had put out from Sydney, N.S. with additional gear and pumps, but radioed that she had had to turn back on account of the weather. Brushett had 17 men in his salvage crew aboard the FORT BOISE and his concern now was to take them off along with the master, chief officer, chief engineer and radio officer of the freighter who had elected to stay aboard.

By now the water stirred up by gale force wind was a cauldron of white surf which made the recovery of the salvage crew particularly dangerous although it was accomplished under the worst of circumstances. The freighter's officers refused to leave their doomed ship as it would effectively amount to a legal abandonment. At least while they remained aboard, the ship was in the legal possession of the owner's representatives.

The FORT BOISE radio officer sent a last despairing message, to the effect that the ship was breaking up. FRANKLIN replied that they should abandon now and try to lay with their boat to a line attached to the leeside of the wreck. The FRANKLIN could see a light aboard the doomed ship but suddenly it was extinguished. She had gone and with her the four souls remaining aboard had perished. In the following days the wreck continued to break up, and the four bodies of her remaining crew were found badly battered further up the shoreline. It was a sad and unsuccessfual end to a herculean effort by the FOUNDATION FRANKLIN and her crew.

Chapter Ten

THE SPECIAL ROLE OF A HALIFAX SHIPPING AGENCY

In this chapter the author wishes to acknowledge the key role of I.H. Mathers & Son Ltd. in securing a large fleet of Canadian war-built ships for operations under both the Canadian and the British flags.

Before going into detail some background on the Mathers company would be appropriate. The firm was founded by the current president's great-grandfather Isaac H. Mathers, a native of Newry in present day Northern Ireland. Mathers joined a Liverpool shipping company and sailed from there for New York in 1870 to open an office in that city for his employers. From there he moved to St. John, New Brunswick to open a Canadian branch. In 1872 he arrived in Halifax and set up his own business.

The port of Halifax in those days was already a busy place with a forest of masts, and both coastal and deepsea ships, to and from a great variety of foreign ports. It was, as it is today, Canada's premier east coast naval and commercial port with a fine sheltered deepwater harbour.

Mathers wasted no time in joining the competitive hurly-burley of a busy port. Competition between numerous shipping agents was very heavy, requiring a great deal of stamina and agility in order to get ahead, and from the beginning the Mathers firm took a leading position in developments. One such was exemplified by a legal notice which appeared in the "Halifax Morning Chronicle" of May 30, 1872:-

"The fine new brigantine, LADY JOSVEN, will be dispatched from
Liverpool on 23rd May for this port. For freight and other particulars,
apply in Halifax to Isaac H. Mathers"

"The fine new brigantine, LADY JOSVEN, will be dispatched from Liverpool on 23rd May for this port. For freight and other particulars, apply in Halifax to Isaac H. Mathers"

A practice resorted to by Mathers was to station a man on Citadel Hill to keep a lookout for inbound ships. When one was seen, the man would race down to the waterfront, and then would row out to the incoming vessel in the hope of securing its agency, and in many instances they were apparently successful. In those days Maritimes and Quebec lumber represented a huge export trade, particularly to Britain, and throughout much of the nineteenth century it had been common practice to build sailing vessels, particularly barques, brigantines and schooners and load them up with lumber where both the ship and cargo were then sold to the highest bidder in a British port. Quite a few British shipowners got their first start by buying Canadian east coast-built vessels, and then putting them into regular trade, much of it with Canada for lumber, and salt-cod.

Mathers was joined in 1890 by his son Isaac Harry, by which time the firm was exporting Nova Scotia lumber and canned lobster. The numbers seem puny today but in 1898 Mathers bought more than 26,000 pounds of canned lobster at an average price of 20 cents per pound, which was exported overseas. It is in this period also that Isaac H. Mathers applied to became local consul for the kingdoms of Denmark, Sweden and Norway. His son Harry later became vice-consul for Czarist Russia in 1899, but following the October Revolution in 1917, the appointment was cancelled by the new Bolshevik regime.

In 1906 Harry Mathers succeeded his father as president of the firm which by then had further diversified into exporting wood pulp, salt fish and importing molasses. To further their trade with the West Indies, Mathers built two sailing vessels, the first of which was the three-masted schooner HELEN MATHERS. They also became agents in Halifax for leading Scandinavian marine insurance firms.

The firm was extremely busy in both world wars acting as agents for great numbers of the ships which came into the port, as it was among the most important single convoy assembly points in the allied convoy system.

With the death of Harry Mathers in 1945 the control of the company passed to his two sons Harry Isaac ll who became president, and his younger brother Evatt who became senior vice-president. This coincided with plans for large scale disposals of Canadian owned war-built ships through the Canadian Maritime Commission. This included the entire Park Steamship Company fleet and many additional vessels on bareboat charter to the British government.

I.H. Mathers & Son Ltd. acting as principals and agents for others, purchased on their behalf, no less than 84-10,000 ton freighters owned by the Canadian government some of which remained Canadian-operated while the rest were placed under the British flag and managed by British operators. This was the largest single transaction involving government steamships and has probably only been exceeded by the deal involving a sale of British government tonnage to Lord Inchcape of the P & O group following the first world war. Inchcape purchased all told 196 ships for resale to British owners, more as a means of quickly getting the British government out of the shipping business in the face of political calls which might have led to a nationalization of the British shipping industry.

There was no danger of the Canadian government wishing to stay in the shipping industry, which would have inevitably led to the Canadian public being saddled with an enormous cost burden as the record for government-owned shipping industries both here and in other countries had been dismal. Memories were still fresh as it was only about 12 years since the Canadian Government Merchant Marine fleet (CGMM) had been finally disposed of with an enormous loss to the taxpayer, as described in chapter 2.

The chairman of the Canadian Maritime Commission was the eminent Vancouver lawyer and later judge, the Hon. J.V. Clyne who was invariably at centre stage in any undertaking with which he became associated, his final appointment being as chairman of McMillan Bloedel, which he piloted through its greatest expansion years. Mr. Clyne has now passed away, but his book *Jack of all Trades: Memories of a Busy Life* is probably the best, most readable and authoritative account of an interesting episode, among the highest levels of government, and the setting of policy in disposing of this fleet. The policy was in fact developed following Mr. Clyne's recommendation, being recalled in more detail in chapter six.

FORT WALLACE
New out of her Burrard, North Vancouver building yard. The familiar distinctive cowl on the funnel can be seen. Like a lid, this contraption was not used in this form except on Canadian war-built ships. From above the exhaust pipe splayed out rather like a flower, shielding the usual platform inside the funnel from weather.

VANCOUVER COUNTY
This photo of the FORT WALLACE after the war, makes a nice comparison with the preceding picture being taken at almost the same angle. Gone are the towering net booms abreast of each mast, as well as all the gun tubs, and the quick release life rafts abreast of each mast.

YARMOUTH ~~VARMOUTH~~ COUNTY
Both this ship and the VANCOUVER COUNTY are Victory type sister ships but examination of the photos will show that at least in the superstructure they differ in matters of detail. Acadia owned the largest East coast fleet of former Park Steamship vessels.

Press reports of the time talked optimistically of Halifax becoming one of the greatest ocean shipping operating centres in the world, and of course the sense of euphoria was also prevalent in Montreal and Vancouver, which with Halifax represented the three great deepsea ship-owning ports of the country. The Mathers connections with the London-based Greeks were particularly strong, and many of the ships purchased within the group of 84 vessels passed to Canadian companies owned or controlled by the London Greeks. Acadia Overseas Freighters Ltd. of Halifax, a Mathers' company, became the second largest shipowner under the Canadian flag with 15 vessels. The largest was Western Canada Steamships with 20, although this latter company purchased three more modern post war-ships as replacements for war-built ships of which it had disposed.

The arguments for and against Canadian owned deepsea shipping are discussed elsewhere in this book, as also are the histories and fleet lists of individual Canadian owners including Acadia, but like other Canadian shipowning operations the Mathers-managed or connected companies declined, and eventually went out of business as an aftermath of international shipping economic trends which eventually destroyed the feasibility of a Canadian deepsea shipowning industry.

I.H. Mathers & Son Ltd. continues today under the leadership of the fourth generation of the family Harry I. Mathers III who took over from his father in 1980. It functions as a shipping agency looking after a growing number of freighters, container ships, passenger liners, and foreign fishing vessels, and in the late sixties started a tugboat business to assist tankers in the Canso Strait area. Mathers moved into the offshore supply vessel business as owners and operators of the ten vessel fleet of Balder Offshore Canada Inc. although this company is believed to be now no longer functioning. It also operates a marine recruitment agency to place trained Canadian officers and seamen on ocean-going vessels as well as a travel agency. Branch offices are located at St. John, N.B. Port Hawkesbury N.S. and St. John's Newfoundland.

The Mathers house flag of a black "M" in a white square on a green ground, has been known around the world's oceans for a good many years now, and today remains as the groups trade mark.

Chapter Eleven

THE FLEET TRAIN

This term was first heard by the author when serving in the British Navy, and being directed at Singapore to take my tank landing craft alongside HMS BUCHAN NESS to have one of our Paxman Ricardo diesels replaced by a re-cycled unit which had been completely rebuilt in the BUCHAN NESS workshops. It was a slick efficient process of refurbishment largely unknown before the war, but now commonplace in many fields as we know when an entire unit or major part of our car engine is lifted out and quickly replaced with a rebuilt component.

Walking the decks of the BUCHAN NESS was also the first occasion when I had been aboard a Canadian-built vessel, and when this was combined with the spit and polish of the Royal Navy, she made for a very smart and immaculate ship. Even to my then young inexperienced eye, I could see that she had been built with great care and was certainly on a par with the best standards to be found in any navy.

Reaching Hong Kong my next visit to Canadian-built ships was to go aboard first the FORT DUNVEGAN and a few weeks later the FORT KILMAR to replenish certain of our ship's stores. This was also my first introduction to Canadian cigarettes with "Sweet Caporal" and "MacDonalds Export", purchased on board.

What all three of these ships represented were typical units in the Fleet Train, designed to in effect be a floating mobile navy base, supplying maintenance, engineering repairs, and goods and services on a scale only to be normally found in a shore navy establishment. When Japan burst so explosively on her path of Pacific and South East Asia conquest, every major naval base west of Pearl Harbour and normally open to the Allies was overrun. The British bases at Hong Kong and Singapore quickly fell, as did the U.S. base at Manila and the Dutch base at Sourabaya in Java. The closest major bases, as distinct from less significant bases, were therefore on a very wide periphery at Pearl Harbour, Sydney NSW and Trincomalee, Ceylon, or modern day Shri Langka, and in each instance too far away to be capable of acting as front line bases. Beyond that line it became a matter of Simonstown in South Africa, San Francisco, Bremerton and Esquimalt, or Britain's home bases. Quite apart from that it was to become a highly mobile war of island hopping requiring close support in a great variety of ways. When the tide of war changed and the Japanese went on the retreat, it also followed that regained bases would be devastated in varying degree and would take time to bring back to a level of efficiency capable of sustaining the offensive.

The Royal Navy did not possess a large fleet of suitable ships except for oil tankers and some submarine depot ships, quite a few of which had already been lost. In normal circumstances with its large network of shore bases it did not need a big fleet of auxiliaries. Quite apart from that it also had its hands full in the Atlantic and Mediterranean. The U.S. Navy on the other hand was quick off the mark and recognised the nature of the Pacific war so that with its huge merchant shipbuilding program already under way with high-class C1, C2 and C3 type ships, it was able to divert many of these ships into the role of navy auxiliaries almost from the time it came into the war.

With British yards having little spare capacity and having arranged for certain new Empire-type ships to be finished as auxiliaries, the Admiralty in London turned to Canada for a substantial fleet of navy auxiliaries. Altogether 21 of the Canadian 10,000 tonners were nominated to be completed as one or other of several different categories of specialist maintenance ships. Of these 16 were completed and commissioned into the Royal Navy, while the remaining uncompleted five were suspended at the end of the Japanese war, and were sold to private owners and completed as merchant ships.

The supply or stores issuing ships numbered 16 of which eight were equipped with refrigeration capacity. The West coast yards built 13 while three came from United Shipyards at Montreal. As the ships made their way to the Far Eastern theatre it is believed that the majority of stores were loaded at Vancouver, with the exception of the three Montreal ships which were designated as ammunition carriers. Ammunition was mostly manufactured in Eastern factories so that they would be relatively close by, for initial loading, although to what extent this might have been a consideration is not known.

One other task was allotted to the prolific Burrard Dry Dock Company. This was to provide two amenities ships as part of the fleet train. For this purpose two Blue Funnel diesel cargo liners, the MENESTHEUS and AGAMEMNON, were sent to Vancouver to be converted. In addition to a movie theatre, games room, gymnasium, and a restaurant, both ships carried a complete brewery capable of making draught beer from distilled sea water. I believe that the AGAMEMNON did not actually go into service as the end of the war halted any further work, but I did go aboard the MENESTHEUS at Hong Kong and among other facilities sampled beer brewed by the ship's brewery. Everyone was used to aeriated bottled beer, but Menestheus draught was by comparison very flat and needed some getting used to. In charge of an experienced brewmaster and brewery staff working under unusual conditions, they did a very good job. Being brewed from distilled sea water any aeration had to be put back into the brew. The flavour was good, the colour was good and once a pint had been consumed to get used to it, it was not a bad brew considering the conditions under which it was made.

After the return of peace MENESTHEUS followed her sister back to her owners. The five incomplete maintenance ships were quickly sold off to private owners and so far as I am aware all conversion work was done at the Vancouver yards of the builders. Certain others as listed in the fleet list which follows, also reverted to merchant ships at later dates after the war. Of the remainder all had careers in the Royal Navy of varying length, and some were altered so drastically as to be unrecognizable. Of the stores issuing ships seven were transferred to the Admiralty and the remainder were converted to peacetime merchant ships.

All told the group of 37 Canadian-built vessels, plus the two converted in Canada for the British constituted a very important fleet in its own right. None were lost due to enemy action and the bulk did not come into service until the war was virtually over.

H.M.S. BEACHY HEAD.

AN UNIDENTIFIED MAINTENANCE SHIP
She looks like a landing craft maintenance ship and may be H.M.S. BUCHAN NESS.

H.M.S. HARTLAND POINT
At anchor in Esquimalt Roads. Before her navy career came to an end her appearance was
to be vastly changed.

FORT SANDUSKY
A fleet train supply ship built by United Shipyards at Montreal, seen at anchor in
Singapore Roads in 1946.

FORT LANGLEY.

FORT ALABAMA.

FORT KILMAR.

LAKEMBA
Converted for W.R. Carpenter & Company of Sydney from the uncompleted H.M.S. SPURN
POINT. Of all the conversions this one departed furthest from the original North Sands design.
Still a steamer, she affected a stumpy motorship funnel and an enclosed bridge with a prominent
raised forecastle, which made her look like a Scandinavina motorship.

NAVY AUXILIARIES

VICTORY Type, all carried names of geographical features around the British Isles

Measurements as with the NORTH SANDS type

Beachy Head	Escort maintenance ship. Blt. Burrard Dry Dock Co. 1945, transferred to Royal Netherlands Navy as VULKAAN, Reverted to R.N under original name 1950, Acquired by R.C.N in 1952 and became HMCS CAPE SCOTT. Now scrapped.
Berry Head	Escort maintenance ship.Blt. Burrard Dry Dock Co. 1945 Stayed on R.N. strength until disposed of for scrapping.
Buchan Ness	Landing craft maintenance ship Blt. West Coast Shipbuilders Ltd 1945. Now scrapped.
Cape Wrath	Coastal craft maintenance ship. Blt. West Coast Shipbuilders 1946.Disposed of for merchant ship conversion. Became MARINE FORTUNE in 1951, SAN MARCOS in 1954, and DITMAR KOEL of the German Hanseatic Line in 1955. Now scrapped.
Dodman Point	Landing craft maintenance ship. Blt. Burrard Dry Dock Co. 1945. Now scrapped.
Duncansby Head	Escort maintenance ship. Blt. Burrard Dry Dock Co. 1945. Stayed on R.N. strength and became a depot ship.
Dungeness	Landing craft maintenance ship. Blt. West Coast Shipbuilders 1945. Disposed of to W.R. Carpenter & Company of Sydney, N.S.E. and converted to merchant ship LEVUKA.
Fife Ness	Landing craft maintenance ship. Blt. Burrard Dry Dock Co. 1945. Became R.A.F. depot ship ADASTRAL in 1947 and then converted to merchant ship GRANHILL in 1953.
Flamborough Head	Escort maintenance ship. Blt. Burrard Dry Dock Co. 1945. Acquired by Royal Canadian Navy. Renamed H.M.C.S. CAPE BRETON. At last report in lay-up at Esquimalt and believed to be the only survivor of the entire Canadian war-built fleet of 10,000 ton freighters.
Girdle Ness	Landing craft maintenance ship. Blt. Burrard Dry Dock Co. 1945. With DUNCANSBY HEAD located at Rosyth, Scotland in 1962 to form depot establishment H.M.S. COCHRANE.

Hartland Point	Landing ship maintenance ship. Blt. Burrard Dry Dock Co. 1945. Became base ship at Hong Kong in 1960. laid up at Portsmouth in 1965. Understood now scrapped.
Mull of Galloway	Escort maintenance ship. Blt. North Van Ship Repairs Ltd. 1945. Launched as KINNAIRD HEAD, but renamed before commissioning. Scrapped at Hamburg.
Mull of Kintyre	Armament maintenance ship. Blt. North Van Ship Repairs Ltd. 1945. Converted to minesweeper maintenance ship.
Mull of Oa	Unclassified as to form of maintenance ship. Blt. North Van Ship Repairs Ltd. 1945. Completed as merchant vessel TURAN.
Orfordness	Unclassified as to form of maintenance ship. Blt. West Coast Shipbuilders. 1945. Completed for W.R. Carpenter & Company of Sydney N.S.W. as merchant ship RABAUL.
Portland Bill	Armament maintenance ship. Blt. Burrard Dry Dock Co. 1945. Sold out of R.N. in 1951 and converted to merchant ship ZINNIA.
Rame Head	Escort maintenance ship. Blt. Burrard Dry Dock Co. 1945. Placed in operational reserve in 1962.
Rattray Head	Unclassified as to form of maintenance ship. Blt. Burrard Dry Dock Co. 1946. Completed as merchant ship IRAN.
Selsey Bill	Armament maintenance ship. Blt. Burrard Dry Dock Co. 1946. Completed as merchant ship WAITEMATA for Union S.S. Company of New Zealand.
Spurn Point	Landing craft maintenance ship. Blt. Burrard Dry Dock Co.1945. Converted in 1947 to merchant ship LAKEMBA for W.R. Carpenter & Co. of Sydney N.S.W.
Tarbat Ness	Unclassified as to form of maintenance ship. Blt. West Coast Shipbuilders, 1945. Converted to merchant ship LAUTOKA for W.R. Carpenter & Co. Sydney, N.S.W.

It is interesting to note that of the ten disposals to private owners, no less than five went to Australian and New Zealand owners. W.R. Carpenter sold their first two acquisitions in 1947 at about the same time as they acquired two further vessels the LAUTOKA and LAKEMBA. The latter vessel became very well known in Vancouver as she operated a regular passenger-cargo service between Sydney and Vancouver until the early sixties.

FLEET TRAIN SUPPLY SHIPS
VICTORY type except for the three vessels which were of the
CANADIAN type, built by United Shipyards Ltd.
Measurements as with the NORTH SANDS type.

Fort Alabama	Blt. Burrard 1944 - Refrigerator capacity. Became merchant ship GULFSIDE.
Fort Beauharnois	Blt. West Coast Shipbuilders, 1945 as the CORNISH PARK. Refrigerator capacity. Became permanent addition to R.N. in 1948.
Fort Charlotte	Blt. West Coast Shipbuilders, 1944 as the BUFFALO PARK. Refrigerator capacity. Became permanent addition to R.N. in 1947.
Fort Colville	Blt. North Van Ship Repairs, 1943. Became air stores issuing ship in 1945. Released from service and became merchant ship LAKE KOOTENAY in 1950.
Fort Constantine	Blt. Burrard Dry Dock Co. 1944. Refrigerator capacity. Became permanent addition to R.N. in 1949.
Fort Dunvegan	Blt. Burrard Dry Dock Co. 1944, Refrigerator capacity. Became permanent addition to R.N. in 1949.
Fort Duquesne	Blt. West Coast Shipbuilders Ltd. 1944, as the QUEENS-BOROUGH PARK. Refrigerator capacity. Became permanent addition to R.N. in 1947.
Fort Edmonton	Blt. Burrard Dry Dock Co. 1944. Refrigerator capacity. Released for merchant ship service in 1947 as FEDERAL VOYAGER.
Fort Langley	Blt. Victoria Machinery Depot 1945, as an air stores issuing ship. 1949 became a permanent addition to the R.N.
Fort Kilmar	Blt. Burrard Dry Dock Co. 1944. Refrigerator capacity. Released for merchant service 1947, became ISLANDSIDE.
Fort McDonnell	Blt. Burrard Dry Dock Co. 1944. Refrigerator capacity. Released for merchant service 1947, became CLIFFSIDE.
Fort Providence	Blt. Burrard Dry Dock Co. 1944. Refrigerator capacity. Released for merchant service 1948. Became EASTWATER and then DUNESIDE 1952.

Fort Rosalie	Blt. United Shipyards Ltd, 1945. Ammunition and heavy stores ship. 1947 became permanent addition to R.N.
Fort Sandusky	Blt. United Shipyards Ltd. 1945. Ammunition and heavy stores ship. 1949 became permanent addition to R.N.
Fort Wayne	Blt. United Shipyards Ltd. 1945. Ammunition and heavy stores ship. 1950 released for merchant service and became ANGUSDALE.
Fort Wrangell	Blt. Burrard Dry Dock Co. 1944. Refrigerator capacity. Released for merchant service in 1948 as EASTWAVE and the LAGOONSIDE in 1952.

LAUTOKA
Another conversion for Carpenter Line. Less altered than LAKEMBA the former H.M.S. TARBET NESS leaves the yard of her builders in False Creek, and eases through the Kitsilano railway swing bridge.

TARBAT

WAITEMATA
Canadian Union Line purchased the incomplete H.M.S. SELSEY BILL from the Admiralty. Her completely enclosed bridge is different again and probably reflects her new owners ideas.

DITMAR KOEL
Started life as H.M.S. CAPE WRATH but was sold out of the Royal Navy in 1951. After two changes of ownership she joined the fleet of the Hanseatic Line of Germany which ran a regular liner service from Germany to North Pacific ports.

Chapter Twelve

A Brief Prosperity: The East Coast Shipowners

This, and the following chapter are intended to review the companies which were established at or near the end of the second world war with the effect of taking Canada's government-built and owned wartime shipping, into the private sector and a peacetime economy.

Chapter 6 sets out the details of the wartime shipbuilding program, the ships it produced, and the considerations applied in laying out a government policy leading to its disposal.

Private owners no matter what the motivations of patriotic idealists might be, have to be a hard-headed lot. Shipping capital like any other in a private enterprise economy seeks profitable opportunity. Sometimes it requires encouragement through enlightened government policies affecting taxation, certain subsidies, a secure legal domicile, a stable labour force and pool of qualified officers and management, and a business climate which with all these factors taken into account, are conducive to a healthy business.

When the war ended Canada was possessed of the third largest navy and the fourth largest merchant marine. It had vastly increased its industrial establishment and pool of skilled labour, possessed a strong hard currency and was generally in the position of being a creditor nation. Moreover its raw material and manufactured products were in heavy demand to cope with world-wide shortages and the need to rebuild following the war.

On the face of things, with a large fleet of modern tonnage, with a long theoretical life ahead of it on account of its recent build, Canadian shipping could not go wrong so long as private owners could be spurred into action. It mattered less as to where the actual capital came from, and more that the ships could derive advantage by being legally owned in Canada. This way they could bring earnings back to the country, create jobs for Canadians and keep a steady flow of repair work coming to Canadian yards. Additionally the flag covenants imposed on new Canadian owners buying good but relatively cheap tonnage ensured that as ships were re-sold to foreign owners, as would inevitably happen with increasing obsolesence, the funds would go into escrow and be utilized for the construction of higher quality, more competitive post war built ships.

The realities of the situation where that by far the largest bulk of capital came from foreign sources. The biggest national block was unquestionably Greek, particularly Greek concerns based in London, they being opportunists who never allowed flag or nationality to cloud the central issue which for them was to take advantage of every and any commercial opportunity as it arose. British, American, Danish and French capital also participated in a smaller more subtle manner. As every company involved was a private concern there was little need for any disclosure as to beneficial ownership so far as the outside public was concerned. If a company was incorporated in Canada and met legal requirements as to directorships and domicile, it was legally a Canadian corporate citizen and that was what counted. It mattered not at all if the beneficial shareholders were domiciled in Athens, Liverpool, Paris or New York, and carried the passport of another country.

Canadian industrial concerns, notably Alcan, Dominion Steel and Coal Corporation, Seaboard Lumber and the H.R. McMillan, the Irving interests and few minor players also participated through their shipping subsidiaries, but as for truly Canadian shipping capital, i.e that which is actually owned by Canadian citizens as opposed to that which could be tapped by a legally incorporated Canadian corporation from its foreign owners, there really was not too much.

Two firms were notable for their roles as being beneficially Canadian owned, Canadian managed companies. They were Acadia Overseas Freighters of Halifax with its close connections with I.H. Mathers & Son Ltd and the wholly Vancouver owned concern, Western Canada Steamships Ltd. both of which are covered in more detail elsewhere in this book. The latter had the distinction of building up the largest individual fleet of the former Park ships, and was one of the longest-lived of the companies which were spawned by the second world war.

Each of the companies is now dealt with on an individual basis, with whatever information is available. All ships comprising their individual fleets are identified as to their type but it is not necessary to quote tonnages and measurements as every vessel has previously been described and listed in Chapter 6 under its war-built name.

NOTE the following list gives the owner's corporate name in alphabetical order, the ship type, the owner's fleet name, the name held while owned by the Canadian government, and the name acquired by the vessel upon resale.

ACADIA OVERSEAS FREIGHTERS LTD. - Halifax
I.H. Mathers & Son Ltd. whose story has already been set out in Chapter 10 appear to have been the driving force in putting together the Acadia Overseas fleets. They were well connected with London Greek shipowners such as Coulouthros Ltd. Fafalios Ltd. Frinton Shipbrokers Ltd Hadjilias & Co. Ltd., C.M. Lemos & Co. Ltd. and P.D. Marchessini & Co. and others, and undoubtedly had a hand in each of the above London firms acquisitions of Canadian freighters as part of the deal whereby Mathers acquired 87 former Canadian Government owned vessels as noted in chapter ten. Mathers' biggest Greek connection appears to have been with the Rethymnis & Kulukundis interests, one of the largest and best established of the Greek ownerships. R & K as it was frequently called, in addition were closely associated with Manuel Kulukundis and Basil Mavrolean, through family and business ties in the operation of Counties Ship Management Ltd becoming one of the largest British operators of tramp shipping, and London & Overseas Freighters Ltd. which became a public company on the London Stock Exchange. Acadia Overseas Freighters Ltd. was established in 1946.

Type	Owner's name	Former name	Later Name
NS	Caribou County	Fort Lennox	Harrow Hill
Vic	Colchester County	Fort Venango	Santa Calli
Vic	Cumberland County	Fort Prudhomme	Corsair
Vic	Digby County	Fort La Baye	Travelstar

Can	Halifax County	Lakeview Park	Canopus
Vic	Hants County	Fort Kaskaskia	Tel Aviv
NS	Inverness County	Kildonan Park	Corsair
Vic	Nanaimo County	Fort Yukon	Haifa
Vic	Pictou County	Fort Brisebois	Archimede
NS	Shelburne County	Riverview Park	Lily
Vic	Vancouver County	Fort Wallace	Akko
Can	Victoria County	Frontenac Park	Canopus
Vic	Westminster County	Fort Kullyspell	Yaffo
NS	Yale County	Fort St. Regis	Sudbury Hill
Vic	Yarmouth County	Fort Astoria	Santa Despo

ACADIA OVERSEAS FREIGHTERS (HALIFAX) LTD.

This company was formed in 1948 again showing as an I.H. Mathers concern, but when large numbers of the Canadian ships were placed under British management and nominal ownership in order to take advantage of lower British manning and other costs, the entire group of the seven following vessels came under the direct management of Counties Ship Management. This is not conclusive evidence of a tie-in to the Rethymnis & Kulukundis interests, but it can be strongly inferred, that R & K had a larger interest in this company than it did in the immediately preceding fleet of Acadia Overseas Freighters Ltd.

NS	Haligonian Baron	Fort Pic	Wembley Hill
NS	Haligonian Duchess	Stanley Park	Malden Hill
NS	Haligonian Duke	Fort Capot Rive	Notting Hill
NS	Haligonian King	Fort Mingan	Streatham Hill
NS	Haligonian Prince	Fort Moose	Tulse Hill
NS	Haligonian Princess	Fort Mattagami	Denmark Hill
NS	Haligonian Queen	Fort Wellington	Muswell Hill

ANDROS SHIPPING CO. LTD. - Montreal
KINGSBRIDGE SHIPPING CO. LTD.
OAKMOUNT S.S. CO. Ltd.

Goulandris Brothers of Andros, Greece, were another large well-established Greek shipping group, with major connections to London and New York where they operated subsidiary companies. They were not part of the group of Greek owners with whom Mathers had extensive connections, working instead through March Shipping Agency of Montreal.

Vic	Bayside	Winnipegosis Park	Aghia Anastasia
Vic	Cliffside	Fort McDonnell	Cavodoro
Vic	^Duneside	Fort Providence	Mar Libero
Vic	Gulfside	Fort Alabama	Anthony
Vic	Islandside	Fort Kilmar	Catherine MS
Vic	^Lagoonside	Fort Wrangell	Lagos Ontario
Can	Lakeside	Lakeside Park	Evgenia MG
Can	Oceanside	Noranda Park	Magdalene
Vic	^Riverside	Fort Biloxi	Doxa
Vic	Rockside	Fort Perrot	Dorion
Can	Seaside	Seven Oaks Park	Rubystar
NS	Kingsbridge (KS)	Withrow Park	scrapped

| NS | Kingsmount (KS) | Fort Nisqually | Kootenay Park |
| NS | ^Surfside (OSS) | Fort Carlton | Theomitor |

The four vessels marked with (^) each carried the names EASTWATER, EAST-WAVE, MARIA G anmd SOREL respectively. It was rare that there should be a Canadian intermediate owner, with transfer to another Canadian owner as happened in these cases.

ARGONAUT NAVIGATION CO. LTD. Montreal

Established in Montreal in 1946, this company was under the management of John C. Yemelos. There was some connection with Constantine Line (Canada) Ltd. an offshoot of the well-known Constantine group from Middlesborough, England. Later records indicate that management passed to A. Lusi Ltd. a sizeable London Greek shipping group.

NS	Argobec	Chippewa Park	Rahiotis
NS	Argodon	Fort Nakasley	Union Metropole
Vic	Argofax	Fort Hall	Strovili
Vic	Argojohn	Fort Marin	Kertis
Vic	Argomont	Fort Saleesh	Corfu Island
Vic	Argovan	Tecumseh Park	Cardamilitis

ARMDALE OVERSEAS FREIGHTERS LTD - Halifax
WINDSOR OVERSEAS FREIGHTERS LTD

These two one-vessel companies were conncetd with the London Greek firm of Nomikos (London) Ltd. Nomikos was one of the smaller such concerns but had been well known since prior to the war.

| NS | Darton (AOF) | Nemiskam Park | Federal Commerce |
| NS | Darfield (WOF) | Fort Highfield | Marine loss 2.28.54 |

BEDFORD OVERSEAS FREIGHTERS LTD. - Halifax

By the name, Marchessini appears to be Italian, although they seemed to be grouped by the shipping industry among the London and New York Greeks. All elements in the group appear to date from 1947. Bedford Overseas was formed in 1950 rather later than most of the other Canadian domiciled companies and certainly after the move was underway to dispose of Canadian flag ships to foreign flags on account of the low shipping rates and the corresponding high costs of 1948. Bedford Overseas showed I.H. Mathers once again as providing the legal address of the company so that it can be inferred that Marchessini was a client of the Mathers firm.

NS	Bedford Earl	Fort Covington	CTL
NS	Bedford Prince	Fort Gloucester	CTL
NS	Bedford Queen	Tweedsmuir Park	Lord Tweedsmuir

BRANCH LINES LTD.- Montreal

Branch Lines was a wholly Canadian owned company operating small tankers in and around the St. Lawrence, the U.S. east coast and the West Indies. It was also a subsidiary of the large shipbuilding concern Marine Industries Ltd. which built a substantial number of the units in the wartime emergency fleet. Marine Industries, controlled by the Joseph Simard interests was the central company in a group which also included Dufresne Construction Co. Ltd., Les Chantiers Manseau Ltee., Sincennes McNaughton Line Ltd., and United Towing & Salvage Co. Ltd.

3600	Elmbranch	Norwood Park	-
3600	Firbranch	Millican Park	-
3600	Poplarbranch	Springbank Park	*Straits Conveyor
3600	Sprucebranch	Otterburn Park	-

The above were all units of the six-vessel group built and known as 3600 tdw tankers.
*Constructive total loss following grounding near Barranquilla, Columbia. Sold to Straits Towing Ltd. Vancouver and converted to a barge.

BRISTOL CITY LINE (CANADA) LTD. - Montreal

This concern was controlled by the historic Bristol shipowning and shipbuilding concern, Charles Hill & Sons which dated back as a company to 1880. Hill had run a direct line of steamers from Bristol Channel ports to Boston and the St. Lawrence ports for many years and developed an interest in Dart Container Line following the demise of conventional freighters on this route.

| CAN | Montreal City | Fairmount Park | Huta Baildon |

BRUNSWICK MOTORS LTD. and KENT LINE - St. John, N.B.

These two companies were part of the K.C. Irving interests of St. John, N.B. Irving Oil was a growing concern in the Maritime provinces and was the main component in establishing a very strong industrial group with broad interests all of which are still controlled by the Irving family.

| Vic T | Irvingdale | Wildewood Park | scrapped |
| 3600 | Irvinglake | Nipiwan Park | c/to barge |

Brunswick Motors Ltd. was the registered owner of the first named vessel and Kent Line Ltd., the second.

CANADIAN NATIONAL STEAMSHIPS (WEST INDIES) LTD. - Montreal

This company was a direct descendent of the Canadian Government Merchant Marine, the crown-owned company operated by the Canadian National Railway, which was finally wound up in 1936. The East Coast to West Indies trade has always been of special interest to Canada, providing one of the traditional and historic markets for salt cod, with ships returning with molasses for the sugar refiners of Eastern Canada.

Canadian National operated the attractive all-white "Lady" liners, consisting of the LADY NELSON, LADY RODNEY and LADY DRAKE, the latter of which became a war loss. Canadian National acquired five of the "Dominion" type of the improved 4,700 tdw class Scandinavian type freighters. Three additional ships where built in Canadian yards in 1946 for the company. Strictly speaking they were a design of their own, and while not part of the wartime program they were obviously designed and projected in the latter months of the war, and are listed following the five Scandinavian type ships, as a matter of record only.

| 4700D | Canadian Conqueror | Sutherland Park | scrapped |
| 4700D | Canadian Highlander | Maissoneuve Park | scrapped |

4700D	Canadian Leader	Lorne Park	scrapped
4700D	Canadian Observer	Westdale Park	scrapped
4700D	Canadian Victor	Cartier Park	scrapped
CN	Canadian Challenger	-	
CN	Canadian Constructor	-	
CN	Canadian Cruiser	-	

In addition to the above vessels Canadian National Steamships, operated the coastal passenger liners which served the coast of British Columbia. Additionally the parent Canadian National Railways operated a fleet of east coast ferries, tugs and a variety of service vessels.

CANADIAN OIL COMPANIES LTD. - Toronto

At one time this company was well known as the vendors of the "White Rose" brand of motor oils and gasoline. The company was absorbed by one of the majors and has now disappeared along with its brand name, but it did acquire one tanker as under.

| 3600 tdw | John Irwin | Eglinton Park | White Rose II |

CANADIAN SHIPOWNERS LTD. - Montreal

This Company was managed by March Shipping Agency Ltd. It appears to have had connections with the Goulandris group as noted under Andros Shipping Co. Ltd. above.

Vic	Marchcape	Fort Sakisdac	Margo
Vic	Marchdale	Dundurn Park	Shahin
Can	Marchport	Portland Park	Mont Clair

For some years March operated an intercoastal service from St. Lawrence ports to Vancouver. March Shipping Agency is still in business as a subsidiary of the Logistec Group of Montreal.

CAPE BRETON FREIGHTERS LTD. - Montreal

This company was affiliated with one of the oldest of the major Greek concerns, S.G. Embiricos Ltd. based in London but founded originally in 1897.

| NS | Alkis | Gatineau Park | Acer |

CHAMPLAIN FREIGHTERS LTD. - Montreal
FORT CARLTON SHIPPING CO. LTD.
FORT ERIE S.S. CO. LTD.
MEGANTIC FREIGHTERS LTD.
MORLAND NAVIGATION LTD.
NORTHEASTERN FREIGHTERS LTD.

All the above companies were legally based in Montreal but the ships were managed from London by the well-known London Greek firm of J.P. Hadoulis Ltd. Hadoulis founded in 1938 managed additional vessels under foreign flags. At the time that they had these Canadian vessels under their management they also had vessels under the flags of Britain, Panama and Costa Rica, which illustrates the well-known Greek propensity for taking advantage of commercial opportunities regardless of flag. The first two vessels were owned by the first named company. One vessel each belonged to the other companies and are named in the order of the above ownerships rather than alphabetically.

NS	Champlain	Prince Albert Park	M.L. 1956
NS	Tarsian	Fort St. Paul	Marika
NS	Mount Royal	Fort Carillon	Monte Rico
NS	Maidenhead	Fort Erie	Aristefs
NS	Assemina K	Fort la Tour	Jean Baptiste
NS	Nimaris	Fort Esperance	Captain Nicos
NS	Commodore Grant	Fort Grant	Sidon

THE COUNTIES GROUP -
ACADIA OVERSEAS FREIGHTERS LTD.
ACADIA OVERSEAS FREIGHTERS (HALIFAX) LTD.
BLACK LION S.S. CO. LTD (Frinton Shipbrokers Ltd)
CANADIAN TRAMP SHIPPING CO. LTD.
FALAISE S.S. CO. LTD.
HALIFAX OVERSEAS FREIGHTERS LTD.
LAURENTIDE S.S. CO. LTD.
NOVA SCOTIA MARINE ENTERPRISES CO. LTD.
VANCOUVER ORIENTAL LINE LTD.

Mentioned elsewhere Counties Ship Management Co. Ltd. was started in London in 1936 as the British branch of the well-known Greek firm of Rethymnis & Kulukundis, one of the largest and longest established of all the major Greek owners. The four Kulukundis brothers and their nephew Basil Mavroleon were to become big names in international shipping, the last named being largely responsible for creating London & Overseas Freighters Ltd. a major postwar British owner of tankers. London & Overseas also acquired the well known S.B. Austin and Wm. Pickersgill shipyards at Sunderland and a shipyard at Appledore in North Devon. The A & P group as they became known were at the forefront of shipbuilding technology and developed the popular SD14 and SD15 Liberty ship replacements, as well as the SD26 bulk-carrier all of which found much favour with both liner and tramp owners.

As with so many of the London Greeks connections with I.H. Mathers & Son Ltd. were very close and eventually many of the ships in the two Acadia fleets listed earlier in this chapter passed into the direct management of Counties. As usual there was a multiplicity of actual shipowning concerns involved, legally domiciled in Montreal or Halifax including in addition to the Acadia companies others whose names are listed above. Vancouver Oriental Line is mentioned in the next chapter as being legally a British Columbia company formed for reasons upon which one can only speculate. Counties also had close connections with other London Greek firms, such as Frinton Shipbrokers Ltd. and Coulouthros Ltd (which see under Laurentian group). Because of the ownership complexities within the group no attempt has been made to do other than list the entire fleet in alphabetical order.

NS	Akti Hill	Fort la Cloche	Cape Drepanon
NS	Alendi Hill	Fort Nottingham	Ho Fung
NS	Beech Hill	Fort Richelieu	Alkon

NS	Bembridge Hill	Hillcrest Park	Elimarie
NS	Cedar Hill	Dentonia Park	scrapped
NS	Denmark Hill	Fort Mattagami	scrapped
	ex Haligonian Princess		
NS	East Hill	Fort Sturgeon	Rio Alto
NS	Elm Hill	Fort la Prairie	scrapped
NS	Fir Hill	Whiteshell Park	Universal Trader
NS	Harrow Hill	Fort Lennox	Silver Peak
	ex Caribou County		
NS	Malden Hill	Stanley Park	Newmoor
	ex Haligonian Duchess		
NS	Maple Hill	Fort Vercheres	scrapped
NS	Marina Hill	Fort Connolly	Fotoulia
NS	Mavis Hill	Fort St. Joseph	scrapped
NS	Mulberry Hill	Fort Brunswick	scrapped
NS	Muswell Hill	Fort Wellington	scrapped
	ex Haligonian Queen		
NS	Notting Hill	Fort Capot River	Cepheus
	ex Haligonian Duke		
NS	Oak Hill	Fort Michipicoten	Agenor
NS	Pine Hill	Fort Henley	Newmoat
NS	Poplar Hill	Rosedale Park	Shienfoon
NS	Streatham Hill	Fort Mingan	scrapped
	ex Haligonian King		
NS	Sudbury Hill	Fort St. Regis	scrapped
NS	Sycamore Hill	Rondeau Park	scrapped
NS	Tulse Hill	Fort Moose	Astronaftis
	ex Haligonian Prince		
NS	Wembley Hill	Fort Pic	Cassiopeia
	ex Haligonian Baron		
NS	West Hill	Fort Musquarro	Rio Doro
NS	Winter Hill	Laurentide Park	Petite Hermine
NS	Woldingham Hill	High Park	scrapped
NS	Wynchwood Hill	Rocky Mountains Park	scrapped

DINGWALL SHIPPING COMPANY LTD. - Halifax

Managed by Quebec S.S. Lines of Montreal, Dingwall Shipping Company was actually based in Halifax. The controlling owner was National Gypsum Company of Buffalo, New York. There were also connections with Ivor Shipping Co. Ltd. a concern controlled by Chandris (England) Ltd. another prominent firm of London Greeks.

Can	Cheticamp	Hampstead Park	Carini
Can	Dingwall	Waverley Park	Rayo
Can	Walton	Montebello Park	Aci

DOMINION SHIPPING COMPANY LTD. - Montreal

This company was a subsidiary of Dominion Steel & Coal Corporation Ltd. (DOSCO) of Montreal. The ships were engaged in the carriage of ore from Wabana, Newfoundland, as well as coal for the parent's business of steel smelting.

| NS | Arthur Cross | Alder Park | |

NS	Louisbourg	Elk Island Park
NS	Wabana	Glacier Park

EASTBOARD NAVIGATION COMPANY LTD. - Toronto

Little is known of this company. It was not in business for long as by 1948 its two ships had been transferred into the Andros Shipping Company fleet detailed above.

Vic	Eastwater	Fort Providence
Vic	Eastwave	Fort Wrangell

ELDER DEMPSTER (CANADA) LTD. - Montreal

Elder Dempster Lines Ltd. of Liverpool, England was one of the major British liner companies heavily involved in the West African trade, where for many years it had enjoyed a dominant position. Dating well back into the previous century, it was one of the huge Royal Mail group companies when the infamous Kylsant financial crash took place in the 1930's. Lord Kylsant was sent to prison for issuance of a fraudulent prospectus, and like all the shipping lines in the group it was sold off being held by a holding company, Liner Holdings Ltd. of Liverpool. Liner Holdings came under the control of Alfred Holt's Blue Funnel line, and following a postwar reorganization Elder Dempster became a wholly owned subsidiary in a new group called Ocean Transport & Trading Ltd. which incorporated all the Holt holdings.

After the first world war Elder Dempster which had earlier sold the Beaver Line to Canadian Pacific, had started a direct line of steamers from the Canadian East Coast and U.S. to West Africa. This was evidently successful but the second world war caused it to be suspended.

After the war the service was restarted by acquiring five ships from Park Steamships Ltd. These were:

Vic	Cabano	Strathcona Park	Happy Voyager
Vic	Cambray	Bridgeland Park	Simeto
Vic	Cargill	Wascana Park	Marine Navigator
Vic	Chandler	Crystal Park	Natale
Vic	Cottrell	Goldstream Park	Santagata

Ocean Transport & Trading is still in business as an industrial conglomerate, but has withdrawn from all forms of ocean shipping.

FAIRVIEW OVERSEAS FREIGHTERS LTD. - Halifax

The London Greek connection in this instance was C.M. Lemos & Co. Ltd. which up to 1950 had been a part of the well known Greek firm of Lyras & Lemos. C.M. Lemos was also another client of I.H. Mathers & Son Ltd.

NS	Johnstar	Algonquin Park	Santhy
NS	Nordicstar	Westmount Park	posted missing 1.23.57
NS	Peterstar	Lafontaine Park	Aspis

FEDERAL COMMERCE & NAVIGATION CO. Ltd. - Montreal

This company dating back to 1944 was founded by an American, Ernest G. Pathy and is now known as Fednav Limited. It is one of the few survivors of the Canadian postwar shipping companies. It is now Canada's largest and most successful ocean shipping group, having prospered where others have withdrawn or retired from business. The company's full story is the subject of chapter 16 which follows. The fleet of war-built vessels is included in this chapter for the sake of uniformity.

NS	^Ernest G. Pathy	Fort Grouard	African Duke
4700	Federal Ambassador	Beresford Park	Gerda Toft
NS	^Federal Commerce	Nemiskam Park	Brasilia
4700	Federal Pioneer	Bell Park	Santa Helena
Can	^Federal Pioneer (2)	Outremont Park	scrapped
4700	Federal Ranger	Taronga Park	Maria Toft
4700	Federal Trader	Landsdowne Park	Provincial Trader
Vic	Federal Voyager	Fort Edmonton	scrapped

^ERNEST G. PATHY purchased from other owners as the SEA CREST.

^FEDERAL COMMERCE purchased from other owners as the DARTON

^FEDERAL PIONEER purchased from other owners as the BRAZILIAN PRINCE

FURNESS (CANADA) LTD - Montreal

Furness Withy was one of the mightiest of the great British shipping groups with world wide interests. It had operated services to both the east and west coast of Canada for many years and controlled other significant interests in this country. Royal Mail Lines to North and South America and Shaw Savill & Albion Line to Australia and New Zealand, Houlder Line and Prince Line were also a part of their extensive shipping interests, but the growth of container traffic required much rationalization including the combining of Royal Mail and Furness Withy services to the North Pacific including Vancouver.

Immediately following the war Furness took advantage of investment opportunities created by disposal of Park Steamship vessels. The following vessels constituted the fleet:

CAN	^Beacon Grange	Albert Park	Constantinos
CAN	Brazilian Prince	Outremont Park	Federal Pioneer
VIC	^Royston Grange (1)	Sapperton Park	Yiannis
NS	^Royston Grange (2)	Fort Ash	Giuan

BEACON GRANGE and ROYSTON GRANGE were purchased from Canadian Transport in 1948 and were previously HARMAC VICTORIA and HARMAC ALBERNI. The following year both were disposed of to foreign owners. The second ROYSTON GRANGE was acquired in 1950 and disposed of in 1952.

IVOR SHIPPING CO. LTD. - Montreal

Originally managed by Quebec S.S. Lines, this company was the Canadian subsidiary of Chandris (England) Ltd. a leading Greek concern, which made a name for itself in the development of emmigrant passenger and cruise liners in the postwar period. There were connections with the Dingwall Shipping Company and National Gypsum Company mentioned above.

NS	Ivor Isobel	Fort Ticonderoga	Novor Isobel
NS	Ivor Jenny	Fort Dease Lake	Novor Jenny
NS	Ivor Rita	Fort Rouille	Novor Rita

LAURENTIAN GROUP - Montreal

Coulouthros Ltd. a London Greek firm were clients of I.H. Mathers, and also seemed to have close working connections with Counties Ship Management and the Rethymnis & Kulukundis group. The vessels were owned in the name of one or other of Laurentian Marine Co. Ltd. Laurentian Overseas Shipping Ltd. and Laurentian Shipping Co. Ltd. all handled by Triton S.S. Co. Ltd. of Montreal. The first three vessels listed below were registered to Ottawa S.S. Company Ltd. c/o I.H. Mathers & Son. Ltd. of Halifax.

NS	Amersham Hill	Rideau Park	Petalon
NS	Andover Hill	Fort Coulonge	Louria
NS	Arundel Hill	Fort Turtle	Cyprinia
NS	Laurentian Forest	Mount Revelstoke Park	Aegean Wave
NS	Laurentian Hill	Fort Brandon	Taygetos
NS	Laurentian Lake	Fort Assiniboine	Olympos
NS	Laurentian Valley	Fort Frontenac	Aegean Sea

LUNHAM & MOORE (CANADA) LTD. - Montreal

Appears to have been closely connected with E.E. Dean & Co. Ltd. ship managers, and shipbrokers Simpson Spence & Young Ltd. both of London. Three former Canadian ships as listed below passed through the fleet, plus very unusually for a Canadian firm, two former U.S. Liberty ships, the ANGUSLOCH ex SAMUEL VERY and ANGUSLAKE ex RODNEY BAXTER.

Can	Angusdale (1)	Fort Wayne	Cape Adan
Vic	Angusdale (2)	Tuxedo Park	Point Aconi
Vic	Angusglen	Fort La Have	Cape Melan

MERSEY PAPER COMPANY LTD. - Liverpool N.S.

This industrial concern based in Liverpool, Nova Scotia was originally founded in 1929. It always operated some tonnage of its own through subsidiary shipping companies which were managed by its shipping arm, Markland Shipping Company Ltd. The two ships acquired from the wartime program were:-

4700	Liverpool Packet	Argyle Park	Westport
Can	Vinland	Champlain Park	Vinkon

MONTSHIP LINES LTD. - Montreal

This company was managed on behalf of its beneficial owners, Buries Markes Ltd. of London, which in turn was a subsidiary of the giant French commodities trading firm of Louis Dreyfus et Cie. of Paris. Montship Lines was another Canadian company which at one period owned ex foreign ships, these being the MONTROSE ex FRANCOIS L.D. owned originally by Louis Dreyfus, built in France in 1938 and MONTCALM ex LA ESTANCIA ex CAPE DUCATO. This latter vessel was one of the U.S. built C1A class ships purchased originally from the USMC by Buries Markes and transferred to its Canadian subsidiary. Even though owned by Montship Lines MONT ALTA and MONT GASPE appeared to be managed through a separate management vehicle, Montreal Shipping Co. Ltd. sharing a common address. Montreal shipping also managed one of the 4700 tdw vessels on behalf of Allied S.S. Lines Ltd.

4700	^Gander Bay	Lansdowne Park	
Can	Mont Alta	Sunalta Park	Georgian Flame
Vic	Mont Clair (1)	Fort Clatsop	Husaini
Can	^Mont Clair (2)	Portland Park	Maria Piera G.
Can	Mont Gaspe	Gaspesian Park	Polyxeni
Vic	Mont Rolland	Fort Island	Maria Paolina G
Can	Mont Sandra	Alexandra Park	Violando
Vic	Mont Sorrel	Fort Orleans	Buys Ballot

^MONT CLAIR (2) acquired from Canadian Shipowners Company as
MARCHPORT.
^GANDER BAY had two intermediate namings under other owners as firstly
FEDERAL TRADER and then PROVINCIAL TRADER.

PAPACHRISTIDIS COMPANY LTD. - Montreal
Unlike most of the Greek interests which hailed from London, the Papachristidis family were immigrants who had been settled in Montreal for some time, being well-known in the city's restaurant business. Today the company now based in London continues as an international shipping concern with ships under a variety of foreign flags including Greece, Panama, and Liberia. Like very few others it can be numbered among the survivors of the postwar Canadian concerns.

NS	^Grande Hermine	Kawartha Park	Canuk Trader
NS	L'Alouette	Fort Romaine	Montrealer
Vic	L'Emerillon	Fort Machault	T.L.
NS	La Fleche	Fort Albany	scrapped
NS	Pantrooper	Fort Wrigley	Royal William
NS	Petite Hermine	Laurentide Park	Canuk Port
NS	^World Trotter	Green Gables Park	Marcos

^GRANDE HERMINE acquired from other owners as HAVERTON HILL.
^WORLD TROTTER held the intermediate name PAPACHRISTIDIS VASSILIOS,
owned within the Papachristidis group
MONTREALER and ROYAL WILLIAM were renamings within the group

PICBELL LTD. - Halifax
Little can be ascertained about this single-vessel company which dated from 1946. The one vessel it owned, the DUFFERIN BELL was lost on May 13, 1951 after going ashore at Framboise Cove, Cape Breton, N.S. during fog while on passage from New Orleans for Dalhousie and Montreal with a cargo of sulphur.

| 4700 | Dufferin Bell | Dufferin Park | T.L. |

REX SHIPPING CO. LTD. - Halifax
This company was connected with long-established London Greeks, Hadjilias & Co. Ltd. who were in turn clients of I.H. Mathers & Son Ltd.

NS	Brookhurst	Belwoods Park	Galicia
NS	Fernhurst	Port Royal Park	Novarra
NS	Midhurst	Mount Robson Park	Andalusia
NS	Oakhurst	Banff park	Catalunia

SAGUENAY TERMINALS LTD. - Montreal
This concern established in 1939 is still in business and functions as the shipping arm of Alcan Ltd. Like other industrial concerns such as Seaboard and Canadian Transport detailed in the next chapter, it now owns no vessels of its own preferring to charter in foreign shipping as required. It operates a number of services but its main concern is in the movement of alumina from Guyana to the parent company's smelters at Kitimat, B.C. and Arvida, Quebec.

4700	Sundale	Bloomfield Park	Amigo
4700	Sundial	Wentworth Park	Celeste
Can	^Sunjarv	Grafton Park	Katerina
Can	Sunjewel	Highland Park	Leefoon
Can	^Sunkirk	Eastwood Park	Ameise
Can	Sunmont	Simcoe Park	Shun Fung
4700R	Sunprince	Shakespeare Park	Salammanna
Vic	Sunrell	Fort Columbia	Sula
Vic	Sunvalley	Fort Panmure	Kally
Can	Sunwhit	Wellington Park	Ceres

^SUNJARV carried the name SUNRAY before the listed name.
^SUNKIRK carried the name SUNAVIS before the listed name

SEAGULL STEAMSHIP COMPANY OF CANADA LTD. - Montreal
Little can be ascertained of this company from available records, except that the company was connected with Papachristidis but was out of business by 1952. Interestingly enough two of its three vessel names were also to be found on North Sands vessels in the Papachristidis fleet minus the "LA" prefix which was part of the names below.

4700	La Grande Hermine	Rockwood Park	Vianna
4700	La Petite Hermine	Kelowna Park	Dharini
4700	Saint Malo	Liscomb Park	Tapagos

LA PETITE HERMINE was sold to the Indian navy and converted into the navy auxiliary DHARINI.

TRITON S.S. CO. LTD. - Montreal
Founded in 1946, this was another company associated with March Shipping Agency of Montreal and Goulandris Brothers of London.

Vic	Triberg	Westend Park	Sevilla
NS	Tricape	Elm Park	Palma
NS	Tridale	Riverdale Park	Harrier

NS	Triland	La Salle Park	Manhatten
Vic	Trimont	Fort Crevecoeur	Eagle
Vic	Triport	Fort Aspin	Heron

WAVERLEY OVERSEA FREIGHTERS LTD. - Halifax

Founded in 1950, this company was controlled by Fafalios Ltd. a London Greek firm who were clients of I.H. Mathers & Son Ltd. of Halifax.

NS	Kenilworth	Sibley Park	Aeolos
NS	Labrador	Fort McPherson	Poseidon

As will be noted only a small number of the above firms could be described as being beneficially owned by Canadian interests. What is illustrated is the international nature of the world's deep sea shipping industries. Shipping capital flows where it finds the greatest opportunities. The foreign-owned, legally Canadian entities quickly withdrew as fast as was legally possible, as owning under the Canadian flag proved unprofitable. That Canadian shipping can survive and prosper to this day is well illustrated in Chapter 16 and some comments supporting this proposition are offered in Chapter 17.

ROCKSIDE ex FORT PERROT.

KINGSBRIDGE ex WITHROW PARK.

DARTON ex NEMISKAM PARK.

ARGOVAN ex TECUMSEH PARK.

4700 ton SCANDINAVIAN type freighters laid up at Yarmouth N.S.
l to r: CANADIAN CONQUEROR ex SUTHERLAND PARK
CANADIAN VICTOR ex CARTIER PARK
CANADIAN LEADER ex LORNE PARK

ALENDI HILL ex FORT NOTTINGHAM.

EAST HILL ex FORT STURGEON.

MARINA HILL ex FORT CONNOLLY.

MULBERRY HILL ex FORT BRUNSWICK.

WEST HILL ex FORT MUSQUARRO
Under charter to T. & J. Harrison of Liverpool with funnel in their colours.

WABANA ex GLACIER PARK.

IVOR JENNY ex FORT DEASE LAKE.

ANGUSDALE ex FORT WAYNE.

ANGUSGLEN ex FORT LA HAVE.

MONTREALER ex L'ALOUETTE ex FORT ROMAINE.

LA FLECHE ex FORT ALBANY.

MIDHURST ex MOUNT ROBSON PARK (1).

SUNKIRK ex SUNAVIS ex EASTWOOD PARK.

SUNRELL ex FORT COLUMBIA.

SUNJEWEL ex HIGHLAND PARK.

TRIMONT ex FORT CREVECOEUR.

TRIDALE ex RIVERDALE PARK.

TRIBERG ex WESTEND PARK.

Chapter Thirteen

A Brief Prosperity:
The West Coast Owners

The West Coast owners were of course entirely based in Vancouver. Fewer in number than their East Coast counterparts where most but not all were controlled or influenced by Greek owners, there was only one West Coast situation which arose where Greek participation was involved (Vancouver-Oriental Line Ltd.). The East Coast owners only included two liner companies in a regular liner trade (Elder Dempster and Furness Withy group), and other than regional heavy industry which set up or owned shipping companies to fit the parent company's need (DOSCO and Alcan), the rest where employed in the general tramping trades.

Of the west coast owners, three (Canadian Australasian and Kerr-Silver Line and Johnson Walton Steamships) came from a liner tradition and in general ran liner services or integrated their tramp operations into the parent's liner services. Two were offshoots of major forest product companies (Seaboard and H.R. McMillan), one (Johnson Walton) represented the only Danish investment on record into Canadian shipping.

The final West Coast company (Western Canada Steamships Ltd.) was unique in several ways. It accumulated the largest single group of ex-Park ships under one ownership, it was locally owned and controlled from Vancouver by a dedicated group of seasoned shipping men, it was the longest lived of the Vancouver companies, and one of only three of the Canadian companies covered in this book which succeeded in replacing, at least in part, its war-built fleet with modern post-war ships.

As a maritime historian and traditional shipping enthusiast I have always felt it to be a matter of deep regret that this last of all Vancouver ocean shipping companies could not have survived and prospered by adjusting to the trends in international trade and shipowning practices, as at least the two East Coast survivors have done, these being Fednav, and Papachristidis, although the latter is now run from London, England and it is not known as to what extent Canadian beneficial ownership continues, if at all. Saguenay Terminals, Canadian Transport and Seaboard Shipping all continue in business but their operations are largely confined to the chartering of foreign tonnage as part of the parent company's shipping requirements, without any actual shipowning being in the picture.

Following the same format as in the previous chapter, the West Coast fleets now follow:

CANADIAN AUSTRALASIAN LINE and CANADIAN UNION LINE - Vancouver

Canadian Australasian Line has roots which extend back into the 1890's. A Mr. Huddart of the Australian firm Huddart Parker, a well-known shipping company in the Australian trades started a service between Sydney and Vancouver in pursuit of the Empire ideal of an "All-red route" as it was popularly called from Britain, across the Atlantic, Canada and then the Pacific to Australia and New Zealand. Mail subsidies were awarded but the financial return and the traffic were not sufficient to ensure viability. The Canadian Australian Royal Mail Line as it was then called, went into receivership in 1897, and the New Zealand Shipping Company as the chief creditor was appointed receiver.

Union Steamship Company of New Zealand then took over the service and by 1913 was able to place the new 13,000 ton NIAGARA on the run. She was joined by the AORANGI a new 18,000 ton motor passenger ship in 1924. To replace the NIAGARA, the AWATEA a 14,000 ton ultra modern passenger liner joined the fleet in 1936.The AWATEA became a war casualty and following the war the AORANGI returned to the service to be joined by four former Park steamers, while Canadian Union Line acquired an additional vessel, the former Royal Navy auxiliary SELSEY BILL. These five ships are listed below:

Vic	Waihcmo	Dominion Park	
Vic	Waikawa	Parkdale Park	Fulda
Vic	Wairuna	Salt Lake Park	Bonna
Vic	Waitomo	Sunnyside Park	Blue Shark
Vic	Waitemata	Selsey Bill (ex R.N.)	

The Canadian-Australasian Line became a joint venture of Union Steamship Company of New Zealand, a member of the giant P & O group, and Canadian Pacific in 1931. Following the war the first ship to go was the AORANGI as by then the trans-Pacific airliner services were killing surface sea travel. The first four ships named above operated a regular cargo liner service from Vancouver to Fiji, New Zealand and Australia, until the last of them the WAIHEMO was disposed of in 1963. The WAITEMATA, so far as is known, never returned once her rebuilding was completed being employed in Union Steamship's other services around the south-west Pacific (a photo of this ship appears in Chapter 11). AORANGI flew the New Zealand flag, and she and her Canadian consorts made a very smart little fleet with their black banded red funnel capped by a black top, white upperworks and bottle green hull with gold band and red boot topping.

CANADIAN TRANSPORT COMPANY LTD. - Vancouver

This firm was originally set up in the 1930's as the chartering arm of H.R. McMillan Export Company Ltd, which grew into the huge McMillan, Bloedel organization of today. Opportunity was taken to acquire several of the former Park Steamship vessels when they came up for disposal, to employ them as carriers of the parent company's forest products. The fleet did not last long as poor trading conditions prevailing in 1948 and 1949 removed any incentive for Canadian Transport to remain as a shipowner so that all six vessels had been disposed of to non-Canadian owners by 1949. Two passed to Houlder Brothers of the Furness Withy group of Britain in 1948 and were kept on the Canadian register only briefly, as by 1949 both had been sold to Greek owners. These two ships were the HARMAC VICTORIA which became BEACON GRANGE and then CONSTANTINOS and the HARMAC ALBERNI which became the ROYSTON GRANGE and then the YIANNIS.

Vic	Harmac Alberni	Sapperton Park	Royston Grange
Vic	Harmac Chemainus	Louisbourg Park	Bombay
Vic	Harmac Crofton	Mewata Park	West Bengal
Can	Harmac Vancouver	Cromwell Park	Amaryllis
Can	Harmac Victoria	Albert Park	Beacon Grange
Vic	Harmac Westminster	Seacliff Park	Panaghia

Today Canadian Transport still functions as the shipping arm of McMillan Bloedel taking foreign vessels on time or voyage charters, to fill the parent company's requirements. However, it is quite a sophisticated operation as time chartered vessels are often cross-traded in order to profitably work them back to British Columbia ports with non-lumber cargoes.

JOHNSON WALTON STEAMSHIPS LTD. - Vancouver.

Originally founded by Captain B.L. "Barney" Johnson one of the most colourful characters to ever grace the Vancouver waterfront, Johnson originally reached these shores as an immigrant sailor from Liverpool, England. He was involved in many marine ventures over a long career including a short spell as commander of one of two submarines which the British Columbia government purchased from a Puget Sound shipyard in 1914, and then turned over to the Canadian government. Johnson was one of the pioneers in log barging forming the Hecate Straits Towing Company for this purpose. The Johnson Walton firm dates back to the early 1930's when it was set up as a steamship agency holding including among other connections the agency for the important Danish East Asiatic Company of Copenhagen.

It also possessed a one man insurance department which later became B.L. Johnson Walton Company Ltd. independent of the steamship department, and one of the largest of the several local marine insurance brokerage firms which enlivened the local shipping and insurance markets after the war. The antics and machinations of these local firms are beyond the scope of this book but could be the basis of an exciting and fascinating story in the future. B.L. Johnson Walton Company is now one of the founding components of the giant international insurance firm of Reed Stenhouse based in London.

The steamship agency department was acquired by Danish East Asiatic at about the time of the end of the second world war, and became Johnson Walton Steamships. East Asiatic had always had a policy of investing in primary commodity producers around the world. This way they were able to control much captive cargo for their ships and additionally they had a position as commodity traders.

In line with this tradition they acquired the Gibson Brothers lumber interests at the end of the war and turned it into the Tahsis Company. Tahsis, through its associate Johnson Walton Steamships, acquired three ex-government steamers listed below, and later went on to build the Gold River pulp mill in the 1950-60's era of greatest expansion in the B.C. Forest industries. Interestingly Johnson Walton was the only west coast company to number an East Coast-built ship in its fleet. This was the TATUK also the only one of the 4700 ton Scandinavian type ships to be acquired by a West Coast owner.

Can	Tahsis	Selkirk Park	Pelops
Vic	Tantara	Whiterock Park	Pelopidas
4700	Tatuk	Victoria Park	Kalo

Johnson Walton Steamships and the East Asiatic interests continue in business to-day as Eacom Lumber Sales.

KERR-SILVER LINES LTD. - Vancouver

This was a joint venture of Kerr Steamship Company of New York and the Silver Line of Britain. Stanley and John Thompson became trampship owners in 1911. They established Silver Line in London in 1925 and immediately commenced the construction of a large fleet of modern motorships for a new high class, round-the-world cargo liner service. From an early date Kerr Steamship became an important shareholder with a stated interest of 31 per cent of the issued stock in 1942. Kerr's Vancouver branch had acted as agents in Vancouver for the Silver Line, from the beginning, so that when the disposals of wartime tonnage took place, they and Silver in a joint venture, acquired four of the ships, and employed them in the general tramp trades. In common with other owners the entire fleet had gone by 1949.

Vic	Manx Fisher	Fort St. Antoine	Al Hasan
Vic	Manx Marine	Bowness Park	Jean
Vic	Manx Navigator	Fort Dearborn	Aloe
Vic	Manx Sailor	Mohawk Park	Vistafjord

SEABOARD SHIPPING LTD. - Vancouver.

Seaboard Lumber Sales, a company owned by a substantial group of independent sawmills was set up in the early 1920's to organize and co-ordinate the export lumber sales of much of British Columbia's sawmill industry. It and H.R. McMillan Export were great rivals and grew on more or less parallel lines. Seaboard Shipping Ltd. was established at about the same time as McMillan's Canadian Transport Company for exactly the same purposes, i.e. to look after time and voyage chartering for the parent company. Like others it took advantage of the prevailing opportunities and acquired six former Park ships. These were:-

Vic	Seaboard Enterprise	Westview Park	Doric
Vic	Seaboard Pioneer	Kootenay Park	Pioneer
Vic	Seaboard Queen	Queens Park	Queen
Vic	Seaboard Ranger	Connaught Park	Ranger
Vic	Seaboard Star	Coronation Park	Classic
Vic	Seaboard Trader	Tobiatic Park	Trader

The last vessel to leave the fleet was the SEABOARD ENTERPRISE which was eventually disposed of in 1957, so as a shipowning concern it lasted longer than most.

VANCOUVER ORIENTAL LINE - Vancouver

This concern was an interest of Counties Ship Management Ltd. a London group of Greeks affiliated with the well-known Greek shipping company, Rethymnis & Kulukundis, and as with all the Counties Canadian interests, connected with I.H. Mathers & Son Ltd. of Halifax. Just why they found it convenient to set up a Vancouver based front company is not recorded, unless they had special reasons for establishing a foothold in the Vancouver shipping market. On the other hand these and most other Canadian ships operated by private owners were strictly tramps which would gain their employment in the international market through such organizations as the Baltic Exchange of London.

NS	Harrow Hill	Fort Lennox
NS	Sudbury Hill	Fort St. Regis

Both vessels had previously been in the fleet of Acadia Oversaes Freighters Ltd. of Halifax as noted in the previous chapter. The first named had been CARIBOU COUNTY and the second YALE COUNTY.

WESTERN CANADA STEAMSHIPS LTD. - Vancouver.

The history of this company is dealt with very fully in Chapter 14, so to maintain consistancy the fleet list only is set out at this point, and available photographs will accompany the history of the company.

Vic	Lake Athabaska	Aspen Park	Agathi
Vic	Lake Atlin (1)	Atwater Park	Halcyon
Vic	Lake Babine	Beaton Park	Mountainside
Vic	Lake Canim	Dorval Park	^Durban Bay
Vic	Lake Chilco	Dunlop Park	Annitsa I
Vic	Lake Chilliwack	Earlscourt Park	^Mossel Bay
Can	Lake Cowichan	Garden Park	Annitsa
Vic	Lake Kamloops	Hastings Park	Lavadara
Vic	Lake Kootenay (1)	Kitsilano Park	Phopho
Vic	Lake Kootenay (2)	Fort Colville	Andros Cygnet
Vic	Lake Lillooet	Leaside Park	Cnosaga
Vic	Lake Manitou	Mount Robson Park (2)	Cliffside
Can	Lake Minnewanka	Princeton Park	Santiago
Vic	Lake Nipigon	Richmond Park	Pontoporos
Can	Lake Okanagan	Rupert Park	Nueva Gloria
Vic	Lake Pennask (1)	Temagami Park	Cygnet
Vic	Lake Shawnigan	Tipperary Park	^Table Bay
Vic	Lake Sicamous	Weston Park	Archipelago
Vic	Lake Sumas	Windermere Park	Katherine
Can	Lake Tatla	Winona Park	^Walvis bay
Vic	Lake Winnipeg	Yoho Park	Americana

In addition the three following vessels, all being modern post war cargo liners were acquired after the war:

Lake Atlin	Jersey Mist	
Lake Burnaby	Llantrisant	T.L.
Lake Pennask	Jersey Spray	

^ Renamings while still in fleet.

WAIKAWA ex PARKDALE PARK.

WAIHEMO ex DOMINION PARK.

WAIRUNA ex SALT LAKE PARK.

WAITOMO ex SUNNYSIDE PARK.

CROMWELL PARK later HARMAC VANCOUVER.

HARMAC CROFTON ex MEWATA PARK.

HARMAC WESTMINSTER ex SEACLIFF PARK.

HARMAC CHEMAINUS ex LOUISBOURG PARK.

HARMAC ALBERNI ex SAPPERTON PARK.

FORT ST. ANTOINE later MANX FISHER.

BOWNESS PARK later MANX MARINE

CORONATION PARK later SEABOARD STAR.

SEABOARD QUEEN ex QUEENS PARK.

SEABOARD RANGER ex CONNAUGHT PARK.

TAHSIS ex SELKIRK PARK.

Chapter Fourteen

A WEST COAST FAMILY TREE

The histories of shipping ventures the world over are peppered with mergers, joint ventures, joint services, and interesting financial deals about which little is ever heard outside of the confines of the average board room or the little publicized shipping industry. Some shipping companies have had long unbroken histories and seem to have sailed regally on like a reigning royal family, others have gone from "rags to riches" in a few short years, and then back to rags and a quick extinction. Many shipping ventures which have long been out of business, leave their mark on history while others are forgotten almost before they have closed their doors.

Shipping is a notoriously speculative and fickle business, sometimes throwing off enormous profits but more frequently capable of creating serious losses for the unwary and unskilled. It is not a business for neophytes, or widows and orphans. As with any business adequate capital, and understanding of the markets and skilled and strong management are two of the prime requisites for success. A capable shipping manager has to be able to say "no" with conviction, but equally has to be able to recognize his opportunities and act upon them most frequently at very short notice.

Except for the two brief periods following each of the two world wars Canada has not been a major deepsea shipowning country although following each period hardy durable shipping men have maintained shipowning enterprises with a surprising degree of longevity, having regard to the difficult conditions in which they operated. After the first world war three such firms sprang into being, one being the Forbes Corporation of Montreal which lasted a few short years following the acquisition of one British vessel built at Coughlin's yard in Vancouver, (see chapter 4). The other two were Coughlin's themselves, a true blue locally owned private enterprise operation, and the Canadian Government Merchant Marine a government enterprise which spread the "Canadian" name around the world's trade routes but cost the Canadian taxpayer an enormous amount of money. By 1936 both were out of business as told in more detail earlier in this book.

Concurrent with the growth of trade a strong group of shipping agents developed in Canadian ports. Some concentrated on representing liner companies, which because of their regularity of service tended to provide a "bread and butter" source of income. Others tended to depend on servicing visiting tramp ships, and when tramp shipping was prosperous so also were the agents, but in times of slump the pickings could be very lean indeed.

There was also another group who acted as chartering agents for large industrial companies in arranging fixtures of vessels particularly for Canadian export cargoes, and while their prosperity also greatly depended on the vicissitudes of international trade, the amount earnable for fixing a tramp-sized cargo of say lumber to South Africa, and acting in many cases as agents in B.C. ports for the ship in addition, was a good deal more profitable than dependence on an agency fee alone.

By the time the second world war broke out the Vancouver international shipping industry, deprived as noted of the local shipowners, was entirely made up of a group of highly skilled shipping and chartering agents. When the war came most of the agencies cut back as so much shipping became subject to government control and direction.

The approaching end of the war brought a resurgence of shipping activity once government shipping controls terminated, and with it came the development of a vast disposal program on the part of the Canadian Maritime Commission of ships which were under bare-boat charter to the British Ministry of War Transport as well as those operated under the Canadian flag by the government owned Park Steamship Company.

At this point our story reverts to the 1920's and the Robert Dollar Company of San Francisco. Robert Dollar himself was a native of Falkirk, Scotland who emigrated to Ontario starting from the beginning as a lumberjack and from there moving down to Michigan and eventually to San Francisco where his first small steam lumber schooner, the NEWSBOY started Dollar off as a shipowner. The Dollar Line had been a substantial firm for many years and its involvement with British Columbia went back to the years before the first world war when it owned and operated a large sawmill at Roche Point, Dollarton near the confluence of the north and south arms of Burrard Inlet. As a steamship owner it had developed a trans-Pacific shipping line which by the early twenties owned some substantial steamers including the ROBERT DOLLAR which with a deadweight of over 16,000 tons ranked as the third largest pure freighter in the world.

One of Robert Dollar's sons was A. Melville Dollar. In fact one of the Robert Dollar fleet carried Melville's name. So far as can be determined Melville Dollar was intent on establishing a separate enterprise, which was to be managed from Vancouver. Dollar's office was located at 425 Howe Street, an address which was right in the heart of Vancouver's financial and shipping agency district.

It is not certain as to exactly when the first three ships were acquired from the Robert Dollar Company, but during the course of the twenties the undernoted vessels entered and made up the fleet, and while owned by an ex-patriate American based in Vancouver, the actual registered owner was the Canadian-American Navigation Co. Ltd. a company which although Canadian, registered its vessels in Hong Kong as British, clearly because it was more economical than a Canadian flag operation.

CHIEF CAPILANO ex-Robert Dollar, ex-Kurland, built in Germany in 1920 and acquired as war reparations by the Americans. On dimensions of 523.5 x 65.7 x 37.5 and with a deadweight tonnage of 16,000 tons, she rated as the biggest vessel in the Melville Dollar fleet.

CHIEF SKIDEGATE ex-Esther Dollar, ex-Parisian, ex-Bethania, built by Alexander Stephen on the Clyde in 1906. Her dimensions were 483.6 x 57.0 x 32 with a gross registered tonnage of 7548. Her notation in Lloyds states that she was equipped to handle pilchard oil in deep tanks, which might have been a special interest of the Dollar firm, although as is widely known the heavily fished pilchard suddenly disappeared from the North Pacific never to return and inevitably this put an end to the rendering of the pilchard for its oil.

CHIEF MAQUILLA ex M.S. Dollar, ex-War King, built by Kawasaki Dockyard Company at Kobe Japan in 1919 as part of the British government program for emergency replacement shipping touched upon in Chapter One. Her dimensions were 475.5 x 61.2 x 30.1, and with a gross tonnage of 9394 she was another big ship for the times. From the Robert Dollar Company she passed to the Melville Dollar interests in 1928 being registered in Hong Kong as being owned by Canadian American Shipping Co. Ltd. She was not to last long in her new ownership being abandoned south of the Aleutians on December 1, 1928 foundering the following day.

Shipping movements to and from the port of Vancouver, between 1924 and 1928 recorded by the Vancouver Merchants Exchange confirm that both the Robert Dollar Company and the Canadian American Shipping Co. were active in handling shipping in this period. Mostly the Dollar Company was concerned with Far Eastern trade, while Canadian-American was particularly active in charters to and from Europe with west coast lumber and grain. It is difficult to determine the relationship between the Robert Dollar Company and Canadian-American in that period as the latter company, which appeared to be at least quasi-independent of the San Francisco concern, also dealt with Far Eastern charters. There were frequent references in the register of ship's arrivals and clearances, to the two locally owned Coughlin ships, the CITY OF VANCOUVER and CITY OF VICTORIA, whose history is dealt with more fully in chapter 3 of this book. They were frequently on charter to either Robert Dollar or Canadian-American. Robert Dollar Company being owners of the Dollarton Mill and operating timber limits, and at least two logging camps on Vancouver Island, were probably more concerned with handling their own export cargo, appearing to more frequently favour American-flag shipping, to service their own trade to the Orient.

Melville Dollar evidently had ambitions to improve his fleet and as a result a new tramp steamer was ordered from the Greenock Dockyard Company at Greenock, Scotland. This ship named the MELMAY sounds as though she was rather special as she carried the combined name of Melville Dollar and his wife May. She first appeared in Lloyds register in 1931 as being owned by the Canadian American Navigation Company. She was smaller and probably handier than the other three preceding vessels and on dimensions of 421.4 x 59.2 x 24.7 she had a gross registered tonnage of 5572.

1930-31 was also right at the worst time in the world-wide depression which followed the New York Stock Exchange crash of 1929. Many industries were virtually in a state of ruin and a great many shipowning companies failed around the world. Melville Dollar who likely made his committment for the ship prior to the crash, based on a supposition of continuing good times, must also have gone through a period of immense personal turmoil such as few can imagine unless they have had the experience, because in 1932 he committed suicide.

Few details are recorded to-day but the short subsequent history of the MEL-MAY indicates something of the personal disaster involved. A local newspaper report of June 23, 1932 indicated that the ship had left Vancouver for West Africa to enter a new trade. The ship's next entry in Lloyds in the following year showed her as being owned by the Melmay Shipping Co. Ltd. and managed by T.L. Duff &

BESSIE DOLLAR
A typical American-built lumber carrier of the twenties. She is flying the red ensign of Hong Kong and her name is expressed on the bow in Chinese characters. Owned by Robert Dollar Company.

CHIEF CAPILANO ex KURLAND
A former German vessel built for Norddeutscher Lloyd and taken by the U.S. as war reparations. Reputed to be the third largest cargo carrier in the world at the time of her construction. Transferred to Melville Dollar interests. Note the distinct list to port due to the vessel's stowage.

MELMAY
The new vessel built on the Clyde. Unfortunately trading conditions went from boom to bust as the depression broke. The conditions, plus the obligations under the construction contract brought about the financial failure of Canadian-American Navigation Co. Ltd. and the suicide of its principal shareholder.

BURCROSS
This tanker owned by British American Oil Company flew the flag of Costa Rica, but was managed by Anglo-Canadian in the late thirties.

LAKE ATHABASKA as ASPEN PARK.

LAKE CANIM ex DORVAL PARK.

LAKE CHILLIWACK ex EARLSCOURT PARK.

Co. of Glasgow. Duff was an old established owner of small tramps, on average about half the size of the MELMAY, and seems to have functioned on behalf of the builders who had probably financed the construction of the vessel through a bank, the collateral during construction being the uncompleted ship, plus an assignment of the owners obligations under his contract. It seems likely that Dollar could not complete his committment to the builder who first of all arranged for the Canadian-American Navigation Co. to have Duff act as manager. I suspect that when Dollar could not clean up his committment, it was then that the ship was re-registered in the name of Melmay Shipping Company, and loss of Dollar's interest and the capital it represented thus perhaps contributed to his suicide.

A local newspaper report in the "Vancouver Province" mentioned that a petition to wind up Canadian-American was entered by Canadian Stevedoring Company, a creditor for about $10,000. At that time the gross liabilities were $411,656 and the assets $396,990 of which all but $10,000 was represented by an amount receivable from the Melville Dollar estate.

Following Dollar's failure a number of his staff found that they were out of jobs at a time when there were very few around. Three of these people, Andy Graham, Bill Aconley and Lorne Richardson then banded together and formed Anglo-Canadian Shipping Co. Ltd, an agency concern which developed strong chartering connections with the U.K. in particular. These men were all experienced shipping people and while there was no financial connection between them and Dollar, they were able to maintain or salvage a sufficient number of the old connections to build upon, sufficiently so that one might say that Anglo-Canadian "grew like a phoenix out of the ashes" of Canadian-American.

Anglo-Canadian's fortune from its establishment, from then on depended upon the recovery of world trade, so that by 1933 clear signs of some degree of recovery were under way and presumably the firm grew in relation to this recovery concentrating in particular on servicing the charter requirements of Seaboard Lumber and H.R. McMillan Export Company. By 1939 Anglo-Canadian was the leading agency in handling trampship cargoes of Western Canadian export cargoes. Additionally the company developed experience as an actual ship manager, in that the tanker BURCROSS was managed on behalf of British American Oil Company during the latter years of the thirties.

While it has nothing directly to do with our story an historical note can be added, the Robert Dollar Company itself drifted into difficulties. The Dollarton Mill functioned through the Second World War while the important and well-known Dollar Steamship Company, following USMC intervention emerged after the war as the American President Line, minus any involvement on the part of the Dollar family.

With the end of the war we now return to the disposal of the wartime Park Steamship vessels previously referred to. The spark in bringing into existance Western Canada Steamships Ltd. was Andy Graham of Anglo-Canadian, the other three initial participants being other local shipping agencies, North Pacific Shipping, Empire Shipping and Canada Shipping. Business was commenced with one vessel chartered from the Canadian Maritime Commission and naturally it made very good money in a period of high freight rates. The securities firm of Wood Gundy & Co. took a major interest in the firm through one of its directors, the late A.H. Williamson who for some years was chairman of the board of Western Canada. The company's banker from the beginning was the Bank of Montreal who proved to be very supportive. All told Western Canada, the largest single fleet to emerge from the second war was to acquire twenty former government vessels and three additional high class postwar vessels, all of which are detailed in the fleet lists in the previous chapter.

My first personal contact with this burgeoning new company was while in the Royal Navy at Hong Kong in 1946. I was crossing the harbour one day by ferry and spotted a strange newly arrived vessel at anchor close by the ferry route. I could tell immediately that she was a Canadian-built Park type vessel, and in fact she was, for the stranger was the ASPEN PARK. She was resplendent with a shiny black hull encircled by a prominent white band, fresh green boot-topping along the water line, white upperworks and an interesting black funnel with two white bands mounted high on the funnel divided by a thin red line, and superimposed on the red line and flooding on to the white bands was an attractive green maple leaf.

At this point Western Canada Steamship Company Limited was a brand new concern, unknown among the international pantheon of shipping companies but if its ships were any indication, it was obvious that it intended to put its best foot forward. The ASPEN PARK looked about as smart as any ship I had ever seen and her funnel colours could not be mistaken for those of any other company. A few days later I was treated to a similar view of the GARDEN PARK which looked every bit as good as her sister. Incidentally while on the subject of colours the house flag was equally attractive, being white with a fishtail upon which was a red St. George's cross and a green maple leaf in the upper quarter against the mast or staff. While at Hong Kong I met the carpenter off the GARDEN PARK and was invited to visit the ship to look her over.

Unfortunately this did not happen as my plans were frustrated by other events on the way over to the landing in Hong Kong harbour where I was to meet the ship's boat at an appointed time. Ten years later, by which time I was a resident of North Vancouver, I took pity on a poor fellow who was walking his way home through a teeming North Shore rainstorm. He was glad to be rescued and as I drove him to his home I immediately remembered that I had met him once before. He was the carpenter off the GARDEN PARK with whom I had formed a brief friendship in Hong Kong. He invited me into his magnificent new home which he had built unassisted with a view to selling, making a fat profit and then moving down to Arizona. I never saw or heard of him after this chance meeting so once again our rendezvous had been as brief and coincidental as the one we had in Hong Kong.

The second occasion of a personal contact with the company occurred in 1952 after my arrival in Vancouver. I was appointed marine insurance manager at the well-known Vancouver firm of Parsons Brown Ltd. More than most, this firm was an aggressive seller of insurance with a large number of salesmen in its employ. Coming from a country where insurance was "transacted" rather than "sold", the Parsons Brown concept was an eye-opener for me. This is not to sell them short in any way as they did in fact have a considerable number of highly trained and capable insurance people on staff. One such was J. Fred Pudney, a likeable extrovert, and a thin intense man with an equally thin mustache. I got on well with Pudney who functioned as sales manager, and then one day he informed me that he had put me down for a Vancouver Board of Trade public-speaking course which was very well thought of among the business community being run by another expert, Dr. Fred Smith of U.B.C.

These sessions in the evening were I think held at the Hotel Vancouver, and through them I came to know Captain J.S. Clarke, president of Western Canada Steamships. Jack Clarke was a true gentleman and first-class shipping man both afloat, and ashore as a ship manager. He felt he needed to improve his public speaking ability, and he occasionally told me interesting items to do with ships within the fleet of Western Canada knowing of my strong interest in such subjects.

Western Canada Steamships came into being as already noted due largely to the efforts of A.B. "Andy" Graham of Anglo-Canadian, and while that company was in no way a financial continuation of the failed Melville Dollar company, Canadian American, it will be seen that in a tenuous way Western Canada grew out of the failure of the one and the establishment of the other in 1932. Western Canada was also unique in another way in that it was very clearly controlled and largely owned and directed by Vancouver people with a robust contingent of dedicated shipping people, who seemed to have a stronger than usual faith in the future of a Canadian shipping company.

Of the six Vancouver-based fleets which emerged after the war, two were offshoots of major forest companies (McMillan and Seaboard) one was a subsidiary of

LAKE COWICHAN ex GARDEN PARK

LAKE KOOTENAY ex KITSILANO PARK

LAKE LILLOOET ex LEASIDE PARK.

LAKE OKANAGAN ex RUPERT PARK.

LAKE SHAWNIGAN ex TIPPERARY PARK.

LAKE SUMAS ex WINDERMERE PARK.

LAKE TATLA ex WINONA PARK.

LAKE WINNIPEG ex YOHO PARK.

a large Danish firm (The East Asiatic Company), one was controlled from New Zealand and Montreal (Union S.S. Company of New Zealand, itself a subsidiary of the giant P & O group, and Canadian) and the fifth was a joint venture of Anglo-American owners (Silver Line of London and Kerr Steamship Company of New York). Seaboard and Canadian-Australasian, the New Zealand-controlled company, were relatively long-lived, the latter managing to continue its trans-Pacific service with the Canadian ships until the container age took over in the early sixties.

In the case of the McMillan ships, owned by its subsidiary Canadian Transport, the Kerr-Silver and the Johnson Walton (E.A.C.) ships they were all disposed of by 1949 as the result of a shipping recession which undoubtedly created a lot of unattractive red ink for them. Western Canada also had to cut back its fleet to some extent, although it did develop the device of transferring four of its ships to the U.K. register and dividing them equally for management purposes between the well known British tramp operators, Sir Robert Ropner & Company of Darlington, England, and the Lyle Shipping Company of Glasgow.

At this point it should be noted that the ships which were sold on attractive terms to the postwar Canadian owners by the Canadian Maritime Commission incurred certain liabilities for their owners, the principal one of which was the flag covenant. If a ship was sold foreign before its deemed economic life under Canadian ownership and registration had expired, the funds which flowed from the sale had to be placed in a special escrow account designed to ensure that such monies would be re-invested in new modern replacement ships.

The requirement in principle was sound as it was meant to sustain an up-to-date privately operated Canadian merchant marine and at the same time give encouragement to Canadian shipyards, but in practice the limitations quickly became apparent as neither Canadian owners or shipbuilders could really compete against cheap foreign flags and highly efficient large scale foreign shipyards. Our merchant marine and shipbuilding industries were mostly a direct outgrowth of the wartime emergency and the attractive immediate postwar shipping rates and opportunities. Once times toughened and became more competitive there remained little attraction to stay in business for most of our Canadian fleets.

Western Canada Steamship Company ran counter to the record of their contemporaries and in fact did acquire three very modern ships starting in 1956 when most of the others had gone out of business. This was an act of faith on the part of Canadian shipping capital but realistically none of the vessels could be brought under the Canadian flag, being managed and registered in Britain where costs were lower, manned by British crews, and operated on behalf of Western Canada, but by 1961 the first two ships remained, the last one to be acquired having been lost by shipwreck in the Philippines.

I have been fortunate in having in my possession annual reports of the company for the years 1956 to 1961 and it is from these that it is possible to develop a fairly full account of the second phase of the history of the Western Canada company when it finally disposed of the last of its Canadian war-built ships, the second LAKE KOOTENAY, until its final demise in 1963 when it was folded into its original founding member Anglo-Canadian Shipping Company. In fact Western Canada, presumably for tax reasons, and with a healthy earned surplus became Anglo-Canadian Shipping Company (1963) Ltd. and the original Anglo-Canadian incorporation was wound up.

Of the three postwar diesel ships which are part of the detailed fleet list in the previous chapter the first two were:-

LAKE PENNASK, ex JERSEY SPRAY. Acquired from Morel Limited, Cardiff, contract of purchase signed March 14, 1956. Purchase price C$ 2,356,305. Vessel built by William Doxford, Sunderland and owned in name of Lake Pennask Shipping Co. Ltd., a B.C. corporation, but the ship itself was registered in the U.K.

LAKE ATLIN ex JERSEY MIST. Acquired from Morel Limited, Cardiff, contract of purchase signed March 20, 1956. Purchase price C$2,344,703. Vessel built by William Doxford, Sunderland and owned in name of Lake Atlin Shipping Co. Ltd., a B.C. corporation, but the ship itself was registered in the U.K.

In the 1956 annual report Captain Clarke explains a little of the intricacies of this transaction. The LAKE PENNASK was purchased partially out of earnings, with the balance made up by way of a loan from the Bank of Montreal. Because no resort was had to tied escrow funds the vessel was not subject to regulation by the Canadian Maritime Commission under the flag covenant.

The position was somewhat different with the LAKE ATLIN as $1,272,931 was utilised from escrow funds with the balance being borrowed from the escrow account, and thus the vessel became subject to Canadian Maritime Commission regulations, which because of this restriction, is possibly the reason why the LAKE ATLIN became the last vessel to be owned by Western Canada or its subsidiaries.The report added that the LAKE PENNASK was delivered to her new owners at Leith on April 11, 1956 and sailed for Hamburg to pick up a full cargo of potash for Japan. The LAKE ATLIN was delivered at Newcastle-on-Tyne July 5, 1956 and sailed July 13 for Norfolk, Virginia to pick up her first cargo of coal, also for Japan.

In 1956 the fleet list included the last of the war-built ex-Park steamers, the TABLE BAY, WALVIS BAY and LAKE KOOTENAY. The WALVIS BAY had sustained a heavy loss due to grounding the previous year which cut into the ship-earning days of the fleet quite severely, but freight rates were bouyant and this almost made up for the loss of the WALVIS BAY earnings by comparison with the previous fiscal year. Gross revenue was $2,902,000 by comparison with the previous year at $2,949,000, but the net profit at $187,979 showed a substantial increase from $39,941 the previous year after all expenses. The report went on to note that a new government policy announcement had liberalised regulations on escrow funds to the extent that such money could now be used for building tankers. With this new regulation to assist, the company also announced that it had sold the balance of its escrow funds of $1,398,376 at a discount of 16 per cent with the net proceeds being used to pay off the balance of funds owing to the bank for the purchase of the LAKE ATLIN.

The 1957 report confirmed the sale of the three remaining warbuilt ships the TABLE BAY, WALVIS BAY and LAKE KOOTENAY at an average price of $1,381,000, the proceeds going back into the previously cleared escrow fund as all three ships were subject to Canadian Maritime Commission regulations. The company did very well out of these three sales as apart from the fact that they had had ten years good service out of the ships, by the time the announcement was noted in

WHAT HAPPENS TO OLD CANADIAN SHIPS
Greek freighter CNOSAGA loads lumber from wooden scows at Vancouver in the early fifties. Formerly the LAKE LILLOOET most of these ships passed to Greek owners, often flying flags of convenience, in this instance Panama. The actual owner was associated with Michael G. Livanos, one of the family who made up Livanos Bros. one of the most powerful in Greek shipping until the group split up into individual units all of whom continued to be related in business.

LAKE PENNASK
One of three modern motorships purchased from British owners in the fifties.

LAKE ATLIN
The second of two sister ships and the last vessel to be owned by Western Canada Steamship Company before it retired from active shipowning.

LAKE BURNABY
This fine looking motorship was the third and last to be acquired and the only one in the fleet to become a total loss. Whatever remains of her lies rusting on a coral reef in the Sulu Sea.

the annual report the market value for similar ships had fallen to under $650,000.

The other major announcement in this year was that a third new vessel had been acquired. This was the m.v. LLANTRISANT, the largest, fastest, and the third diesel ship the company was to own. With a deadweight capacity of 10,800 tons and a speed of 13.5 knots, she had been built for Evan Thomas & Radcliffe Ltd. of Cardiff in 1952. Delivery was actually effected in Seattle on May 13, 1957 and Radcliffe's managed her back to the U.K. where her name was changed to LAKE BURNABY with management then going to Ropner's one of the two favoured U.K. managers. In the case of this third vessel it was not placed into the ownership of a subsidiary, the parent Western Canada Steamship Company assuming ownership in its own name.

Once again the Bank of Montreal financed the purchase pending receipt of the proceeds of sale of the above three warbuilt ships, which taken together almost equalled the purchase cost of the LAKE BURNABY.

The buyers of the escrow funds mentioned above as having been sold the previous year turned out to be Imperial Oil who used them to build coastal tankers. As later events unfolded much similar escrow money found its way into such investments as re-engining and rebuilding a variety of B.C. tugs, as well as new fishing vessels.

The company also announced the securing of a five-year contract to carry bulk alumina from Japan to the Columbia River and as Captain Clarke stated it would assist in bringing their vessels back to the B.C. coast in many cases. Despite best efforts it was very difficult to return a vessel from Japan to the west coast with a paying cargo.

This was a bad period for major losses. The LAKE ATLIN touched a coral reef in the Celebes Sea on October 24, 1957. Fortunately she was not holed and she was able to proceed to the U.K. with her full cargo of copra after temporary repairs at Singapore. On arrival at Hull she was drydocked and found to have sustained severe bottom damage.

The big news in the 1959 report was the untimely loss of the LAKE BURNABY, which after loading a full cargo of copra at several Philippine ports left her final port of departure at Zamboanga on November 3, 1958 for ports in the Rotterdam/Hamburg range. While crossing the Sulu Sea she ran aground on a coral reef. The weather was deteriorating before the salvage ships from Manila could arrive and the vessel started to break up. By November 18 there remained only one course which was to tender notice of abandonment to the underwriters. Salvors removed whatever they could, and fortunately there was neither loss of life or injury, the crew being flown home to England arriving December 2, 1958, while the master and chief engineer stood by in case they could be of assistance to the salvors but by January 19, 1959, they also left for England.

Oddly enough this vessel the last to be acquired, was the company's first and only total loss.

The report commented that with the loss of this ship the directors would continue to watch for fresh opportunities to replace with another vessel, but this was not to happen as events turned out. Freight rates were high but so also were ship replacement costs and it was clearly only a matter of time before both came down following the usual cycles. Owners would always try to buy a second-hand replacement ship at as near to the bottom of a cycle as they could judge, with the expectancy that they would catch the next cycle of rising freight rates.

A big disappointment was that the five-year contract for the carriage of alumina from Japan to Portland was cancelled unilaterally by the charterers after one delivery on the grounds of the unsuitability of the vessels placed on the berth. One wonders how the charterers could have been so mislead, as the company's ships were fully documented in Lloyds Register of shipping. Quite apart from that it was usual when negotiating contracts of this nature for the owner or his broker to submit general arrangement plans for the charterer's information and approval. Frustration of a charter on some technical grounds was not unknown as a device when a long-term committment such as a five-year contract indicated to the charterer that he was caught with a high freight rate committment in a falling market. Frustrating the contract in this manner might well prove cheaper, even though commercially dishonest, but when comparing the results which would flow from legal action and a negotiated settlement, with paying a higher rate for five years ahead, some hard-nosed charterers could be relied upon to adopt such tactics.

The report for 1960 was of a very routine nature. Freight rates were low and the company made a loss of $251,422, but there was a note that an acceptable out of court settlement was expected in the matter of the alumina contract.

When the 1961 report appeared it was confirmed that the settlement of the breach of contract action in regard to the alumina contract was received, but the amount was not mentioned in the president's statement or specifically recorded in the statement of operating income unless it was buried in an item of $44,254 under miscellaneous operating revenue. Reading between the lines the outcome was clearly not one that Western Canada could derive much satisfaction from, and it was probably a matter of making the most out of a bad job.

Captain Clarke noted in the previous year's report that the British seamen had received increases in wages amounting to 20 per cent which impacted on operating costs. For a second time within the year a further increase was awarded which boosted manning costs by a further 15 per cent, and compounded the problems of operating ships competitively under the British flag which was starting to increasingly take on the uneconomic aspects of Canadian and American flag operations in competition with cheaper foreign flags, and thus going out of business or flagging out under flags of convenience.

Looking back historically this point in time also probably represented the high-water mark in the British merchant marine, and from the early 1960's the slow decline in British flag shipping got under way, with many old-established owners finding that this was when they should sell their ships to foreign owners and retire.

There were by now also signs that Western Canada Steamship was in the process of making a change in direction. The increasing popularity of the single deck bulk-carriers was making inroads at the expense of the typical two-deck tramps of the type of the LAKE ATLIN and LAKE PENNASK, while the growth of container traffic was to ensure the demise of the traditional cargo liner, and thus a previously strong charter market for many owners of good class tramp type ships. By this time however the Canadian Maritime Commission flag covenant restrictions had expired, and while nothing is said in so many words about the disposal of the last two vessels, it was now clear that the ships could be disposed of without restriction when a favourable opportunity arose. The first to go was LAKE PENNASK and soon after the LAKE ATLIN followed.

As events unfolded this was to be the end of Western Canada as a shipowning concern but by now its affairs were more closely linked to those of Anglo-Canadian than ever before as the other significant shareholders had all been bought out over the years. Co-inciding with the large scale removal and scrapping of war-built, ex-Park and Liberty ships from first-class ownerships on account of age, Anglo-Canadian had been encouraging the B.C. forest product producers to package their lumber and pulp into convenient size parcels. The basic idea was that with new types of ships and cargo handling equipment packaged product could be more speedily and conveniently handled. With new large scale lumber assembly docks, modern methods could load a ship with more cargo a lot more quickly when compared to the old methods using several loading points and ship's gear which had not changed in any essential way since the beginning of the century when twin boom union-purchase gear came into common use.

Around the mid-sixties and probably not too long after the last Western Canada ship had been disposed of, Anglo-Canadian was approached by a representative of the large Swedish shipping concern, Brostroms of Gothenburg to enquire as to the interest of Anglo-Canadian in taking under charter new ships to be constructed, which would meet with Anglo's ideas and specifications for the movement of B.C. forest products.

Anglo-Canadian's ideas called for a type of bulk-carrier described as the "open hatch" design, equipped with high speed electric cranes of the Hagglund or similar type. Described simply, an open hatch ship had huge sliding steel hatches which would open up the entire length and breadth of the hold, while the side ballast tanks were arranged vertically in such a way that the hold formed a near perfect box. This made for fast and easy stowage with no significant wasted space when loading prepackaged cargo. Not only was this type of ship faster and more economical in both loading and discharge but the common speed now became 14 knots by comparison with the old standard which seldom exceeded 11 knots with the conventional tramps. The most critical factor was the economics of scale created by loading a ship with say a deadweight of 27,000 tonnes or more, compared to a slower conventional trampship loading about a third of that tonnage, and with the modern vessel manned by a smaller crew.

In any event Anglo-Canadian's requirements had a material bearing on the formation of the Scanscot bulk-carrier consortium, an eight-vessel group of sister ships, three under the British flag, three Swedish and two Norwegian. Of these the Swedish COLUMBIALAND of 1967 and VICTORIA of 1968, and both of 26,420 deadweight tons, honoured both the province of B.C. and the provincial capital at Victoria. It was in these two vessels that Anglo-Canadian for a period of time was a part-owner.

Scanscot was a product of the period in the sixties and seventies when British, Scandinavian and other European owners were busily forming consortiums to jointly own the new generation of larger and vastly more expensive ships then coming into vogue. With the passage of time and the massive shift of shipowning capital to flags

178

of convenience often controlled from the Orient, the greater number of the consortiums of that period have drifted into extinction which proves that shipping is always a changing often fast-moving business, with little of the old stability remaining which saw household names in shipping last for a century and more. Modern shipping is more likely to be a faceless, traditionless exercise in balance sheet economics, having little relationship to companies of even such recent vintage as Western Canada Steamship Company Ltd. a British Columbia-owned company in which local ship-lovers could take genuine pride. Regretably we are unlikely to see the likes of such a Canadian-flag concern again.

Anglo-Canadian is now the sole survivor of the three companies whose histories have been outlined here. It has also prospered for sixty years as a chartering concern whose place in international shipping remains secure. Ownership of the company shifted from the founders to an in-house group along with a locally-based international investment concern, Hastings West Investments Ltd. Then for a period from 1981, Hastings held sole ownership after the in-house group had more or less reached retirement age. In 1991 the present internal management purchased the business from Hastings West, which returned the company back to purely local ownership. Born at the height of the depression, the sixty years which have elapsed have successfuly taken the company through the second world war, and several major trade recessions. It is now reasonable to wish the firm every success over the next sixty years.

Chapter Fifteen

WHAT OF THE CANADIAN SHIPYARDS?

The origins and industrial growth brought on by both world wars in the country's shipyards have already been described elsewhere in this book. The purpose in this chapter is to focus on the actual shipyards, to measure individual impact and to look at where the survivors may be today.

Before recalling history let us look at the world shipbuilding picture and compare it with the relative position in years gone by.

Up until the first world war Britain was the undisputed leader among the world's shipbuilding industries. Germany probably had the most shipbuilding muscle after Britain followed by the United States, with lesser but important industries growing in countries like Japan, France, Italy, Sweden and Denmark. Among the British Dominions, Canada and to a lesser extent Australia were the only ones with a potential for great expansion in shipbuilding although this was considered most unlikely in 1914.

The first world war was to upset many things including Britain's leading position as a shipbuilding and shipowning country. Germany was temporarily knocked out of the picture although much of her industrial capacity remained, while the United States took giant leaps forward through its demonstrated ability to build a large fleet in a very short period of time. The three main shipbuilding countries Britain, the U.S.A. and Germany all possessed large coal mining and steel-making facilities, both necessities to support the industrial effort required to build large naval ships and the huge passenger liners which were the forerunners of the airline industry of today.

The war was of great advantage to Japan even though her participation was limited to taking over German possessions in the Orient while she received large orders for munitions including new ships built for Britain. Japan was able to demonstrate her capability very quickly and from thereon her industrial and military capacity grew unabated until December 7, 1941 when she attacked Pearl Harbour and the Pacific war commenced.

The 1920's and 30's saw a resurgence of shipbuilding in Germany which not only built many high-class vessels for her own decimated merchant marine, but also became a major supplier of new ships to other countries in particular Norway and even Britain. The USSR also started to show signs of becoming a significant shipbuilding country in the 1930's, but the war was a set-back which saw most of her shipbuilding industry laid waste. Following the war, the USSR and other iron curtain countries notably Poland and East Germany accomplished a huge resurgence in their industries.

The shipbuilding industries in Sweden, Denmark, France and Italy made big strides between the wars, but for the most part that of the U.S. remained in the doldrums until 1936 when the U.S. Maritime commission instituted a steady program of building new high-class freighters and tankers as well as producing new modern warships, all of which proved to be a god-send when the U.S. came into the war.

When the British position at sea was so bad during both wars, it was the spark needed to get huge shipbuilding programs under way to augment the output of Britain's own hard-pressed shipyards, the principle contributor in both cases was the United States, and to a lesser extent Canada in keeping with her smaller industrial infrastructure. In terms of postwar peacetime requirements there were unfortunately too many tramp-type ships built which quickly demonstrated their inability to compete against new modern postwar shipping, and while efforts were made to maintain a strong nucleus of merchant ship-building in both countries, the shipbuilding industry quickly deflated, the first yards to close usually being those whose reason for existance was wholly based on the wartime emergency.

All the yards set up during the 1914-18 war to build wooden steamers, were among those which folded up very quickly with the return to peace. All of these had been set up by lumber manufacturing and civil engineering and construction companies to fill a need during the wartime emergency. A few had built schooners prior to the commencement of the steamer building program for the Imperial Munitions Board. The schooners built in British Columbia appear to have been the result of a program initiated by the B.C. provincial government, under the B.C. Shipping Act, where Victoria in a limited way sought to fill the role usually reserved for the federal government. The aim of the shipping act was to encourage the building of a fleet of schooners capable of looking after the export shipping requirements of the B.C. lumber industry which had been hampered by the severe shortage of shipping, primarily British, which was normally available to local industry. Of all the wooden shipbuilders only Wallace in North Vancouver had a long tradition in the wood shipbuilding art. It also was the only one to have a long life ahead, becoming eventually Burrard Dry Dock Company which played such a significant role in the Second World War.

After the 1939-45 war some yards managed to hang on for a number of years obtaining sufficient peacetime work to fill the local market for, ferries, naval vessels, tugs, barges and other types of specialist craft. Others survived and continue to this day mostly as ship repairers, and yet others particularly in the St. Lawrence succeeded in obtaining significant Canadian Navy and foreign orders, a prime market being France.

However, while the Canadian government adopted an enlightened policy in the early post-war period in terms of both disposals of war-built ships and encouraging a continuation in shipbuilding activity through the application of shipbuilding subsidies and attractive tax write-offs, this has not warded off the demise of a large number of the yards which contributed to our war effort. One of the prime contributors to this has been the Canadian government itself, which has consistantly and short-sightedly favoured East coast yards on the grounds that the West coast, with its higher costs, cannot compete. This is true, the West coast does have higher costs and that in turn is part of the national reality. How quickly the massive contribution of the West coast in two world wars is conveniently forgotten, and how quickly would West coast industry be expected to respond once again should a similar emergency ever arise!

From the perspective of local history in the various shipbuilding towns on both coasts, once a yard had closed, its old location and identity usually disappeared very

CANADIAN CONSTRUCTOR
At a more advanced stage alongside the fitting out wharf at Burrard. For a completion photograph
see chapter two.

RISING ON THE WAYS AT BURRARD
CANADIAN CONSTRUCTOR, an
immediate postwar freighter built for
Canadian National Steamships.

WEST COAST SHIPBUILDERS LTD.
This historic yard previously run by J. Coughlin & Son in the first world war, built a large fleet during the second war. The site along with adjoining industrial developments is now occupied by a large condominium development.

YARROWS at ESQUIMALT
The Yarrows yard is to the left with a B.C. ferry alongside. The entrance to the Esquimalt Graving dock is at lower left while the R.C.N. depot Esquimalt is to the right. The vessel with the white helicopter pad near the centre of the picture is HMCS CAPE BRETON the last of all the Canadian-built freighter hulls built for the second war. Photo taken in 1987.

PRINCE RUPERT DRY DOCK CO. LTD.
The large floating dock appears to be ready to receive an incoming vessel at lower left. The fitting out wharf is at left centre with a stiff-leg and mobile crane visible. Post second world war photo.

PRINCE RUPERT DRY DOCK CO. LTD.
A 10,000 ton hull lays alongside the fitting out berth. The stiff leg crane in the previous photo is visible behind the tall tree trunk at the centre of the picture.

NORTH VAN SHIP REPAIRS LTD. formerly PACIFIC DRY DOCK CO. LTD.
Three freighters are visible. FORT GROUARD at centre is close to launching date. Cates Towing
Company with several of its tugs is to the right. The steam tug is almost certainly the last such unit
owned by Cates, having been built by famed local tugboat builder Arthur Moscrop as MOONLIGHT.

A SIGHT WHICH WILL NEVER BE REPEATED
Aerial view of Burrard Dry Dock in its heyday. All told a total of 22 vessels are visible. There is a
cluster of ten naval vessels at the right. Three French collier four-hatch hulls are on the building
ways. Viewing from the left the freighters are a French collier, a Canadian-Australasian, a Silver
Line ship raised in the dry dock, three French colliers, a Western Canada, another French collier
and a U.S. Liberty Ship with bow into an empty building ways. Burrard's successor company
Versatile Pacific Shipyards closed permanently in Sept. 1992.

quickly, the only evidence being found in old fire maps, the memories of old timers and if the site has not been redeveloped in such a manner that all clues of a past existance have been eliminated, in a few old pilings or piles of unidentifiable debris.

Take Vancouver as an example as this is the only place where the author has been able to witness redevelopments on a daily basis and even go on the sites whether active or derelict shipyards. Burrard's wartime south yard has given way to the Vanterm Container terminal and the company's now inactive North Vancouver yard seems destined for eventual real estate development on a grand scale. A little to the west, on the other side of the foot of Lonsdale Avenue, at the site of the old Pacific Dry Dock Company and its successor North Van Ship Repairs, the large Lonsdale Quay development of stores and offices, has turned a dreary industrial wasteland into a glistening real estate development. Further to the west again few could identify the old W. Lyall S.B. Company, for decades the site of some tumbledown sawmills and acres of old sawdust fill, but now a modern warehouse development at the foot of Fell Ave. Over in False Creek a huge condominium development occupies the site of West Coast Shipbuilders and its associated Vancouver Iron Works, this also being the site in the First World War of the historic J. Coughlan yard. The story is roughly the same in many locations on both sides of the country.

Following is a list of individual yards and their output of the ships in each war, which are the subject of this book. The wood-building yards have been placed in their appropriate alphabetical order, the only division being that the West coast yards have been separated from those of the Great Lakes and East Coast yards.

British American Shipbuilding Company, Welland, Ontario
This first war yard built three steel steamers of the 3,500 type, followed by two similar ships for the CGMM and then ceased operations upon completion of its contracts in 1920.

War Badger	War Raccoon	War Weasel
Canadian Otter	Canadian Squatter	

Canadian Allis Chalmers, Bridgeburg, Ontario
An operation of the well known engine builders of the same name, built four steel steamers of the 3,500 ton type, and then closed upon completion of its contracts in 1920.

War Magic	War Vixen	War Wallaby
War Wombat		

Canadian Vickers Ltd. Montreal, Quebec
This large shipyard was established as a subsidiary of the well-known British firm of Vickers Armstrong before the first world war. It became independent of its British parent between the wars, building a substantial fleet of both merchant ships and warships during the second war. It is now a part of the Versatile group under the name Versatile Vickers. (for final comments see the end of this chapter.)

WW1 Output
The first two ships named were building under contract for Westfal Larsen of Norway and were acquired by the Shipping Controller before completion.

Porsanger	Samnanger	War Duchess
War Earl	War Faith	War Joy
Canadian Commander	Canadian Conqueror	Canadian Leader
Canadian Miller	Canadian Navigator	Canadian Pioneer
Canadian Planter	Canadian Ranger	Canadian Seigneur
Canadian Spinner	Canadian Victor	Canadian Voyager

WW2 Output
NORTH SANDS type

Fort Ville Marie	Fort Nipigon	Fort Louisbourg
Fort Abitibi	Fort Senneville	

NORTH SANDS type tanker

Point Pelee Park

Collingwood Shipbuilding Company, Collingwood, Ontario
This yard built two ships of the 2,900 ton type for British account and ten of similar size for the CGMM in the first war program. In the second war it built three of the 3.600 ton tankers and four of the "C" type coasters. The yard was always closely associated with building Great Lakes carriers, and is now a subsidiary of Canadian Shipbuilding & Engineering Ltd. based in Collingwood, Ontario. (for final comments see the end of this chapter.)

WW1 Output
War Wizard	War Witch	Canadian Beaver
Canadian Coaster	Canadian Farmer	Canadian Gunner
Canadian Observer	Canadian Pathfinder	Canadian Recruit
Canadian Rover	Canadian Signaller	Canadian Warrior

WW2 Output
3.600 tanker type

Nipiwan Park	Norwood Park	Springbank Park

"C" type coaster

Ottawa Mayhill	Ottawa Mayrock	Ottawa Maytor
Ottawa Maybrook		

Davie Shipbuilding Co. Sorel, Quebec
This large concern only lists three vessels for the CGMM and then became a larger builder of standard ships in the second war. It was also the only major yard to build 10,000 tdw, 4.700 tdw, and the tiny "C" type coasters of 300 tons deadweight. This company was for many years a part of the Canada Steamship Lines group, but later became a part of the Versatile group operating as Versatile Davie. (for final comments see the end of this chapter.)

WW1 output

Canadian Challenger	Canadian Hunter	Canadian Trapper

WW2 output

Fort Albany	Fort Brunswick	Fort Carillon
Fort Cataraqui	Fort Chambly	Fort Concord
Fort La Maune	Fort Mingan	Fort St. Francois
Fort Tadoussac	Banff Park	Chippewa Park
Gatineau Park	High Park	Jasper Park
Point Pleasant Park	Prince Albert Park	Riverdale Park
Riverview Park	Dufferin Park	Lansdowne Park
Mayfair Park	Baldwin Park	Willow Park
Bell Park	Cartier Park	

"C" type coaster

Ottawa Maycrest	Ottawa Mayfall	Ottawa Mayhaven
Ottawa Mayspring	Ottawa Maythorn	

Dominion Shipbuilding Company, Halifax N.S.

This was strictly another First World War yard. It lists two steel vessels only for CGMM, both of which were among the first to be disposed of by this owner.

Canadian Artificer	Canadian Engineer

Foundation Company, Victoria, B.C.

This concern was an offshoot of the well known Foundation Group of companies based in Montreal. Its yard was set up to participate in the wooden shipbuilding program of the First World War following which it closed. Five ships were built.

War Babine	War Camchin	War Masset
War Nanoose	War Songhee	

Foundation Maritime Ltd. Pictou, N.S.

This was a second war shipbuilding venture of the Foundation Group. Foundation Maritime Ltd. actually dated back to 1928 and became famous as a successful deep-sea salvage concern, owning among other vessels the veteran FOUNDATION FRANKLIN so well-known for many epics of salvage. This yard was the largest builder of the 4,700 tdw Scandinavian type freighters.

Ainslie Park	Avondale Park	Beresford Park
Cataraqui Park	Chignecto Park	Confederation Park
Crescent Park	^Hector Park	Kelowna Park
Kensington Park	Liscomb Park	Manitou Park
Montmorency Park	Rockcliffe Park	Taber Park
Victoria Park	Wentworth park	Woodland Park

^This ship was one of several which were planned to be turned over to the British Ministry of War Transport, all with names carrying the prefix "Camp". HECTOR PARK was renamed CAMP DEBERT during construction, and was the only such vessel turned over to the British government.

Fraser, Brace & Co. Montreal, Quebec

This company were constructional engineers whose yard came into being to build WW1 wooden vessels at a site which was set up on the south side of the Lachine canal, in the district of Cote St. Paul. Four vessels were built for the British Imperial Munitions Board.

War Erie	War Huron	War Niagara
War Ottawa		

Grant & Horne, Courtenay Bay, St. John, N.B.

Yard set up for building wooden steamers.

War Fundy	War Moncton

Great Lakes Dredging Company, Fort William, Ontario

Yard Set up for building wooden steamers.

War Nipigon	War Sioux

Halifax Shipyards Ltd. Halifax, N.S.

This company built four of the large 8,800 tdw type for the CGMM following the first war. There is no record of merchant shipbuilding in the second war and it appears that the company was confined to naval and repair work, as it was still in business for some years after the war, and later became Halifax Industries with repair and dry dock facilities at Halifax and Dartmouth.

Canadian Constructor	Canadian Cruiser	Canadian Explorer
Canadian Mariner		

T.M. Kirkwood & Co. Trois Rivieres, Quebec

This wartime yard built only one wood steamer.

War Mingan

Marine Industries Ltd. Sorel, Quebec

Part of the Simard group of companies with interests in various marine-based industries as mentioned in chapter 12 under Branch Lines Ltd. This major shipbuilding firm is still in business, though now nationalized. (for final comments see end of this chapter.)

Fort Beausejour	Fort Frontenac	Fort la Cloche
Fort la Tour	Fort Lennox	Fort Mattagami
Fort Michipicoten	Fort Missanabie	Fort Musquarro
Fort Nottingham	Fort Pic	Fort Richelieu
Fort St. Joseph	Fort St. Paul	Fort St. Regis
Belwoods Park	Champlain Park	Eglinton Park
Elm Park	Frontenac Park	Kawartha Park
Lakeview Park	Millican Park	Mount Revelstoke Pk
Otterburn Park	Rocky Mountains Park	Stanley Park
Tweedsmuir Park	Yamaska Park	

Midland Shipbuilding Company, Midland, Ontario
This yard built three steel steamers of the 3,500 tdw type although gross tonnages were very variable between each of the three vessels. A successor company under the name Midland Shipyards Ltd. built tugs during the second world war.

War Fiend	War Fury	War Leveret

Moreton Engineering & Dry Dock Co. Ltd. Quebec
This yard built four of the 4,700 tdw type during the second war as well as five of the "C" class coasters. It became St Lawrence Metal & Marine Works Inc. following the war.

Hamilton Park	Maissoneuve Park	Rockland Park
Westdale Park	Ottawa Maybank	Ottawa Maycliff
Ottawa Mayglen	Ottawa Maymere	Ottawa Maystar

Nova Scotia Steel & Coal Company, New Glasgow, N.S.
This company built two vessels for the Imperial Munitions Board and three similar ships for CGMM. The yard became defunct following completion of these vessels.

War Bee	War Wasp	Canadian Miner
Canadian Sapper	Canadian Sealer	

Polson Ironworks Ltd., Toronto, Ontario
This was a well-known company, building ships in the 3,500 tdw class for the Imperial Munitions Board. The company was not awarded any contracts from the CGMM. The first two vessels were ordered by Norwegian owners but requisitioned by the Shipping Controller,

Asp	Tento	War Algoma
War Halton	War Hamilton	War Hydra
War Taurus	War Timiskaming	

Port Arthur Shipbuilding Co., Ltd. Port Arthur, Ontario
Now a part of Canadian Shipbuilding & Engineering Ltd. along with Collingwood Shipyards, this company built the following,

War Dance	War Fish	War Hatbor
War Horus	War Isis	War Karma
War Osiris	Canadian Adventurer	Canadian Carrier
Canadian Runner	Canadian Sailor	Canadian Sower
Canadian Trader	Ottawa Maybird	Ottawa Maycove
Ottawa Mayferry		

Quebec S.B. & Repair Company, Quebec, P.Q.
This building yard finished two wooden steamers. Out of business by 1919.

War Quebec	War Sorel

Quinlan & Robertson, Quebec, P.Q.
The output of this yard was four wooden steamers. Like the others building the type, it was out of business by 1919.

War Gaspe	War Matane	War Mohawk
War Seneca		

Saint John Dry Dock Co. Ltd. St. John, N.B.

This yard controlled by the K.C. Irving interests built eight of the 4,700 Scandinavian type vessels and a few "C" class coasters. It is one of the few Canadian yards enjoying a satisfactory level of prosperity today as it is the prime builder of the R.C.N's current program of destroyer replacements. It has the capability of building ships to 100,000 tdw, although this was not the case during the war.

Argyle Park	Bloomfield Park	Dartmouth Park
Fawkner Park	Oakmount Park	Rockwood Park
Shakespeare Park	Taronga Park	Ottawa Maybeech
Ottawa Maycloud	Ottawa Mayview	

Southern Salvage Company, Liverpool N.S.

This company built one of the wooden steamers in 1918 and then went out of business as a shipbuilder.

War Halifax

Three Rivers S.B. Co. Trois Rivieres, Quebec

This yard, formerly known as T.M. Kirkwood, built one of the wooden steamers, but a second was evidently cancelled.

War Radnor

Tidewater Shipbuilders Ltd. Trois Rivieres, Quebec

This yard built a number of 4,600 tdw steel steamers for CGMM as listed.

Canadian Fisher	Canadian Forester	Canadian Rancher
Canadian Settler		

Toronto DD & SB Company, Toronto, Ontario

Another wood building yard, responsible for two steamers in the 1918 program.

War Ontario   War Toronto

United Shipyards Ltd. Montreal, Quebec.

This was a large wartime yard laid out at Montreal to greatly add to emergency shipbuilding output in that region. It was operated jointly by Dominion Bridge Company Ltd. the leading Canadian heavy steel fabricator and bridge builder, together with the Montreal civil engineering firm of Fraser, Brace & Co. The latter firm had operated a wood-building shipyard in the first world war, mentioned earlier in this chapter. United ceased operations upon completion of its contracts.

Fort Coulonge	Fort Covington	Fort Crevier
Fort Erie	Fort Esperance	Fort Henley
Fort la Prairie	Fort Longueuil	Fort Maissoneuve
Fort Moose	Fort Norfolk	Fort Remy
Fort Romaine	Fort Rosalie	Fort Rouille
Fort Sandusky	Fort Ticonderoga	Fort Vercheres
Fort Wayne	Fort Wellington	Alder Park
Alexandra Park	Dentonia Park	Eastwood Park
Elk Island Park	Grafton Park	Hampstead Park
Hillcrest Park	Kildonan Park	Lafontaine Park
La Salle Park	Mount Orford Park	Noranda Park

Outremont Park	Portland Park	Rideau Park
Rondeau Park	Rosedale Park	Runnymede Park
Sibley Park	Sunalta Park	Wellington Park
Westmount Park	Whiteshell Park	Withrow Park

* * * * *

Burrard Drydock Company Ltd. North Vancouver, B.C.

Established around the turn of the century by Alfred Wallace as a builder of small wooden fishing craft for the canneries, this enterprise started as Wallace Shipyards at a small yard in False Creek and grew into the largest shipbuilding concern on the west coast. In terms of output during the second world war, it was also the most prolific builder of the merchant vessels which are the subject of this book. In addition it built and converted naval vessels. Its first ventures into large wooden shipbuilding saw the firm building a number of the five masted schooners constructed in the first war under the B.C. Shipping Act. It sold this yard to W. Lyall in 1916 who continued with the construction of wood hulled steamers.

In and after the second war it first purchased the assets of its neighbour Pacific Dry Dock Company in 1944 and continued construction there of 10,000 ton freighters renaming the company North Van Ship Repairs Ltd. In 1946 Burrard acquired the assets and undertaking of Yarrows Ltd. at Esquimalt, the merged firms then becoming Burrard-Yarrows. In 1971 the controlling Wallace family sold out to Cornat Industries, a rising conglomerate with an array of interests, which in turn became Versatile Corporation. (for conclusion see end of this chapter.)

During the second world war, Burrard opened a second yardon the Vancouver side of Burrard Inlet, naming the subsidiary Vancouver Dry Dock Company. Hulls were constructed here and towed over to the North Vancouver yard for completion. Between the two yards and with the addition of the North Van Ship Repairs, the group outstripped by a broad margin the output of all other yards in the construction of *North Sands, Canadian* and *Victory* types.

It built the largest number of the stores issuing or fleet train vessels and the navy maintenance ships for the British Admiralty, as well as converting all 19 of the pocket aircraft carriers transferred from the U.S. Navy to the Royal Navy. Even though North Van Ship Repairs has been numbered in the group the output of this yard has been listed separately as there was of course output from this concern when owned by its previous owners as Pacific Dry Dock Company.

WW1 output at Wallace Shipyards

War Dog	War Power	War Storm
Canadian Highlander	Canadian Raider	Canadian Skirmisher
Canadian Trooper	Canadian Volunteer	

WW2 output - As Burrard Dry Dock Co. North Vancouver Yard

NORTH SANDS type

Fort Ash	Fort Assiniboine	Fort Athabaska
Fort Bedford	Fort Bell	Fort Brandon
Fort Buckingham	Fortt Churchill	Fort Connolly

Fort Fork
Fort Kootenay
Fort Lawrence
Fort McMurray
Fort Pitt
Fort Spokane

Fort Fraser
Fort Lac la Ronge
Fort Livingstone
Fort Meductic
Fort Poplar
Fort Vermillion

Fort Howe
Fort Lajoie
Fort McLoughlin
Fort Nashwaak
Fort St. James

VICTORY type
Fort Bellingham
Fort Columbia
Fort Machault
Fort Wallace
Kootenay Park
Tobiatic Park

Fort Biloxi
Fort Dearborn
Fort St. Nicholas
Beaton Park
Mewata Park
Westend Park

Fort Brisebois
Fort la Have
Fort Sakisdac
Coronation Park
Strathcona Park

VICTORY Fleet Train ships
Fort Dunvegan
Fort McDonnell

Fort Edmonton

Fort Kilmar

CANADIAN type
Cromwell Park

Garden Park

Rupert Park

VICTORY type - R.N. Maintenance Ships
Beachy Head
Duncansby Head

Berry Head
Portland Bill

Dodman Point
Selsey Bill

"B" type - China coasters
Ottawa Page
Ottawa Pangis

Ottawa Pageant
Ottawa Parade

Ottawa Palmer
Ottawa Patience

WW2 output - Vancouver DD Company, (Burrard Dry Dock Co.) South Yard

NORTH SANDS type
Fort Aklavik
Fort Caribou
Fort Cumberland
Fort Ellice
Fort Good Hope
Fort Kootenay
Fort Pine
Fort Reliance
Fort Yale

Fort Anne
Fort Charnisay
Fort Dauphin
Fort Gaspereau
Fort Halkett
Fort La Reine
Fort Qu'appelle
Fort Thompson

Fort Cadotte
Fort Chesterfield
Fort Dease Lake
Fort George
Fort Jemseg
Fort Pembina
Fort Rae
Fort Wedderburne

VICTORY type
Fort Island
Fort Orleans
Fort Yukon
Dunlop Park
Mohawk Park (2)
Tipperary Park

Fort Massac
Fort St. Croix
Aspen Park
Green Hill Park
Sapperton Park
Wascana Park

Fort Prudhomme
Fort Venango
Bowness Park
Louisbourg Park
Seacliff Park

VICTORY Fleet Train ships

Fort Alabama	Fort Constantine	Fort Providence
Fort Wrangell		

CANADIAN type

Albert Park	Fairmount Park	Princeton Park

VICTORY type - R.N. Maintenance Ships

Fife Ness	Flamborough Head	Girdle Ness
Hartland Point	Spurn Point	

Cameron Genoa Mills, Victoria, B.C.
A wooden shipbuilder set up to participate in the wooden steamer building program of 1918. The yard was a subsidiary of the well known Cameron Lumber Company of Victoria.

War Haida	War Skeena	War Stikine
War Yukon		

J. Coughlan & Son Ltd. Vancouver, B.C.
The story of this most prolific company from the First World War has been fully set out in chapter 3. The ability of the shipyard to turn out ships in record time says much for the management and the work crew. In a newspaper report in the Vancouver News-Herald of June 8, 1942, it was stated that Coughlan's record of 66 1/2 days from keel laying to trials in English Bay was never beaten, Within 91 days this vessel the INDUS, was loading in Tacoma for her maiden voyage. It was claimed as a Canadian record not excelled even in the second war when Burrard, arguably the most efficient and productive of all Canadian yards reduced its building time to a record 112 days from keel-laying to completion of trials.

WW1 output
8,800 TDW type

Alaska	War Camp	War Cavalry
War Charger	War Chariot	War Chief
War Column	War Company	War Convoy
War Noble	Canadian Exporter	Canadian Freighter
Canadian Importer	Canadian Inventor	Canadian Prospector
Canadian Transporter	Indus	Braheholm
Margaret Coughlan	City of Vancouver	City of Victoria

Harbour Marine Company, Victoria, B.C.
Was a company set up by interests associated with Victoria Machinery Depot (see below). V.M.D. as a supplier of engineering services and products obtained a contract from the Canadian Government Merchant Marine to build an initial two of the 8,800 tdw type of freighter built by Coughlan's in particular, but was so located that it could not build them itself. Harbour Marine Company Ltd. was set up for the purpose and a site acquired near Ogden Point upon which many ships were to be built in the subsequent history of Victoria Machinery Depot. The two vessels were increased to a total of four, viz,

Canadian Armourer   Canadian Composer   Canadian Traveller
Canadian Winner

W. Lyall SB Company, North Vancouver

This yard was set up and owned by W. Lyall Construction Company a large civil construction firm originating from Montreal. The yard located near the foot of Fell Avenue had originally been set up by Wallace Shipyards to build wooden schooners. Wallace with a long tradition of wooden ship and boat building disposed of the yard to Lyall consequent upon its decision to concentrate on steel shipbuilding. Lyall, which had first built six schooners for Belgian interests, was originally awarded ten building contracts but while all keels were laid only six were completed, viz,

War Atlin   War Cariboo   War Cayuse
War Nicola   War Puget   War Suquash

New Westminster SB & Eng Co. New Westminster, B.C.

Located at Poplar Island, New Westminster this company completed four wooden steamers in 1918, viz,

War Comox   War Edensaw   War Ewen
War Kitimat

North Van Ship Repairs Ltd./Pacific D.D. Company

The origins of this company grew from the acquisition of B.C. Salvage Company, owners of salvage tugs based in Victoria, and originally founded by Bullen's, predecessors of Yarrows in the operation of what became the well-known Victoria yard, Yarrows Ltd. Arthur and Norman Burdick were investors who had a number of business interests particularly in real estate development. After acquisition of B.C. Salvage they acquired property just west of the foot of Lonsdale Avenue, North Vancouver on the site of the present day Lonsdale Quay.

Because of their success in bringing in damaged or disabled ships the development of repair facilities became a logical extension to their towing activities, and thus Pacific Dry Dock Company came into being. They do not appear to have been responsible for any large shipbuilding projects until the need for wartime emergency shipping became apparent in 1941.

Pacific Dry Dock was later acquired by Burrard Dry Dock Company, but the entire output is listed below. At this point in time it is not possible to allocate which vessel building contracts solely benefitted the Burdick interests, and which went to Burrard. Suffice to say that the company was taken over as a going concern with contracts in hand and work at various stages on vessels under construction. Burrard renamed the firm North Van Ship Repairs Ltd.

NORTH SANDS type

Fort a la Corne	Fort Alexandra	Fort Augustus
Fort Babine	Fort Battle River	Fort Bourbon
Fort Buffalo	Fort Capot River	Fort Carlton
Fort Cedar Lake	Fort Drew	Fort Fairford
Fort Fidler	Fort Frederick	Fort Frobisher
Fort Gibraltar	Fort Grahame	Fort Grouard

Fort Jasper	Fort la Montee	Fort McPherson
Fort Paskoyac	Fort Simpson	Fort Steele
Green Gables Park	Mount Robson Park (1)	

VICTORY type

Fort Clatsop	Fort Hall	Fort Marin
Fort Panmure	Fort Saleesh	Fort St. Antoine
Buffalo Park	Bridgeland Park	Connaught Park
Crystal Park	Dorval Park	Dundurn Park
Goldstream Park	Kitsilano Park	Leaside Park
Richmond Park	Temagami Park	Westbank Park
Whiterock Park	Yoho Park (2)	

CANADIAN type

| Highland Park | Selkirk Park | Simcoe Park |

VICTORY- R.N. Maintenance Ships

| Mull of Galloway | Mull of Kintyre | Mull of Oa |
| Rame Head | Rattray Head | |

"B" class China coasters

| Ottawa Panda | Ottawa Parapet | Ottawa Patrol |

VICTORY Fleet Train ships
Fort Colville

Pacific Construction Company, Coquitlam, B.C.
This was a large civil contracting firm. Its yard built two only of the wooden steamers in 1918.

| War Sumas | War Tyee |

Pacific Drydock Company Ltd. (see North Van Ship Repairs Ltd.)

Prince Rupert Dry Dock Company, Prince Rupert, B.C.
Of all the shipyards in Canada no single one probably owes more for its existence and continuation over almost half a century to politicians. The project was conceived as part of the terminal operations at Prince Rupert of the Grand Trunk Pacific Railway. It was part of a grand plan to turn Prince Rupert into a huge port possessing the advantage of being several hundred steaming miles closer to the Orient, than was Vancouver or Seattle.

The yard was a white elephant which passed into the orbit of Canadian National Railways when it absorbed Grand Trunk Pacific. During the first war a number of ships were built there as below. After the war the CGMM took over management and was able to divert some of its own maintenance and other government business to the yard, but with the end of CGMM the yard was more or less inactive until the Second World War shipbuilding program got under way.

The yard was not a cost-effective proposition and depended fairly heavily throughout its history on its relationship with Burrard Dry Dock who supplied technical help.

WW1 ships
Canadian Britisher   Canadian Harvester   Canadian Reaper
Canadian Scottish   Canadian Thrasher

WW2 ships
NORTH SANDS type
Fort Acton   Fort Mumford   Fort Rupert
Fort Stikine   Fort Turtle   Nemiskam Park

VICTORY type
Fort Aspin   Fort Perrot   Earlscourt Park
Westview Park   Winnipegosis Park

CANADIAN type
Elgin Park   Gaspesian Park

"B" Type China coaster
Ottawa Paget   Ottawa Palette

Victoria Machinery Depot Ltd.

VMD's connection with Harbour Marine has already been explained above. By the time of the Second World War, the company was in a position to fully participate in the wartime shipbuilding program. The company continued as an active builder of ferries and other craft until the 1960's when it was closed down for lack of orders. It also had the distinction of being the only Canadian yard to build one of the massive offshore oil exploration rigs.

NORTH SANDS type
Fort Camosun   Fort Douglas   Fort Hudson's Hope
Fort Liard   Fort Sturgeon   Fort Tremblant
Fort Walsh   Fort Wrigley   Yoho Park (1)

VICTORY type
Hastings Park   Mission Park   Salt Lake Park

VICTORY type tankers
Brentwood Bay Park   Clearwater Park   Cypress Hills Park
Mount Maxwell Park   Mount Royal Park

VICTORY type Fleet Train ships
Fort Langley

CANADIAN type
Lakeside Park   Seven Oaks Park

"B" Type China Coasters
Ottawa Painter   Ottawa Pandora   Ottawa Parian
Ottawa Pasqua

Wallace Shipyards Ltd. North Vancouver, (See Burrard D.D. Co. Ltd)

West Coast Shipbuilders Ltd. Vancouver
This yard occupied an historic site, as in the First World War it had been occupied by the J. Coughlan shipyard. It lay idle for many years until acquired by Vancouver businessmen Frank Ross and Colonel Victor Spencer. Arthur McLaren joined the company as an expert shipbuilder having built vessels for the Union Steamship Company of B.C. at his own yard Coaster Construction Company at Montrose in Scotland.

The yard was virtually ready and available when the Second World war program was initiated. For some years after the war it functioned as Allied Builders until the site was purchased for a major housing redevelopment project. During the war it was the largest merchant shipbuilder after Burrard on the West coast. Allied Builders now operates a modern yard in North Vancouver and with the near demise of Burrard's North Vancouver site, is with Vancouver Shipyards of the Seaspan group, one of the few surviving yards still capable of building larger self-propelled vessels.

NORTH SANDS type

Fort Brule	Fort Chilcotin	Fort Chipewyan
Fort Confidence	Fort Enterprise	Fort Finlay
Fort Fitzgerald	Fort Franklin	Fort Glenlyon
Fort Glenora	Fort Gloucester	Fort Grant
Fort la Trait	Fort Maurepas	Fort Nakasley
Fort Norman	Fort Rampart	Fort Slave
Fort Souris	Fort Stager	

VICTORY type

Fort Astoria	Fort Boise	Fort Crevecoeur
Fort Kaskaskia	Fort Kullyspell	Fort la Baye
Atwater Park	Dominion Park	Mount Robson Park
Parkdale Park	Queens Park	Sunnyside Park
Tecumseh Park	Tuxedo Park	Weston Park
Windermere Park		

VICTORY type tankers

Arlington Beach Park	Moose Mountain Park	Mount Bruce Park
Silver Star Park	Wildewood Park	Willowdale Park

VICTORY Fleet Train ships

Fort Beauharnois	Fort Duquesne

CANADIAN type

Montebello Park	Waverley Park	Winona Park

Western Canada Shipyard, False Creek, Vancouver, B.C.

One of the larger wood steamer yards. Six vessels were completed which put it on a par with Lyall. Like the other wood builders it closed as quickly as possible with the end of hostilities in 1918.

War Casco	War Chilcat	War Nootka
War Selkirk	War Tanoo	War Tatla

Yarrows Ltd. Esquimalt, B.C.

This was the leading large ship repairer in British Columbia utilizing the government graving dock at Esquimalt for many major jobs over the years. Originally founded as Bullen's Shipyard it was, as noted acquired by Sir Alfred Yarrow a highly regarded Scottish shipbuilder well-known for his prowess as a builder of torpedo boats and destroyers for navies around the world. During the First World War it did not participate in building merchant ships for either the British government, or the Canadian Government Merchant Marine, being mainly engaged in repair work. In the Second World War it was a big builder of vessels for the Canadian Navy and only built two Forts and no Parks, both of which became war losses. These ships were,

NORTH SANDS Type
Fort McLeod   Fort Pelly

The Position Pertaining Today

My purpose in this postscript is to sum up the position in Canadian shipbuilding today and how the larger wartime yards have fared.

The country appears to be carved up into four shipbuilding districts. This is largely the result of geography and economics and needless to say some of these districts have fared better than others.

On the east coast, St. John Dry Dock & Shipbuilding Company, at St. John, N.B. which is controlled by the dominant K.C. Irving interests, has prospered and continues to prosper as the result of Canadian Navy contracts. The only other yard with a capacity for building larger ships in the region is Halifax-Dartmouth Industries, part of a group led by FENCO a division of SNC-Lavalin of Montreal, which is also engaged in navy work.

In the St. Lawrence-Montreal region, aside from United whose fate has already been described, the three other big yards were Davie Shipbuilding & Repairing Company Ltd. at Lauzon, Marine Industries Limited at Sorel and Canadian Vickers Ltd. at Montreal.

Headed by Vancouver financier Peter Paul Saunders, Versatile Corporation of Toronto, an industrial conglomerate with broad interests, formerly known as Cornat Industries Ltd. sought to bring about a regrouping under its umbrella, having already brought Burrard-Yarrows under its wing as Versatile-Pacific Shipyards. Davie became Versatile Davie and Canadian Vickers became Versatile Vickers. Versatile Corporation at this point thus controlled the major segment of the larger yards across the country, but it was weighted down with a bad economy in its other investments, notably its farm tractor manufacturing division, a most difficult heavy industry for Canadian companies with their need to compete for the larger market in the U.S.

Versatile Corporation was dismanted and the Davie and Vickers divisions absorbed into MIL Group Inc. a public company which already operated the Marine Industries yard, and had been taken over by the Quebec government, along with Geo. T. Davie & Sons, a smaller near neighbour of Davie S.B. & R. Company. The latter was known locally as "Big Davie" to distinguish it from the former known as "Little Davie".

In the Great Lakes region, Canadian Shipbuilding & Engineering operates facilities at St. Catherines, Port Weller, and Thunder Bay, Ontario. One of the most successful of the yards was that of Collingwood Shipyards at Collingwood, Ontario. This yard built a great reputation for competitive efficiency, in the construction of large lakes-type bulk-carriers, but in the rationalization which followed in the form of Canadian S & E, Collingwood was eliminated.

Meanwhile on the west coast Versatile Pacific had passed into the control of a Toronto financial group. With government assistance it had acquired a large new floating dock built in Japan. This was meant to keep it abreast of American and foreign competition in handling repairs in larger ships up to "Panamax" size, meaning a vessel with a deadweight of about 75,000 tonnes. It still has full access to the Naval graving dock, which was neighbour to the Yarrows division at Esquimalt, with its capability of handling even larger vessels.

The former Burrard yard was closed by its new owners in September 1992. The floating dock repair facility was taken over by a partnership of Vancouver Shipyards, a division of Seaspan International Ltd. one of the two major west coast tug and barge operators, and Allied Builders Ltd. While no announcement has been made, the drydock will probably be eventually moved to a new location which will permit redevelopment of the Burrard site.

Of the wartime yards, this now leaves Yarrows as the sole west coast survivor. However shipbuilding is far from dead on the west coast even though it does not enjoy the political benefits of the eastern half of the country, or the economic support afforded by federal government or Royal Canadian Navy work. The promised Polar icebreaker contract awarded to Versatile Pacific at their North Vancouver yard, would have been a big shot in the arm, but it does appear to have been a sop to west coast sensitivities after having been cut out of naval work. As has been noted before it is a national reality that west coast costs are higher, but equally it has been a national reality, than when the need arose in two world wars, the west coast yards rose like champions to do more than their fair share.

Outside of the currently depressed coastal transportation business, hurt by the downturns in the forest industries, the biggest west coast customer for large new ships is the B.C. Ferry Corporation, which happily keeps its business at home. Two mid-size ferries have recently been built by Vancouver Shipyards Ltd. while a consortium of Yarrows, Allied and the Vito shipyard (Pacific Rim Shipyards) in Delta, B.C. a successful builder of small vessels and of more recent vintage, have each contributed to two major new ferries which will be the largest ever built in this country. Yarrows and Allied each contracted to build half the hulls. These two components were joined at the Esquimalt graving dock. The hull was towed back to Pacific Rim who in the meantime had been fabricating the superstructure, which was moved in three huge modules onto the hull. The first vessel is nearing completion while work proceeds on the second.

Between these two contracts with a value of $267 million the work has been spread out equitably by the prime contractor, Integrated Ferry Constructors Ltd. formed for this purpose by B.C. Ferry Corporation. This has done much to ensure the survival and prosperity of shipbuilding in British Columbia notwithstanding the tough times through which the industry is passing.

I am indebted to my friend Andrew N. McLellan of Toronto, for clarifying and updating the position on the eastern shipyards. In this vast country what goes on elsewhere in our land can sometimes be very foggy when viewed at a distance.

Chapter Sixteen

Fednav Limited: The Story of a Canadian Enterprise

This chapter deals with Fednav Limited, which not only grew like the others mentioned in this book out of the war, but has since survived, diversified and prospered on a scale, unknown in any other Canadian deepsea shipping organization. With justification, the company describes itself as the largest ocean-shipowning and chartering group in Canada, at last report with assets of US$385 million and group revenues of US$395 million. The company currently owns 18 specialized vessels, and charters an average of 60 at any given time from other owners. On a world scale it ranks among the "bigs" of the international shipping business. It has successfully done what others have tried and failed to do, and for this there can only be one main reason. That is the quality of leadership and inspired management which it has brought to bear, and a philosophy which will become apparent as one reads on.

However, readers may point to Canadian Pacific as being a larger concern, but it should be remembered that Canadian Pacific's now greatly reduced shipping activities are part of a vastly larger multi-faceted entity, which has since grown into one of the largest North American conglomerates of which both the railway and shipping activities are but a relatively small part, even though they remain at the core of its operations. At the time of writing the company is out of ocean shipping and west coast coastal services are now largely confined to a limited railcar barge operation.

Fednav was founded in Toronto in 1944. The company moved its head office to Montreal in 1953. Under the original name of Federal Commerce & Navigation Company, the first ship acquired was named the ERNEST G. PATHY after the founder. Built as the FORT GROUARD this was the first of a number of ex-Canadian government vessels as listed in Chapter 12. The late Mr Ernest Pathy's nephew, Mr Lawrence G. Pathy, is today the president and chief executive officer of the group.

From the early years the company sought contract business and quickly established a position for itself as the main contractor for supplying Arctic bases and settlements. This grew as the Arctic and its resources were opened up, and in some years the supply expedition was a multi-vessel convoy made up of vessels supplied by Federal Commerce or chartered in by them. It has now supplied this service continuously for almost 40 years, and also today brings out export cargoes of minerals from Arctic mining developments.

In more recent years the parent company was renamed FEDNAV LIMITED and under its umbrella the group's activities now embrace, shipowning and chartering, bulk freight operations, liner services, marine terminals, stevedoring and ship agency work. Other divisions specialize in Arctic transportation, offshore supply and support services, ship finance, oil and gas production drilling and new business development. The broad range of the group's activities is illustrated by the list of subsidiaries and associates set out at the end of this chapter.

The group's transportation policies are based on the principle that vessels will be chartered in from other owners for those conventional trades which do not require specialized vessels, while it can devote its own resources to building and operating its own fleet of specialized vessels which service long term contracts or work in areas of the world which call for their own techniques and expertise, such as the Canadian Arctic.

Among the owned fleet there is a series of eight 35/38,300 tdw bulk carriers, specially designed for the carriage of maximum deadweight cargoes through the St. Lawrence Seaway. These vessels have a greater length to breadth ratio and shallower draft than regular equivelent ocean-going deadweight vessels. As a result they can handle 25 per cent more cargo through the St. Lawrence Seaway, and are really ocean going laker-type vessels. These eight ships are FEDERAL SCHELDE, FEDERAL RHINE, FEDERAL CALUMET, FEDERAL ST. CLAIR, FEDERAL THAMES, FEDERAL DANUBE, FEDERAL OTTAWA and FEDERAL MAAS. Six other vessels are chartered/controlled on a long term basis.

These ships operate in the Transatlantic trades carrying steel and general cargo from Europe into the Great Lakes, and grain and bulk cargoes outward. Known as the "FALLINE Service", this acronym describes the Federal-Atlantic-Lakes Line, along with the Arctic services, another core activity on which the group has been built. FALLINE serves the entire Great Lakes from Duluth, Minnesota east down the St. Lawrence to the European Northern Range ports, including Antwerp, Brake, Bremen and Hamburg, plus Aviles and Bilbao in Northern Spain. The route up the English Channel and along the north European coast could be described as the busiest shipping main street in the world. Europe generally possesses exceptional comprehensive transportation links and a distribution structure, by coastal ship, rail, road, canals and rivers. The ability to collect and distribute is second to none and for this reason Fednav maintains agencies in European countries as far flung from its central main shipping route as Italy, Sweden, Norway and Portugal.

There are geared bulk-carriers of 30,350 tdw which are ice-strengthened to Lloyds Ice Class 1, enabling them to trade year-round to St. Lawrence ports and to the Arctic during the summer. These are the FEDERAL St. LAURENT and FEDERAL SAGUENAY.

The company owns a series of 148,000/165,000 tdw bulk carriers designed specially for the carriage of large bulk cargoes, such as grain, ore, and coal. These include the FEDERAL SKEENA and FEDERAL HUNTER.

Fednav is a shareholder in Oceanex which has a fleet of three roll-on/roll-off (ro-ro) type vessels, ASL SANDERLING and CICERO and CABOT which serve the Maritime provinces and St. Lawrence, carrying containers, vehicles and trailers between Halifax, Montreal and Newfoundland, plus tugs and barges committed to offshore activities in support of oil exploration in the Mackenzie Delta, Beaufort and North Seas.

The Fednav Group's freight operations include a broad range of bulk cargoes, as well as general cargoes including steel, containers, agricultural and construction equipment, road vehicles, newsprint and forest products. Specialized cargo such as large fabricated modules, oil drilling rigs, pressure vessels and other heavy or awk-

ERNEST G. PATHY ex SEA CREST ex FORT GROUARD
Named after the founder of Federal Commerce & Navigation. This vessel is also illustrated
elsewhere in this book while on the ways at her builders yard.

FEDERAL VOYAGER ex FORT EDMONTON
Originally one of the Victory type used as part of the Fleet Train.

FEDERAL RHINE
A member of the first group of oceangoing Lakers inward bound from European ports in the Gulf
of St. Lawrence. She will proceed via Montreal and Lakes ports as far west as Duluth.

FEDERAL MAAS
One of the second group of oceangoing Lakers specially built to carry maximum tonnages through
the Seaway locks in the Federal-Great Lakes service to and from Northern Europe. She carries a
complete train of rail passenger cars. Long and narrow their breadth to length ratio is roughly
10:1 compared to a more usual 7 or 8:1.

FEDERAL ST. LAURENT
This Ice Class 1 geared bulk carrier and her sister FEDERAL SAGUENAY are part of the fleet
employed by the Fedcom division in servicing the annual Arctic lift as well as the requirements of
Arctic mines. When not working the Arctic they are engaged in world-wide trade. 30,350
deadweight tonnage.

FEDERAL SKEENA
Seen here delivering a cargo of 137,500 tons of Australian coal to a Japanese port. Her sister ship
is the FEDERAL HUNTER, named for the Australian river of that name. Both vessels would be
described as being gearless bulk carriers.

WORKING IN THE ARCTIC ICE
Tug/supply vessels operated by associated company Arctic Transportation Ltd. engaged in a vessel
drydocking in the Beaufort Sea. Photo gives some idea of the severe conditions mostly met
with in this region.

ward materials are a feature. Something of a speciality is the carriage of small craft such as yachts, a Fednav bulker being able to carry a veritable fleet on deck in addition to a full load of containers or other cargo.

Terminal operations are a big part of the Fednav Group's activities. Development of such projects have been central to the group's development strategy since the early years. Through subsidiary Federal Marine Terminals, Fednav operates bulk and general cargo terminal facilities at Montreal, Quebec City, Port Cartier, Sorel, St. John, N.B., Toronto amd Hamilton.

Its American subsidiary Federal Marine Terminals Inc. operates similar facilities at Chicago, at Eastport, Maine, and through a joint venture at Burns International Harbour, Indiana.

The company owns 50 per cent of CSL Investments Ltd. which holds the non-bulk shipping interests of CSL Ltd. formerly known as Canada Steamship Lines Ltd.

A major investment is its holding in Navios Corporation of Greenwich, Connecticut, which like Fednav operates a large fleet of ocean-going bulk carriers, some owned but others chartered in. Because of chartering activities the fleet ranges in size between 35 and 50 vessels. It was established in 1954 as the shipping subsidiary of U.S. Steel. Navios operates a range of agency offices handling all aspects of ship representation in ports along the U.S. East Coast and the U.S. Gulf.

Fedmar International offices and agencies are located throughout the Great Lakes, but in addition the Fednav Group maintains business offices in London, Antwerp, Hamburg, Rio de Janeiro, Hong Kong and Tokyo.

Fednav vessels function under a number of flags including Canada, Liberia, Cyprus, Luxemburg, USA and the Bahamas. Connections with Belgium have always been particularly strong, several vessels having been built in Belgian shipyards while Belcan N.V. of Antwerp, a subsidiary is the registered owner of six of the fleet bulk carriers.

Fednav's corporate philosophy and business strategy is fully described by the company itself in the following words:-

"FEDNAV has for many years specialized in solving unusual transportation and cargo handling problems. Its philosophy has been to work directly with its existing and potential customers to satisfy their requirements in a flexible and innovative way.

The projects and business development group was formed to continue and broaden this area of activity with a view to expanding and diversifying the shipping and shipping related interests of the FEDNAV group as a whole. It comprises a nucleus of individuals of wide technical, commercial and financial experience with a mandate to develop opportunities outside and beyond the areas already covered by established lines of business.

This small group functions as a team, one member of which will assume responsibility for a particular project, drawing on the specialized skills of the others and of the field offices worldwide as required. It seeks to approach each customer's needs with imagination, but without preconceived ideas"

THE FEDNAV LIMITED GROUP
DIVISION

Federal Marine Terminals	Terminal operators	Montreal
		Quebec City
		Hamilton
		Toronto

SUBSIARIES

Fednav International Ld.	Ocean freighting division	Montreal
		Halifax
		Saint John
		St. Johns
		Vancouver
Belcan N.V.	Shipowners	Antwerp
Burnett S.S. Co. Ltd.	Shipowners	London
Burris Drilling Company	Oilfield drilling services	Denver
Carlton S.S. Co. Ltd.	Shipowners	London
Federal Marine Terminals Inc.	Terminal operators	Chicago
		Eastport
Federal Pacific (Liberia Ltd.)	Shipping operations	Greenwich
Fednav Asia Ltd.	Group operations	Tokyo
Fednav (Hamburg) Gmbh	Group operations	Hamburg
Fedmar International, division of Federal Marine Terminals, Inc.	Terminal operators	Chicago
		Cleveland
		Detroit
		Duluth

Fednav Europe Limited	Group operations	London
Fednav (UK) Ltd.	Group operations	London
Fednav (USA) Inc.	Group operations	Detroit
Pacific & Atlantic Ltd	Group operations	Bermuda
Piute Energy & Transportation Company	Oil producers	Denver
Sandaliotis Shipping Cp.	Shipping operations	London
Tamarack Energy, Inc.	Oilfield exploration	Denver

ASSOCIATES

Atlantic Searoute Ltd Partnership	Ship operators	Halifax
Amsbach Group Ltd.	Shipping operations	Singapore
Arctic Transportation Ltd	Tug and barge operators	Calgary
Canartic Shipping Co. Ltd	Shipowning joint venture	Ottawa
Navios Corporation	Ship owning and ship operations group	Greenwich
Corporacion Navios Secursal Uruguaya	River Plate Transfer Station for bulk shipping	Montevideo
Navios Ship Agencies	Shipping agencies	New Orleans Houston Mobile Morrisville Tampa Baltimore Charleston Norfolk/ Newport News
Newocean Contractors Ltd.	Offshore developments	St. John's
Oceanic Finance Corpn.	Ship finance	Bermuda

CURRENT FLEET LIST

An active group like Fednav is always subject to ongoing change in both its corporate empire and in the vessels it owns or operates under different types of charters. The following list was up to date as at September 1992.

LONG TERM CHARTERS

	Dw(mt)	B.H.P.	Built
Bulk Carriers			
Federal Agno	29,643	9500	1985
Federal Fraser	36,248	10,880	1983
Federal Fuji	29,531	9,500	1986
Federal Inger	29,212	12,000	1978
Federal Kumano	45,750	10,680	1990
Federal Mackenzie	36,248	10,880	1983
Federal Manitou	28,192	10,500	1983
Federal Matane	28,214	8,640	1984
Federal Nord	29,466	11,400	1981
Federal Oslo	29,462	8,388	1985
Federal Polaris	29,536	9,500	1986
Island Gem	28,000	9,600	1984
Lake Charles	26,209	6,662	1990
Mosdeep	49,000	13,200	1981
Saskatchewan Pioneer	36,248	10,880	1983

OWNED FLEET

*Associated Partnership Company
+Bareboat Charter

THE CARLTON STEAMSHIP CO. LTD.

Off-shore Supply/Anchor Handling Vessel

	Dw(mt)	B.H.P.	Built
Arctic Nanook	520	6400	1982

*OCEANEX LIMITED PARTNERSHIP

Ro-Ro Vessels

	Dwt(mt)	B.H.P.	Built
ASL Sanderling	14,689	18,980	1977
Cabot	7,089	14,600	1979

*CYGNUS LIMITED PARTNERSHIP

	Dwt(mt)	B.H.P.	Built
Thekwini	14,545	18,980	1977

BELCAN N.V.

Bulk Carriers

	Dwt(mt)	B.H.P.	Built
Federal Danube	38,294	11,600	1980
Federal Hunter	164,891	18,400	1984
Federal Maas	38,294	11,600	1981
Federal Ottawa	38,294	11,600	1980
Federal Skeena	164,891	18,400	1983
Federal Thames	38,294	11,600	1981

FEDERAL PACIFIC (LIBERIA) LTD.

Bulk Carriers

	Dwt(mt)	B.H.P.	Built
Federal Calumet	38,568	10,400	1977
Federal Rhine	38,568	10,400	1977
Federal Saguenay	29,531	10,400	1978
Federal St. Clair	38,450	10,400	1978
Federal St. Laurent	29,531	10,400	1978
Federal Schelde	38,568	10,400	1977

CIONA LTD.

Bulk Carriers

	Dwt(mt)	B.H.P.	Built
Orinoco	140,784	18,400	1982

*ARCTIC TRANSPORTATION LTD.

Tugs

	Dwt(mt)	B.H.P.	Built
Arctic Ivik	1,565	7,200	1985
Arctic Nanabush	879	7,200	1984
Arctic Nutsukpok	841	6,500	1982
Arctic Surveyor	736	1,700	1978
Arctic Tuktu	719	3,280	1972
J. Mattson	307	2,250	1973

Air Cushion Vehicle

Laurus

	Dwt(mt)	Size	Built
Barges			
Arctic Breaker	8,930	316' x 104'	1977
Arctic Immerk Kamotik	11,295	375' x 105'	1982
Arctic Kiggiak	10,000	375' x 105'	1983
Arctic Tuk	10,800	346' x 105'	1980
Floating Dry Dock			
ARD-31			
Arctic Kibvayok	9,500	312' x 111'	1983

THE BURNETT STEAMSHIP COMPANY LIMITED

	Dwt(mt)	B.H.P.	Built
+Cicero	7,132	14,600	1978

Chapter Seventeen

WILL CANADA EVER AGAIN BE A DEEPSEA SHIPOWNING COUNTRY?

This is a question which has been asked many times, and not unnaturally there are differing answers depending on which point of view has one's sympathies. The politician can be for or against the proposition with great vehemence, but politically motivated viewpoints can lead people into treacherous quicksands. Union people sometimes become very vocal as they see a Canadian merchant marine as a means of creating jobs which would be true if the considerations went no further. Maintaining union gains, which in the eyes of some is the equivelent of featherbedding, and greedy short-term objectives, for which the Canadian maritime unions were infamous in the years that followed the war, contributed to the demise of the merchant marine. To all this it can be added that our shipyards would want to keep their building berths full and reap the benefits of an ongoing repair industry, but in the last analysis it is, and can only be the shipowner, risking his own capital, who makes the final decision.

It is after all the shipowner who assesses the economic benefits to himself and by extension to the country. In the process he has to convince others such as investers and bankers who either by way of equity investment, bank loan or ship's mortgage are going to take an interest either in the ship or the owning company.

In order to answer the question it is necessary to firstly take a look as to how and why Canada has on three separate occasions in the past 200 years become a major shipping power only to see its position deteriorate in such a way that the thought of a fourth such cycle now seems more unlikely than ever.

When this country was born and in the years which followed up to the outbreak of the second world war a wood shipbuilding industry grew up in the Maritime provinces and in the lower reaches of the St. Lawrence. Immigration had brought its share of shipwrights from the British Isles, France and others from among the United Empire Loyalists, and later from other European countries such as Scandinavia with a strong shipbuilding tradition. Wood shipbuilding on the Atlantic coast of sizeable ocean-going schooners and larger barques and barquentines was really one big indigenous industry starting on the north shore of the St. Lawrence and stretching through Maine south into the other New England States.

Wooden shipbuilders from Cheticamp, Baddeck, Lunenberg, North Sydney and a host of other small ports built thousands of wooden craft of all sizes. The larger vessels were run in overseas trade by local owners carrying such cargoes as saltcod and lumber on routes which took them to Northern Europe, the Mediterranean and Caribbean. Often newly-built speculative vessels would be loaded at such places as Rimouski and Chedebucto and sailed to Britain. As soon as the lumber cargo was sold the vessel would be offered on the market most frequently being sold by auction. Some British owners started in a small way in the middle years of the last century, through purchase of one or more of these Canadian-built vessels and progressed through their history into becoming major shipping companies. Examples of two such Scottish concerns were the famous Ben Line of Leith and the equally well-known Hogarth's Baron Line of Ardrossan.

This first Canadian shipbuilding and shipowning cycle, grew with the country, was long-lived and thrived through natural economic forces, the biggest of which was probably a ready abundance of prime softwood timber close at hand to the ship-yards and an abundance of first-class shipwrights. As economical sailing and steamships of steel became more prevalent, the larger wooden shipyards gradually declined but many were still turning out fine fishing and trading schooners well into this century, being given a boost by the demand created through the first world war. With small craft the activity still exists although aluminum, fibreglass and steel have largely taken over.

The wartime boom in wood shipbuilding was particularly important in British Columbia whose yards turned out a range of schooners and wooden steamers mostly as part of the war effort and for government account, but few of these vessels had a long life as under wartime conditions they were largely built of unseasoned lumber.

The next two cycles grew out of the wartime emergencies of the first and second wars. They differed from the first cycle in that they were the result of the unusual conditions created by war, where in the circumstances the ships were built to fill a pressing need, without too much attention being given to the sophisticated economics which could be expected in normal peacetime trading conditions. In other words the emphasis was on quantity rather than quality although as matters developed these ships turned out to be surprisingly fine vessels, within the limitations of their design and simple old-fashioned machinery.

With the end of both wars, Canada found itself in possession of large fleets of tramp-type freighters, but the method of disposal differed in both cases. Chapter 2 gives an account of the Canadian Government Merchant Marine into which some 67 government owned vessels were vested, and run in competition with foreign lines on several major foreign trade routes.

The indications are that the Canadian government of the day having recently consolidated three transcontinental railways into the Canadian National Railways was imbued with the idea that it could quickly create a marine arm for the railway and placed the CGMM under railway management. Contemporary thinking in Canada always seemed to couple railway development with ancillary shipping services. Doubtlessly this grew out of the need to control shipping as a feeder to the railway operation both of which had to be "forced fed" given the nature of the country, the highly speculative nature of early railway development, and the general dearth of available risk capital, for which in those days Canada had to largely turn to Britain which had many other claims on its resources.

Canadian Pacific is the prime and most successful example of early Canadian need coupled with British capital, and the quickly perceived rationale of coupling shipping operations with those of the parent railway. Canadian Northern and Grand Trunk System both got into the shipping business as did their successor Canadian National.

The theory which gave rise to the CGMM was good but the practice left much desired. There is evidence that many inexperienced personnel were employed both ashore and afloat and while the company did manage to stay in business for far more years than most of its critics ever thought possible, by 1936 it was out of business. Among the last ships it owned, some were reorganized into Canadian National Steamships, while six became the initial fleet owned by Aristotle Onassis, who went on to become one of the foremost shipping magnates of the mid-twentieth century. The accumulated loss of about $86 million, accelerated by the depression, was enormous and it all had to be born by the taxpayer.

At least one owner from the private sector, the Coughlin Line from Vancouver (see Chapter 3), managed to stay in business with similar ships to the CGMM vessels in foreign trade, also until 1936. This concern received no government assistance but following the loss of one of its last two vessels by shipwreck it was evidently decided that it created the opportunity for a prudent withdrawal from the shipowning business.

In the second world war the shipbuilding program was far bigger. All told 353 -10,000 d.w.ton freighters were built along with a further 43 ships of 4,700 d.w. ton ships. These constituted the two main classes although there were other classes of smaller ships as more particularly described in Chapter 6. At the end of the war the Canadian Maritime Commission therefore had the task of disposing of several hundred large freighters, but this time having learned the lesson of the CGMM they avoided the mistake of setting up a crown corporation to compete with the private sector or foreign flags. The ships were in fact managed by Park Steamship Company, a crown corporation for Canadian flag operation, or bareboat chartered to the British government, but in neither case was there a desire to perpetuate these wartime arrangements.

Instead the preferred method was to sell the ships for cash at roughly half their original building cost. A favourable tax regime and good write-offs coupled with the immediate post-war freight rates meant that new owners could get off to a good start. There were some flag restrictions governing ownership of these cheaply acquired steamers, in that sale proceeds if sold prior to the period during which Canadian ownership and flag were required, had to be held in an escrow account for re-investment into new vessels to be built in Canadian yards. The theory was reasonable, but impractical as Canadian owners came up against the realities of operating as part of a high-cost economy in competition with cost-effective cheaper flag foreign competition.

Moreover official policy discouraged Canadian investment in foreign flag shipping using the "flag of convenience" device. I am uncertain that it was as rigid as British policy in this regard which forbade the movement of British shipping capital to cheap flags such as Panama, Liberia or Honduras, for whom the term "PanHonLib" was devised by the shipping press as a convenient descriptive handle. Somewhat later Britain did create cheap registers in Bermuda, Gibraltar and the Isle of Man, and at least one Canadian owner, Canadian Pacific Bermuda Ltd. did put its postwar bulk-carrier shipping under the Bermudan flag.

As described in chapter 12, one owner, Western Canada Steamship Company, did make an effort to develop a postwar fleet with some degree of success but by the early sixties it became apparent that the incentives for a continuation were eroding away. Transfer of Canadian ships to the British flag only had a limited attraction as it became apparent by the sixties that British union activity was turning operations under that flag into a high cost proposition, in much the same way as militant Canadian union activity did the same in the previous decade of the forties.

Incentives had they existed might have included a free flow of Canadian shipping capital into cheaper flag operation, but as noted this was restricted, the exception being transfer to the British national flag or the British "flag of convenience" in Bermuda, Gibraltar or the Isle of Man. While this course was pursued and many Canadian vessels operated advantageously under the British flag, this was only cost-effective so long as British manning costs remained competitive. In chapter 12 reference is made to two successive wage increases awarded to British crews after serious disruption in British shipping through strike action. The effect of these increases was to move Britain from a cost-competitive flag to one of high cost which ensured the slow demise of the British shipping industry, particularly over the past twenty years.

By the time these increases took place in the early sixties, there was an additional factor which had been mounting ever since the ships were built. Essentially they were out of date when they were built, and while they were good well-found vessels, they were war-built emergency ships, built to fill a need, but with many new ships pouring out of the yards of Japan and Europe the Canadian ships became economically obsolescent, for which as time went on, there was only one ship resale market, i.e. to cheaper flags such as Greece, Italy, Cyprus and flag-of-convenience countries, or for scrapping.

As mentioned above Western Canada Steamship Company did start to acquire a good quality type of diesel tramp purchasing three such vessels from South Wales owners, which were built in the early fifties. This roughly co-incided with the development of the single-deck bulk-carrier which quickly supplanted the conventional tramp such as Western Canada had purchased. Not only that but operating these new bulk-carriers often under flags-of-convenience was rendered even more cost-effective through the economics of scale afforded by rapidly increasing deadweight tonnages, without a proportionate growth in individual crews. New technologies on board ship meant that larger ships could be handled by smaller crews.

This does not imply that the only people who understood this were forward thinking Greek owners and Japanese builders. Maritime countries quickly grasped these trends as no doubt did Canadian owners. What Canada lacked was a national shipping policy which should have recognized that shipping is in reality an international industry and all that the setting up of narrow national restrictions did was to create unnatural boundaries, supportable only by subsidies which put the taxpayer back into shipowning, and played into the hands of militant unions of which Canada has had its fair share.

It is fine to have a union and to secure high rates of pay and ideal working conditions, but if Canadian ships were to compete successfully as part of the structure of international shipping, owners needed to be able to compete on a "level playing field". This needed a suitable tax climate within which to function, including good tax shelteres, such as fast write-offs against capital cost, to encourage capital into the industry and thus help offset proportionately higher operating costs. A provision allowing offshore shipping profits only to be taxed upon repatriation to Canada which used to be the case, would be another assistance, instead of as at present where Canadian citizens and corporations operating overseas, have to declare all world-wide income in their tax return.

I know that these suggestions are neither new or original. In fact they have already been tried in Canada with excellent results, and encouraged the massive rebuilding and expansion of the British Columbia coastal transportation industry from the fifties on. Also any suggestion that tax-shelters and the like be adopted, brings on protests from certain sections of the populace, who fail to recognise that the creation of the new capital which follows, results in eventual benefits to everyone. The process returns benefits to the national treasury by way of new taxes on increased earnings from more efficient companies, as well as individual earnings of personnel.

There are two types of direct subsidy, the first being a shipbuilding subsidy, by which suitable vessels receive a contribution to their capital cost. This is a one-shot deal, in other words there is no ongoing liability to subsidize beyond the one single act of assisting building cost. The benefit flows in two directions, in that it assists the shipyard to competitively provide a vessel at an attractive first cost to the owner, ensuring maintenance of a viable shipbuilding industry including a core of skilled management and a capable labour nucleus for this purpose, and thus also a level of profit and wages which again will see tax flowing back to the government.

The other type of subsidy is an operating subsidy by which a proportion of operating and management costs are paid directly to the shipowning entity. The disadvantage of operating subsidies must always be that they encourage inefficiency and stifle the normal competitive factors of the market place. Business inefficiency usually leads to abuse of sources of assistance, and an operating subsidy can quickly become a form of corporate welfare. This in turn saps the morale and incentive to succeed by one's own effort, because that crutch is always there. The United States in the name of national strategic interest, awarded operating subsidies over the years to many of its shipping companies providing regular liner services on what it called strategic trade routes. I am not suggesting that the process was necessarily abused because I do not know if this was the case or not, but it was a perpetual bleed of taxpayers funds amounting to billions of dollars.

In short there is proven value in shipbuilding subsidies which do not remove the need for the shipbuilders to compete among themselves, and at the same time ensure the creation of income earning capital assets in the form of new ships. Operating subsidies for reasons already given should be avoided as they constantly bleed the taxpayer.

There are other forms of less direct subsidy, which have been and still are employed in other countries. One is to provide govenment backed financing to owners for new ships at subsidised interest rates. A typical example arises where an owner is required to put up a down payment of say 20 per cent of capital cost on a new ship, and an institution puts up the balance, secured by a first ship mortgage and assignment of charter monies. The institution might be a government agency merely acting as the funnel for government funds or it might be a combination of both government and private institutional money. In the latter case a proportion of government money might be provided at a low rate of interest while the private institution charges a higher rate in keeping with its own market committments. The private institution acts effectively as fiscal agent for the government and is able to blend the government rate of interest with its own higher rate to provide an overall attractive and competitive rate to the shipowner.

As a tool easier financing is used as a means by which a national shipbuilding industry is able to compete more effectively with that of other countries in securing shipbuilding orders from shipowners whether they be from the shipbuilder's own country or foreign nationals usually alert to any possibilities wherever they may find them. However it can only be fully effective if shipbuilding costs in the country offering the attractive finance are competitive in the first instance, with or without shipbuilding subsidies. There is also a point where financing new vessel contracts becomes overproductive, and at times in the past this has encouraged irresponsible builders and inexperienced financiers and shipowners to excesses which through oversupply into the shipping market have proven costly to all.

At one point Canada did offer facilities along these lines, to gain foreign business during the fifties and sixties and had some limited success in its east coast yards, but this was during periods when foreign shipbuilders had not fully recovered from the war, and rather later when an international shipbuilding boom saw foreign yards with a huge backlog on their order books. In both examples there can be an earnings advantage to a shipowner who can secure early delivery of a ship even if it costs more, and as much as anything that was a consideration in Canadian east coast yards securing such orders from French owners in the early seventies.

From the foregoing it will be obvious that high labour rates coupled sometimes with poor productivity, out of date technology, inadequacy of tax incentives, uncompetitive interest rates, and a lack of interest on the part of successive Canadian governments to formulate an effective national shipping policy, have effectively kept real progress out of the reach of the bulk of Canadian deepsea operators and investors who might be interested in the ocean shipping business. However matters have not all been negative and there is proof that Canadians can effectively function in this competitive international field.

Canada had for the most part been a shipping agency economy in terms of the shipping industry. Vancouver, Montreal and Halifax as our three main traditional foreign trade seaports prior to the opening of the St. Lawrence seaway have always functioned with a network of shipping agencies some of whom are experts in the chartering field. As such the industry possessed adequate management expertise except in one area, which is actual shipowning, although the post second world war period saw a nucleus of capable shipowning entities formed which could no doubt be reorganized if there was ever an incentive to do so. This could be achieved through drawing on its own pool of talent or hiring foreign nationals for the purpose as happened in both shipbuilding and shipowning during and after the second world war.

At least one company functions effectively today in the competitive international shipowning field. This is Fednav Ltd. based in Montreal whose story was told in the previous chapter. Its fleet of ships are mostly operated under foreign flags, including Belgium, Cyprus, Liberia, and the Bahamas. Fednav has had or still has ships under both the Canadian and the U.S. flag, but where this arises it has to be assumed that there are special advantages, probably associated with domestic trade restrictions, where the ships concerned are not seriously exposed to foreign flag competition. U.S. flag operation is restricted to minority foreign participation by the provisions of their Jones Act, but presumably Fednav can legally circumvent this restriction, as certain of its principals may still be American and can therefore hold a beneficial investment interest.

There is another factor which has to be taken into account. In the last few years Vancouver gained the status of an international banking and finance centre. The idea was that because of our stable democratic political climate and other factors associated with the concept of the Canadian "way of life", we should be able to attract foreign banks and corporations to establish here, including offshore shipping enterprises owned by foreign nationals.

This would be a form of foreign investment in Canada, which should contribute to local employment, although there must always be some question as to just how valuable this is, as the foreign interests can be expected to import their own key operatives. It will not create any shipbuilding opportunities, and probably little repair work unless the ships visit Vancouver which might never happen. What it will do is create opportunities in the service sector such as legal and accounting services, insurance and similar white collar opportunities. Assuming that Vancouver functions ever more effectively as an international banking centre, there should be an increasing volume of international banking transactions from shipping operations which will benefit Canadian banks generally.

As an international banking centre one presumes that an attraction will be that foreign corporations establishing here will be able to avoid the ever hungry tax-collecting activities of our federal government in its unceasing thrust to cut off all tax loopholes. In this case the move to international banking has been fostered by the federal government, through special provisions of the Finance Act, in conjunction with the B.C. provincial government, to effectively circumvent circumstances largely fostered by government itself in the past.

There are indications that this new type of activity has enjoyed some success and at least one international shipping concern, Teekay Shipping founded by Norwegian-American Torsten Karlshoej, has in fact moved its world operations headquarters to Vancouver to take advantage of these helpful provisions. Typically this company is mostly interested in large tankers so to what extent its vessels would bring any actual ship operating advantages to Vancouver is a matter for conjecture, as they would not normally be the type of ship we see.

To what extent these advantages are similarly available to Canadian interests cannot be stated with certainty, although presumably an offshore company could be set up by Canadian capital and still find it in its interest to function out of Vancouver to derive whatever advantage it can out of its legal status as a "foreign offshore company". However the idea of using Vancouver as an offshore banking centre with the same advantages as we confer on foreigners appears to be negated by the fact that our income tax laws are framed in such a way that all world-wide income of a Canadian citizen is declarable and taxable, whether it is returned to Canada or not. To this author there is something highly contradictory when we as a nation create financial advantages for foreigners which we are not prepared to fully grant to our own citizens.

To me there is a little too much emphasis on the importation of foreign capital for ill-defined objectives of creating jobs for Canadians which do not actually materialize in the way that our politicians blythely assume. One can be forgiven for thinking that there are times we are willing to sell anything for a "mess of pottage", without sometimes remembering that when we do so we gradually also permit the gradual remoulding of our country and its society into something which may be rather different to our cherished ideals. There is a price to pay for everything!

I suppose the justification may be that if a Canadian citizen forms a Panamanian corporation and runs it from the Vancouver international banking centre, the corporation's income will not be taxable unless it disburses it to its Canadian owner, who is then deemed to be subject to Canadian income tax as with any other world-wide income from which he may benefit.

In dealing with the question, "will Canada ever again be a deepsea shipowning country?" we can start with this matter of international banking and financial centres. Is there any response to developing interest on the part of Canadians in investing in offshore foreign flag shipping enterprises? That it can be done is demonstrated by the references to Fednav Ltd. That this concern is not a fly-by-night operation is demonstrated by the fact that they have been in successful business for a sufficient number of years, in fact since second world war days.

One consideration which cannot be overlooked has to do with the training of competent personel. A Canadian-owned foreign flag ship might well have an entirely foreign crew, whereas up until the demise of British shipping there were always a proportion of young Canadians in training for officer qualifications aboard many British ships. This trend has probably died out completely so that we are not geared now to man our own ships. Even on coastal ships many positions are filled by immigrant officers and crew. Many countries are having difficulty in manning their ships with competant officers, so that training schemes have now had to be instituted to provide people to replace the large numbers of trained Europeans who used to be in plentiful supply due to the reductions in their own national fleets. This particularly applies to such owners as the Hong Kong Chinese. Britain is the perfect example of reduced human output as it and other countries are not deliberately training their people for the purposes of manning foreign ships.

The recognition has also obviously been made that international shipping as opposed to purely domestic shipping is a highly fluid industry where capital flows freely from one flag or jurisdiction to another. As an industry which is integral to the global village it is and must remain thus in order that its participants can remain competitive. National concepts have become out of date in creating a healthy climate for national shipping unless these factors are recognized and allowed for, and the narrower concepts of patriotism and the national interest as exemplified by the national flag flying from the stern of a ship has been largely swept under the carpet in the new pragmatic age in which we live.

The truth is that if enough foreign shipping interests prosper by adopting this highly fluid process then the rest must also do so in order to survive. The Americans started it in devising the Panamanian flag of convenience, the Greeks embraced the project as their own, and today Norwegian and German owners use the flags of Cyprus and Singapore, the Dutch use the Netherlands Antilles, and the British, as noted, Bermuda and elsewhere. Republics such as Croatia, part of former Yugoslavia, are registering their ships in St. Vincent, W.I. and the Russians are using Malta for a similar purpose, which in the latter two cases may also be political to shelter these ships from domestic upheavals.

Taxation policies here and elsewhere have done much to distort the business of shipowning from a national proposition, to one where the bulk of shipping capital takes refuge in low tax, or tax free havens, and if it is prevented from free flow then it moves out of the shipping industry entirely. It can also be added that there has been much abuse of crews by certain unscrupulous foreign owners, and a lack of supervision and inspection of ships by some of the "flag of convenience" countries. In no way can this be excused and is not advocated by anything stated in this book. Equally it is wrong to assume that all ships which fly such flags are badly managed, poorly maintained, and undermanned with abused crews because such is not the case.

With all these factors taken into account I think the answer to the question which forms the title of this chapter must indeed be negative. Unless an entire new spectrum of circumstances develops, which at present cannot be foreseen, Canada will never again be a deepsea shipowning country, i.e. flying the national flag, although Canadian nationals can be expected to benefit from overseas investment in shipping whenever they follow the example of other maritime communities.

A MUTE MEMORY
Possibly the only identifiable remaining artifact of the large
fleet of Canadian-built 10,000 tonners. The boom standing at an
angle points north in Sechelt Inlet, Sechelt, B.C. It is one of the
lofty upright net booms that these ships carried on either side
of their masts, and was last used for lifting logs out of the
water to the derelict sawmill it once worked for.

APPENDIX 1

List of Canadian Maritime Museums and/or Archives with Marine Collections, and Ship Research Organizations.

British Columbia Archives & Records Service (corporate records)
865 Yates Street, Victoria, B.C. V8V 1X4.

Collingwood Museum (The), Box 566, Memorial Park, St. P:aul St.
Collingwood, Ont. L9Y 4B2

Haida Inc. (HMCS Haida Preservation Project, Ontario Place, 955
Lake Shore Blvd. West, Toronto, Ont. M6K 3B9.

Marine Archaeology Section, Archaeological Research Branch,
Canadian Parks Service, 1600 Liverpool Court, Ottawa, Ont K1A OH3.

Marine Transporation Section, National Museum of Science &
Technology, P.O. Box 9724, Ottawa Terminal, Ottawa, Ont K1G 53A.

Maritime Museum of the Atlantic 1675 Lower Water Street, Halifax, N.S. B3J 1S3.

Maritime Museum of British Columbia, 28 Bastion Square, Victoria, B.C. V8W 1H9.

Maritime Museum of Manitoba, Selkirk, Manitoba.

Maritime Museum of Upper Canada, Exhibition Place, Toronto, Ont. M6K 3C3.

Musee David M. Stewart, CP 1024, Succ. A, Montreal, Quebec H3C 2W9.

Musee Maritime Bernier, L'islet-sur-Mer, Quebec GOR 2BO.

Museum of the Great Lakes, 55 Ontario Street, Kingston, Ontario K7L 2Y2.

National Archives of Canada, 395 Wellington St. Ottawa K1A ON3.

New Brunswick Museum (The), 277 Douglas Ave. Saint John, NB E2K 1E5.

Newfoundland Museum (The), Historic Resources Section,
285 Duckworth St. Newfoundland B3J 1S3.

North Vancouver Museum & Archives, 333 Chesterfield Ave.
North Vancouver, B.C. V7M 3G9.

Prince Rupert City & Regional Archives, P.O. Box 1093,
Prince Rupert, B.C. V8J 4H6.

Queens University Archives, Queens University, Kingston, Ont.

Vancouver City Archives, 1150 Chestnut Street, Vancouver, B.C. V6J 5E5.

Vancouver Maritime Museum, 1905 Ogden Ave, Vancouver, B.C. V6J 1A3.

World Ship Society (Canadian Branch of WSS England)
P.O. Box 3096, Vancouver, B.C. V6B 3X6.

Yarmouth County Museum, P.O. Box 39, 22 Collins St. Yarmouth, NS B5A 4B1.

Note: The objectives of individual museums, collections and archives will vary greatly. Some do not maintain archives, while others possess for example, large book and photo collections. In some instances museum book stores provide a valuable additional facility, while in others it is usually possible to obtain prints from their photo collection for a fee.

BIBLIOGRAPHY

Asian Dream (The) - Donald MacKay
    (Douglas & McIntyre, Vancouver, B.C. - 1986)

British Standard Ships of World War 1 - W.H. Mitchell &
    L.A. Sawyer (Sea Breezes, Liverpool, England - 1968)

Economics of Tramp Shipping, (The) - B.N. Metaxas
    (Athlone Press, London - 1971)

Empire of Wood - Donald MacKay
    (Douglas & McIntyre, Vancouver, B.C. - 1982)

Grey Seas Under - Farley Mowat,
    (McLelland & Stewart, Toronto 1980)

Jack of All Trades: Memories of a Busy Life - J.V. Clyne
    (McLelland & Stewart, Toronto 1985)

Oceans, Forts & the Parks, (The) - W.H. Mitchell and
    L.A Sawyer (Sea Breezes, Liverpool, England - 1966)

Progress - (Published privately by Burrard
    Dry Dock Co. Ltd, North Vancouver B.C.-1946)

Shipyards of British Columbia - G.W. Taylor
    (Morriss Publishing, Victoria B.C. 1986)

Tramp Shipping - Hector Gripaios
    (Thomas Nelson & Sons Ltd - London 1957)

PHOTO CREDITS

All photographs reproduced herein and listed by page number are the copyright of the person/s or organization/s listed below, and whose names are set out opposite the applicable page number. In some instances copyright in terms of the original negative has expired, but no reproduction may be made without infringing the general copyright applicable to this book, and without the express permission of the person or organization to whom the photograph has been credited. (U=upper, L=lower)

A. Duncan, Gravesend, England   175L

Fednav Limited, Montreal, P.Q   205U, 205L, 206U, 206L, 207

Maritime Museum of the Atlantic   31U, 32L, 35U, 107L, 108, 136L, 139L
Halifax N.S.

North Vancouver Museum &   14U, 15L, 16L, 17, 20U, 20L, 61U, 185U, 185L
Archives, North Vancouver.

Prince Rupert City & Regional   18U, 18L, 19U, 184U, 184L
Archives, Prince Rupert, B.C.

Vancouver Maritime Museum,   14L, 15U, 25U, 25L, 27U, 27L, 28U, 28L, 29U,
Vancouver, B.C.   29L, 30U, 30L, 31L, 32U, 33U, 33L, 34U, 34L,
35L, 40U, 40L, 41U, 41L, 44U, 44L, 45U, 45L,
48U, 48L, 52U, 52L, 53U, 53L, 55, 60L, 61L, 62U,
66U, 66L, 67U, 67L, 68U, 68L, 69U, 69L, 74U,
75U, 76U, 96U, 96L, 100U, 107U, 112U, 112L,
113U, 114L, 115U, 115L, 119, 120U, 134, 135U, 13
136U, 137U, 137L, 138U, 138L, 140U, 140L, 141U,
141L, 142U, 142L, 143U, 143L, 144U, 144L, 145U,
145L, 153U, 153L, 154L, 155U, 155L, 156U, 156L,
157U, 157L, 158, 162U, 162L, 163U, 163L, 164U,
164L, 165, 168U, 168L, 169U, 169L, 170U, 170L
171U, 171L, 175U, 182U, 182L, 183U, 204U, 204L.

Versatile Pacific Shipyards   100L, 101U, 101L, 102

Author's collection   15U, 60U, 62L, 63U, 63L, 74L, 75L, 76L, 113L,
114U, 120L, 139U, 151U, 151L, 152U, 152L, 174U,
174L, 183L, 220.

ACADIA OVERSEAS FREIGHTERS LTD.
122,127
ACADIA OVERSEAS FREIGHTERS
  (HALIFAX) Ltd. 123, 127
ACONLEY, Wm. "Bill" 165
Adastral, R.A.F. 116
Agamemnon 111
Ainslie Park 86, 188
Akti Hill 127
Alaska 12, 194
Albert Park 85, 130, 194
ALCAN LTD. 133
Alder Park 82, 128, 191
Alendi Hill 127, 137
Alexandra Park 85, 132, 191
Algonquin Park 82, 129
Alkis 126
ALLIED BUILDERS LTD. 36
Amersham Hill 131
Andover Hill 131
ANDROS SHIPPING CO. LTD. 123
ANGLO-CANADIAN SHIPPING CO. LTD. 165
Angusdale 131, 140
Angusglen 131, 140
Anguslake 131
Angusloch 131
Aorangi 147
ARCTIC TRANSPORTATION LTD. (ATL) 207
Argobec 124
Argodon 124
Argofax 124
Argojohn 124
Argomont 124
ARGONAUT NAVIGATION CO. LTD. 124
Argovan 124, 134
Argyle Park 87, 131, 191
Arlington Beach Park 85, 198
ARMDALE OVERSEAS
  FREIGHTERS LTD. 124
Arthur Cross 128
Arundel Hill 131
ASAHI SHOJI K.K. 38
ASK Sanderling 203
Ashby Park 87
Asp 12, 190
Aspen Park 84, 150, 166, 193
Assemina K 127
ATLANTIC S.S. CO. 37
Atlanticos 47
Atwater Park 84, 150, 198
AUSTIN & PICKERSGILL LTD. 127
Avondale Park 71, 86, 90, 188
Awatea 147

Baldwin Park 87, 188
BALLANTYNE Hon. J.M. 21
Banff Park 82, 131, 188
BANK OF MONTREAL 166
Bayside 123

B.C. SHIPPING ACT, 192
Beech Hill 127
Beachy Head, H.M.S. 112, 193
Beacon Grange 130
Beaton Park 84, 150, 193
Bedford Earl 124
BEDFORD OVERSEAS
  FREIGHTERS LTD. 124
Bedford Prince 124
Bedford Queen 124
BELAIRE SHIPYARDS LTD. 46
Belwoods Park 82, 131, 189
Bell Park 87, 130, 188
Bembridge Hill 128
Beresford Park 86, 130, 188
Berry Head, H.M.S. 116, 193
Bessie Dollar 162
BLACK LION S.S. CO. LTD. 127
Bloomfield Park 86, 133, 191
Bluefin, U.S.Submarine 38
BLUE FUNNEL LINE 21, 38, 129
Bowness Park 84, 98, 149, 156, 193
Braheholm 37, 194
BRANCH LINES LTD. 124
Brazilian Prince 130
Brentwood Bay Park 85, 197
Bridgeland Park 84, 129, 196
BRIDGES, Capt. Trevor W, 37
BRISTOL CITY LINE (CANADA) LTD. 125
BRITISH AMERICAN OIL COMPANY 163
BRITISH AMERICAN S.B. CO. LTD. 186
BRITISH CANADIAN STEAMSHIPS LTD. 38
BRITISH INDIA S.N. Co. Ltd 22
BRITISH MINISTRY OF WAR
  TRANSPORT 70
BROCKLEBANK, T & J. 73
Brookhurst 133
BROSTROM GROUP OF SWEDEN 37, 178
BRUNSWICK MOTORS LTD. 125
Buchan Ness, H.M.S. 110
Buffalo Park 84, 196
Burcross 163
BURDICK, Arthur & Norman 195
BURIES MARKES LTD. 131
BURRARD DRY DOCK
  CO. LTD. 46, 192

Cabano 129
Cabot 203
Cambray 129
CAMERON GENOA MILLS LTD. 194
Camp Debert 86, 188
CANADA SHIPPING COMPANY LTD. 166
CANADA STEAMSHIP LINES 207
Canadian Adventurer 24, 190
CANADIAN ALLIS CHALMERS LTD. 186
CANADIAN AMERICAN
  NAVIGATION CO. 39, 160
Canadian Armourer 23, 195

Canadian Articifer 24, 188
CANADIAN AUSTRALASIAN LINE 146
Canadian Aviator 23, 32, 55
Canadian Beaver 24, 51, 52, 187
Canadian Britisher 23, 197
Canadian Carrier 23, 190
Canadian Challenger 23, 188
Canadian Challenger (1946) 123
Canadian Coaster 24, 187
Canadian Commander 23, 187
Canadian Composer 23, 195
Canadian Conqueror 23, 25, 125, 136, 187
Canadian Constructor 23, 189
Canadian Constructor (1946) 35. 126, 182
Canadian Cruiser 23, 189
Canadian Cruiser (1946) 126
Canadian Engineer 24, 188
Canadian Explorer 23, 25, 189
Canadian Exporter 23, 194
Canadian Farmer 24, 33, 187
Canadian Fisher 23, 191
Canadian Forester 23, 191
Canadian Freighter 23, 26, 194
CANADIAN GOVERNMENT MERCHANT
   MARINE 21, 72
Canadian Gunner 24, 187
Canadian Harvester 23, 197
Canadian Highlander 23, 26, 125, 192
Canadian Hunter 23, 188
Canadian Importer 23, 27, 194
Canadian Inventor 23, 194
Canadian Leader 23, 126, 136, 187
Canadian Logger 24
Canadian Mariner 23, 189
CANADIAN MARITIME
   COMMISSION 71, 106, 177
Canadian Miller 23, 27, 187
Canadian Miner 24, 190
CANADIAN NATIONAL RAILWAYS 21, 126
CANADIAN NATIONAL STEAM-
   SHIPS (WEST INDIES) LTD. 22, 123, 126
Canadian Navigator 23, 187
CANADIAN NORTHERN RAILWAY 21
CANADIAN OIL COMPANIES LTD. 126
Canadian Observer 24, 34, 126, 187
Canadian Otter 23, 186
CANADIAN PACIFIC RAILWAY 21, 147
Canadian Pathfinder 24, 187
Canadian Pioneer 23, 28, 187
Canadian Planter 23, 28, 187
Canadian Prospector 23, 29, 194
Canadian Raider 23, 192
Canadian Rancher 23, 191
Canadian Ranger 24, 29, 187
Canadian Reaper 23, 197
Canadian Recruit 24, 187
Canadian Rover 24, 34, 187
Canadian Runner 23, 32, 190
Canadian Sailor 24, 190
Canadian Sapper 24, 190
Canadian Scottish 18, 23, 197

Canadian Sealer 24, 190
Canadian Seigneur 23, 30, 187
Canadian Settler 23, 191
CANADIAN S.B. & ENG. LTD 187
CANADIAN SHIPOWNERS LTD 126
Canadian Signaller 24, 187
Canadian Skirmisher 23, 192
Canadian Sower 24, 190
Canadian Spinner 23, 187
Canadian Squatter 23, 186
CANADIAN STEVEDORING CO. LTD. 165
Canadian Thrasher 23, 197
Canadian Trader 24, 190
CANADIAN TRAMP SHIPPING LTD. 127
CANADIAN TRANSPORT
   COMPANY LTD. 147
Canadian Transporter 23, 30, 194
Canadian Trapper 23, 188
Canadian Traveller 23, 195
Canadian Trooper 23, 192
CANADIAN UNION LINE 146
CANADIAN VICKERS LTD 186, 199
Canadian Victor 23, 31, 126, 136, 187
Canadian Volunteer 20, 23, 33, 192
Canadian Voyager 23, 187
Canadian Warrior 24, 187
CANADIAN WESTERN STEAM-
   SHIPS LTD. 37
Canadian Winner 23, 31, 195
Cape Breton, H.M.C.S. 99, 116
CAPE BRETON FREIGHTERS LTD 126
Cape Scott, H.M.C.S. 99, 116
Cape Wrath, H.M.S. 116
Capilano 77
Cargill 129
Caribou County 122
Cartier Park 87, 126, 188
Cassiar 77
Cataraqui Park 86, 188
Cathcart 24, 35
Cavalier 24
Cedar Hill 128
CGMM 21, 72
Champlain 127
CHAMPLAIN FREIGHTERS LTD. 126
Champlain Park 85
Chandler 129
CHANDRIS (ENGLAND) LTD. 128, 130
CHARLES HILL & SON 125
Cheticamp 128
CHEVRIER, Hon. Lionel 71
Chief Capilano 160, 162
Chief Maquilla 161
Chief Skidegate 160
Chignecto Park 86, 188
Chilcop 38
CHILE S.S. CO. INC. 38
Chilkoot 77
Chippewa Park 82, 124, 188
Chomedy 24
Cicero 203

City of Vancouver 38, 42, 45, 52, 53, 161, 194
City of Victoria 38, 41, 44, 161, 194
CLARKE, Capt. J.S. "Jack" 167
Clearwater Park 75, 85, 197
Cliffside 123
CLYNE, Hon. J.V. 71, 106
Cnosaga 174
Colchester County 122
Colborne 24
COLLINGWOOD SHIPYARDS LTD. 187
Columbialand 178
Commodore Grant 127
COMMONWEALTH OF AUSTRALIA 59
Confederation Park 86, 188
Connaught Park 84, 149, 196
Connector 24
CORNAT INDUSTRIES LTD 199
Cornish Park 84
Cornwallis 24
Coronation Park 84, 149, 156, 193
Cottrell 129
COUGHLAN J. & SONS 36, 194
COUGHLAN, JOHNNY, LINE 39
COULOUTHROS LTD. 127, 131, 161
COUNTIES SHIP MANAGEMENT
  LTD. 122, 127
Crescent Park 86, 188
Cromwell Park 85, 153, 193
Crystal Park 84, 129, 196
CSL LTD. 207
Cypress Hill Park 85, 197
Cumberland County 122

DANISH EAST ASIATIC COMPANY 148
Darfield 124
Dartmouth Park 86, 191
Darton 124, 134
Dauntless 94
DAVIE SB & REPAIRING
  COMPANY 187, 199
Denmark Hill 128
Dentonia Park 82, 128, 191
DICKINSON, J, & Sons 39
Digby County 122
Dingwall 128
DINGWALL SHIPPING COMPANY LTD. 128
Ditmar Koel 116
Dodman Point, H.M.S. 116, 193
DOLLAR, Melville 39, 160
DOLLAR, Robert, interests 39, 160
DOLLARTON MILL 39, 160
DOMINION BRIDGE COMPANY 191
Dominion Park 84, 147, 198
DOMINION SHIPBUILDING COMPANY 188
DOMINION SHIPPING CO LTD. 128
Dorval Park 84, 150, 196
DOXFORD Economy Tramps 39
DREYFUS, LOUIS et Cie 131
DUFF, T.L. & Co. 161
Dufferin Bell 86, 132
Dufferin Park 86, 132, 188

DUFRESNE CONSTRUCTION CO. 125
Duncansby Head, H.M.S. 116, 193
Dundurn Park 84, 126, 196
Duneside 123
Dungeness, H.M.S. 116
Dunlop Park 84, 150, 193
Durban Bay 150

Earlscourt Park 84, 150, 197
EASTBOARD NAVIGATION
  COMPANY LTD. 129
East Hill 128, 137
Eastwater 124, 129
Eastwave 124, 129
Eastwood Park 85, 133, 191
Edmunston, H.M.C.S. 94
Eglinton Park 87, 126, 189
ELDER DEMPSTER (CANADA) LTD. 129
Elgin Park 85, 197
Elk Island Park 82, 129, 191
Elmbranch 124
Elm Hill 128
Elm Park 82, 133, 189
S.G. EMBIRICOS LTD. 126
EMPIRE SHIPPING CO. LTD. 166
Empress of Asia 42
Ernest G. Pathy 61, 130, 204
Evangeline Park 87
EVANS THOMAS & RADCLIFFE LTD. 176

FAFALIOS LTD. 134
Fairmount Park 85, 125, 194
FAIRVIEW OVERSEAS FREIGHTERS
  LTD. 129
FALAISE S.S. CO. LTD. 127
Fawkner Park 86, 191
Federal Ambassador 130
Federal Calumet 203
Federal Commerce 130
FEDERAL COMMERCE &
  NAVIGATION CO. LTD. 130
Federal Danube 203
Federal Hunter 203
Federal Maas 203, 205
Federal Ottawa 203
Federal Pioneer 130
Federal Ranger 130
Federal Rhine 203, 205
Federal Saguenay 203
Federal Schelde 203
Federal Skeena 203, 206
Federal St. Clair 203
Federal St. Laurent 203, 206
Federal Thames 203
Federal Trader1 130
Federal Voyager 130, 204
FEDNAV LIMITED 130, 209
FEDNAV current fleet list 209, 210
FEDNAV group companies 208
FENCO Division of SNC-LAVALIN 199
Fernhurst 131

Fife Ness, H.M.S. 116, 194
Firbranch 125
Fir Hill 128
Flamborough Head, H.M.S. 99, 116, 194
Flags of Convenience 212
Fleet Train ships 70
FORBES CORPORATION 47
Fort a la Corne 60, 80, 90, 195
Fort Abitibi 80, 187
Fort Acton 80, 197
Fort Aklavik 62, 81, 193
Fort Alabama1 14, 118, 123, 194
Fort Albany 81, 188
Fort Alexandra 80, 193
Fort Anne 80, 193
Fort Ash 81, 130, 192
Fort Aspin 83, 134, 197
Fort Assiboine 66, 81, 131, 192
Fort Athabaska 90, 97, 192
Fort Astoria 83, 123 ,198
Fort Augustus 80, 195
Fort Babine 80, 90, 195
Fort Battle River 80, 90, 195
Fort Beauharnois 118, 198
Fort Beausejour 81, 189
Fort Bedford 81, 192
Fort Bell 81, 192
Fort Bellingham 83. 90, 193
Fort Biloxi 83, 123, 193
Fort Boise 83, 90, 103, 198
Fort Bourbon 89, 195
Fort Brandon 81, 131, 192
Fort Brisebois 83, 123, 193
Fort Brule 80, 198
Fort Brunswick 71, 81, 128, 188
Fort Buckingham 80, 90, 192
Fort Buffalo 81, 195
Fort Cadotte 81, 193
Fort Camosun 80, 94, 197
Fort Capot River 81, 123, 128, 195
Fort Caribou 81, 193
Fort Carillon 81, 127, 188
Fort Carlton 61, 81, 124, 195
FORT CARLTON SHIPPING CO. LTD. 126
Fort Cataraqui 80, 188
Fort Cedar Lake 80, 90, 195
Fort Chambly 80, 188
Fort Charlotte 118
Fort Charnisay 80, 193
Fort Chesterfield 63, 81, 193
Fort Chilcotin 80, 90, 198
Fort Chipewyan 80, 198
Fort Churchill 80, 192
Fort Clatsop 83, 132, 196
Fort Columbia 83, 133, 193
Fort Colville 118, 150, 196
Fort Concord 80, 90, 188
Fort Confidence 80, 90, 198
Fort Connolly 74, 81, 128, 192
Fort Constantine 118, 194
Fort Coulonge 81, 131, 191

Fort Covington 81, 124, 191
Fort Crevecoeur 83, 134, 198
Fort Crevier 81, 90, 97, 191
Fort Cumberland 67, 81, 193
Fort Dauphin 81, 193
Fort Dearborn 83, 149, 193
Fort Dease Lake 81, 131, 193
Fort Douglas 80, 197
Fort Drew 80, 195
Fort Dunvegan 110, 118, 198
Fort Duquesne 67, 118, 198
Fort Edmonton 118, 130, 193
Fort Ellice 80, 193
Fort Enterprise 81, 198
Fort Erie 81, 127, 191
FORT ERIE S.S. CO. LTD. 126
Fort Esperance 81, 127, 191
Fort Fairford 80, 195
Fort Fidler 81, 195
Fort Finlay 80, 198
Fort Fitzgerald 80, 90, 198
Fort Fork 80, 193
Fort Franklin 80, 90, 198
Fort Fraser 80, 193
Fort Frederick 80, 195
Fort Frobisher 68, 80, 195
Fort Frontenac 81, 131, 189
Fort Gaspereau 80, 193
Fort George 80, 193
Fort Gibraltar 80, 195
Fort Glenlyon 81, 198
Fort Glenora 81, 198
Fort Gloucester 81, 124, 198
Fort Good Hope 80, 90, 193
Fort Grahame 80, 195
Fort Grant 68, 81, 127, 198
Fort Grouard 61, 81, 130, 195
Fort Halkett 80, 90, 193
Fort Hall 83, 124, 196
Fort Henley 82, 128, 191
Fort Howe80, 90, 193
Fort Hudson's Hope 80, 187
Fort Island 83, 132, 193
Fort Jasper 80, 196
Fort Jemseg 80, 90, 193
Fort Kaskaskia 83, 123, 198
Fort Kilmar 110, 115, 118, 123, 193
Fort Kootenay 80, 193
Fort Kullyspell 83, 123, 198
Fort la Baye 83, 112, 122, 198
Fort la Cloche 63, 82, 127, 189
Fort la Have 83, 193
Fort la Maune 80, 91, 188
Fort la Montee 80, 91, 97, 196
Fort la Prairie 82, 128, 191
Fort la Reine 80, 91, 193
Fort la Tour 69, 82, 127, 189
Fort la Traite80,198
Fort Lac la Ronge 80, 91, 193
Fort Lajoie 80, 97, 193
Fort Langley 114, 197

Fort Lawrence 80, 193
Fort Lennox 82, 112, 122, 128, 189
Fort Liard 80, 197
Fort Livingstone 80, 193
Fort Longueuil 80, 91, 191
Fort Louisbourg 80, 83, 187
Fort Machault 83, 193
Fort Maissoneuve 82, 91, 191
Fort Marin 83, 124, 196
Fort Massac 83, 91, 193
Fort Mattagami 82, 123, 128, 189
Fort Maurepas 80, 198
Fort McDonnell 80, 118, 123, 193
Fort McLeod 80, 91, 199
Fort McLoughlin 69, 80, 193
Fort McMurray80,193
Fort McPherson 82, 134, 196
Fort Meductic 80, 193
Fort Michipicoten 82, 128, 189
Fort Mingan 82, 123, 128, 188
Fort Missanabie 82, 91, 189
Fort Moose 82, 123, 128, 191
Fort Mumford 80, 91, 197
Fort Musquarro 82, 128, 189
Fort Nakasley 82, 124, 198
Fort Nashwaak 80, 193
Fort Nipigon 80, 187
Fort Nisqually 82, 124
Fort Norfolk 82, 91, 191
Fort Norman 80, 198
Fort Nottingham 127, 189
Fort Orleans84, 132, 193
Fort Panmure 84, 133, 196
Fort Paskoyac 80, 196
Fort Pelly 80, 91, 199
Fort Pembina 80, 193
Fort Perrot 84, 123, 197
Fort Pic 82, 123, 128, 189
Fort Pine 80, 193
Fort Pitt 80, 193
Fort Poplar 80, 193
Fort Providence 118, 123, 129, 194
Fort Prudhomme 84, 112, 193
Fort Qu'appelle 80, 91, 193
Fort Rae 80, 193
Fort Rampart 80, 91, 198
Fort Reliance 80, 193
Fort Remy 80, 191
Fort Richelieu 82, 127, 189
Fort Romaine 82, 191
Fort Rosalie 119, 191
Fort Rouille 82, 131, 191
Fort Rupert 80, 197
Fort St. Antoine 84, 149, 155, 196
Fort St. Croix 84, 193
Fort St. Francois 75, 80, 188
Fort St. James 71, 82, 193
Fort St. Joseph 82, 128, 189
Fort St. Nicholas 84, 91, 193
Fort St. Paul 82, 127, 189
Fort St. Regis 123, 128, 189

Fort Sakisdac 84, 126, 193
Fort Saleesh 84, 124, 196
Fort Sandusky 113, 124, 191
Fort Senneville 80, 187
Fort Simcoe 98
Fort Simpson 80, 196
Fort Slave 80, 198
Fort Souris 80, 198
Fort Stager 80, 198
Fort Steele 80, 196
Fort Stikine 80, 91, 93
Fort Sturgeon 74, 82, 128, 197
Fort Tadoussac 80, 188
Fort Thompson 80, 193
Fort Ticonderoga 82, 131, 191
Fort Tremblant 66, 80, 197
Fort Turtle 82, 131, 197
Fort Venango 84, 112, 122, 193
Fort Vercheres 82, 128, 191
Fort Vermillion 80, 193
Fort Ville Marie 77, 82, 187
Fort Wallace 84, 107, 123, 193
Fort Walsh 80, 197
Fort Wayne 119, 191
Fort Wedderburne 80, 193
Fort Wellington 82, 123, 128, 191
Fort Wrangell 119, 123, 129, 194
Fort Wrigley 82, 197
Fort Yale 80, 91, 193
Fort Yukon 84, 123, 193
FOUNDATION COMPANY 188
Foundation Franklin 103
FOUNDATION MARITIME LTD. 103, 188
FRASER BRACE & CO. 189, 191
FRINTON SHIPBROKERS LTD. 27
Frontenac Park 85, 123, 189
FURNESS (CANADA) LTD. 130
FURNESS WITHY & CO. LTD. 38

Gander Bay 132
Garden Park 86, 150, 166, 193
Gaspesian Park 86, 132, 197
Gatineau Park 82, 126, 188
Girdle Ness, H.M.S. 116, 194
Glacier Park 82, 129
Goldstream Park 84, 129, 196
GOULANDRIS group 126, 133
Grafton Park 86, 131, 191
GRAHAM, A.B. "Andy" 165
GRAND TRUNK RAILWAY 21
GRAND TRUNK PACIFIC RAILWAY 21
Grande Hermine 132
GRANT & HORNE 189
GREAT LAKES DREDGING CO. 189
Green Gables Park 82, 196
Green Hill Park 84, 91, 97, 193
GREENOCK DOCKYARD COMPANY 161
Gulfside 123

HADOULIS J.P. Ltd 126
Hake, U.S.Submarine 49

Halifax County 123
HALIFAX-DARTMOUTH INDUSTRIES 199
HALIFAX OVERSEAS FREIGHTERS 127
HALIFAX SHIPYARDS 189
Haligonian Baron 123
Haligonian Duchess 123
Haligonian Duke 123
Haligonian King 123
Haligonian Prince 123
Haligonian Princess 123
Haligonian Queen 123
HALLIDAY MACHINERY COMPANY 47
Hamilton Park 87, 190
Hampstead Park 86, 128, 191
Hants County 123
HARBOUR MARINE LTD. 194
Harmac Alberni1 48, 155
Harmac Chemainus 148, 154
Harmac Crofton 148, 153
Harmac Vancouver 148
Harmac Victoria 148
Harmac Westminster 148, 154
Harrow Hill 128, 150
Hartland Park, H.M.S. 113, 117, 194
Hastings Park 84, 150, 197
HASTINGS WEST INVESTMENTS
   LTD. 179
HECATE STRAITS TOWING CO. 148
Hector Park 188
Helen Mathers, s.v. 106
Henry Foss 95
High Park 82, 128, 188
Highland Park 86, 131, 196
Hillcrest Park 82
HINDUSTAN SHIPYARD, India 59
HOLT, ALFRED, & COMPANY 21, 129
HUDDART PARKER & CO. 146
HYDE PARK DECLARATION 70

I-25, Japanese submarine 94
Imo, 97
IMPERIAL MUNITIONS BOARD 10
Indus 37, 194
INTERCOLONIAL RAILWAY 21
Inverness County 123
Iran 117
Irvingdale 125
Irvinglake 125
IRVING, K.C. interests 125
Islandside 123
Ivor Isobel 131
Ivor Jenny 131, 140
Ivor Rita 131
IVOR SHIPPING CO. LTD. 128, 130

J.H. Carlisle 98
Jasper Park 82, 91, 188
Jersey Mist 150, 173
Jersey Spray 150, 173
Jessie Norcross, s.v. 14
John Irwin 126

JOHNSON, Capt. B.L. "Barney" 148
JOHNSON WALTON STEAMSHIPS
   LTD. 148
Johnstar 129
Justitia 97, 100

KARLSHOEJ, Torsten 216
Kawartha Park 82, 189
Kelowna Park 86, 133, 188
Kenilworth 134
Kensington Park 86, 188
KENT LINE LTD. 125
KERR-SILVER LINES LTD. 149
KERR STEAMSHIP COMPANY 149
Kildonan Park 82, 123, 191
KING, T.K. 38
KING, W.L. MacKenzie 71
Kingsbridge 123, 135
Kingsmount 123
Kinnaird Head, H.M.S. 116, 193
Kinshu Maru, Kinsyu Maru 47
KIRKWOOD T.M. & CO. 189
Kitsilano Park 84, 150, 196
Kootenay Park 82, 84, 149, 193
Kriegsmarine 58
KULUKUNDIS BROTHERS 127
KYLSANT, Lord 129
Kyokusei Maru 38

Labrador134
La Crescenta 56
La Grande Hermine 133
La Petit Hermine 133
La Salle Park 83, 134
Lady Drake 24, 125
Lady Josven, s.v. 105
Lady Nelson 24, 125
Lady Rodney 24, 125
La Fleche 132, 142
Lafontaine Park 82, 129, 191
Lagoonside 123
Lagos Michigan 99
Lake Athabaska 150, 164
Lake Atlin 150, 175
LAKE ATLIN SHIPPING CO. LTD. 173
Lake Babine 150
Lake Burnaby 150, 175
Lake Canim 150, 164
Lake Chilco 150
Lake Chilliwack 150
Lake Cowichan 150, 168
Lake Kamloops 150
Lake Kootenay 150, 168
Lake Lillooet 150, 169
Lake Manitou 150
Lakemba 117
Lake Minnewanka 150
Lake Nipigon 150
Lake Okanagan 150, 169
Lake Pennask 150, 173, 174
LAKE PENNASK SHIPPING CO. LTD. 173

Lake Shawnigan 150, 170
Lake Sicamous 150
Lakeside 123
Lakeside Park 86, 123, 197
Lake Sumas 150, 170
Lake Tatla 171
Lakeview Park 86, 123, 189
Lake Winnipeg 150, 171
L'Alouette 132
LAND, Admiral Emory S. 73
Lansdowne Park 86, 130, 133, 188
La Salle Park 83, 191
Laurel Whalen, s.v 14
LAURENTIAN GROUP 131
Laurentian Forest 131
Laurentian Hill 131
Laurentian Lake 131
Laurentian Valley 131
Laurentide Park 83, 128
LAURENTIDE S.S. CO. LTD. 127
Lautoka 119
Leaside Park 84, 150, 196
L'Emerillon 132
LEMOS, C.M. & CO. LTD 129
Levuka 116
LINER HOLDINGS LTD. 129
Liscomb Park 87, 133, 188
Liverpool Packet 131
Llantrisant 150, 176
LONDON & OVERSEAS
  FREIGHTERS LTD. 127
Lorne Park 87, 126
Louisbourg 129
Louisbourg Park 84, 193
LUNHAM & MOORE (CANADA) LTD. 131
LUSI, A & Co. 124
LYALL, W., S.B. COMPANY 195
LYLE SHIPPING COMPANY 46, 172

Mabel Brown, s.v. 14
Maidenhead 127
Maissoneuve Park 87, 125, 190
Makalla 77
Malden Hill 128
Manitou Park 87, 188
MANSEAU, Les Chantiers Ltee 125
Manx Fisher 149
Manx Marine 149
Manx Navigator 149
Manx Sailor 149
Maple Hill 128
MARCH SHIPPING AGENCY LTD. 126, 134
Marchcape 126
Marchdale 126
MARCHESSINI, P.D. & Co. 124
Marchport 126
Margaret Coughlan 37, 40, 41, 194
Maria G. 124
Marina Hill 128, 138
Marine Fortune 116
MARINE INDUSTRIES LTD. 124, 189, 199

MARINE INSURANCE ACT, 1906, 50
MARKLAND SHIPPING CO. LTD. 131
MATHERS, I.H. & Son 105, 122, 127, 134
Mavis Hill 128
MAVROLEAN, BASIL 127
Mayfair Park 87, 188
MAZAGON SHIPYARD, India 59
McKENZIE MARINE WAYS LTD. 46
McMILLAN BLOEDEL LTD. 71, 147
McMILLAN, H.R., EXPORT COMPANY 166
MEGANTIC FREIGHTERS LTD. 126
Melmay 161, 163
MELMAY SHIPPING COMPANY 165
Menestheus 111
MERSEY PAPER COMPANY LTD. 131
Merton 58
Mewata Park 84, 193
Midhurst 131, 142
MIDLAND S.B. CO. 190
MIL GROUP Ltd 200
Millican Park 87, 125, 189
Mission Park 84, 197
Mohawk Park 83, 84, 149, 193
Mont Alta1 32
Mont Blanc 97
Montcalm 131
Mont Clair 132
Montebello Park 67, 86, 128, 198
Mont Gaspe 132
Montmorency Park 87, 188
Montreal City 125
MONTREAL SHIPPING CO. 131
Montrealer 132, 141
Mont Rolland 132
Montrose 131
Mont Sandra 132
MONTSHIP LINES 131
Mont Sorrel 132
Moose Mountain Park 85, 198
MOREL LIMITED 173
MORLAND NAVIGATION LTD. 126
MORTON ENG & D.D. CO. LTD. 190
Mossel Bay 150
Mount Bruce Park 85
Mount Douglas Park 83, 91
Mount Maxwell Park 85
Mount Orford Park 83
Mount Pentilikon 47
Mount Revelstoke Park 83
Mount Robson Park 83, 84
Mount Royal 126
Mount Royal Park 85
Mulberry Hill 128, 138
Mulgrave Park 87
Mull of Galloway, H.M.S. 117
Mull of Kintyre, H.M.S. 196
Mull of Oa, H.M.S. 117, 196
Muswell Hill 128

Nanaimo County 123
NATIONAL GYPSUM CORPORATION 128

NAVIOS CORPORATION 207
Nenamook, H.M.C.S. 95
Nemiskam Park 83, 130, 197
Newsboy 160
NEW WESTMINSTER SB. & ENG. CO. 195
Niagara 147
Nimaris 127
Nipiwan Park 87, 125, 187
NOMIKOS & Co. 124
Noranda Park 86
Nordicstar 129
North Coaster 77
NORTH EASTERN FREIGHTERS LTD. 126
NORTH PACIFIC SHIPPING CO. 166
North Pioneer 77
NORTH VAN SHIP REPAIRS
  LTD. 46, 185, 192, 195
Norwood Park 87, 125
Notting Hill 128, 187
NOVA SCOTIA MARINE 127
  ENTERPRISES CO. LTD.
NOVA SCOTIA STEEL & COAL CO. 24, 190

Oak Hill 128
Oakhurst 131
Oakmount Park 87, 191
Oceanside 123
Ocean Angel 78
Ocean Athlete 78
OCEAN CARRIERS INC. 39
Ocean Courage 78, 92
Ocean Courier 78
Ocean Crusader 78, 92, 93
Ocean Faith 78
Ocean Fame 78
Ocean Freedom 78
Ocean Gallant 78
Ocean Glory 78
Ocean Gypsy 78
Ocean Honour 78, 92
Ocean Hope 78
Ocean Hunter 78, 92
Ocean Justice 78, 92
Ocean Liberty 78
Ocean Merchant 78
Ocean Messenger 78
Ocean Might 78, 92
Ocean Peace 78, 92
Ocean Pilgrim 78
Ocean Pride 78
Ocean Rider 78
Ocean Seaman 78, 92
OCEAN SHIPPING CO. LTD. 39
Ocean Stranger 79
Ocean Strength 79
Ocean Trader 79
OCEAN TRANSPORT & TRADING
  Plc 129
Ocean Traveller 79
Ocean Vagabond 79, 92
Ocean Vagrant 79

Ocean Valentine 79
Ocean Valley 79
Ocean Valour 79
Ocean Vanguard 79
Ocean Vanity 79
Ocean Vanquisher 79
Ocean Vengeance 79
Ocean Venture 79, 92
Ocean Venus 79, 92
Ocean Verity 60, 79
Ocean Vesper 79
Ocean Vestal 79
Ocean Veteran 79
Ocean Viceroy 79
Ocean Victory 79
Ocean Vigil 79
Ocean Vigour 79
Ocean Viking 79, 92
Ocean Vintage 79, 92
Ocean Virtue 79
Ocean Viscount 79
Ocean Vision 79
Ocean Vista 79, 92
Ocean Voice 79
Ocean Volga 79
Ocean Volunteer 79
Ocean Voyager 79, 92
Ocean Vulcan 79
Ocean Wanderer 79
Ocean Wayfarer 79
ONASSIS, Aristotle 22
Orfordness, H.M.S. 117
Ottawa Maybank 88, 190
Ottawa Maybeech 88, 191
Ottawa Maybird 88, 190
Ottawa Maybrook 88, 197
Ottawa Maycliff 88, 190
Ottawa Maycloud 88, 191
Ottawa Maycove 88, 190
Ottawa Maycrest 88, 188
Ottawa Mayfall 88, 188
Ottawa Mayferry 88, 190
Ottawa Mayglen 88, 190
Ottawa Mayhaven 88, 188
Ottawa Mayhill 88, 187
Ottawa Maymere 88, 190
Ottawa Mayrock 88, 187
Ottawa Mayspring 88, 188
Ottawa Maystar 88, 190
Ottawa Maythorn 88, 188
Ottawa Maytor 88, 187
Ottawa Mayview 88, 191
Ottawa Page 76, 87, 193
Ottawa Pageant 87, 193
Ottawa Paget 87, 197
Ottawa Painter 87, 197
Ottawa Palette 88, 197
Ottawa Palmer 88, 193
Ottawa Panda 88, 196,
Ottawa Pandora 76, 88, 197
Ottawa Pangis 88, 193

Ottawa Parade 88, 193
Ottawa Parapet 88, 196
Ottawa Parian 88, 197
Ottawa Pasqua 88, 197
Ottawa Patience 88, 193
Ottawa Patrol 88, 196
Otterburn Park 87, 125, 189
Outremont Park 86, 130, 192

PACIFIC CONSTRUCTION CO. 196
PACIFIC D.D. CO. 192,195
Pantrooper 132
PAPACHRISTIDIS CO. LTD. 132
Papachristidis Vassilios 132
PARK, Capt. John 47
PARK STEAMSHIP CO. LTD 82, 106
Parkdale Park 84, 147, 198
PATHY, Ernest G. 202
PATHY, Lawrence G. 202
PERMANENTE METAL CORPORATION 64
Peterstar1 29
Petite Hermine 132
Phaeax II 99
PICBELL LTD. 132
Pictou County 123
Pine Hill 128
Point Pelee Park 85, 187
Point Pleasant Park 83, 92, 188
P & O Group 147
POLSON IRONWORKS LTD. 190
Poplar Hill 128
Poplarbranch 125
Porsanger 12, 187
PORT ARTHUR S.B. CO. LTD. 190
Portland Bill, H.M.S. 117,193
Portland Park 86, 126, 132, 192
Port Royal Park 83, 131
Prince Albert Park 83, 127, 188
Prince David 24
Prince George 24
Prince Robert 24
Prince Rupert 24
PRINCE RUPERT DRY DOCK
  COMPANY 22, 184, 196
Princeton Park 86, 150, 194

QUEBEC S.B. & REPAIR CO. 190
QUEBEC S.S. LINES 128, 130
Queens Park 84, 149, 198
Queensborough Park 84
Quesnel, H.M.C.S. 94
Quetico Park 85, 198
QUINLAN & ROBERTSON 190

Rabaul 117
Rame Head, H.M.S. 117, 196
Rattray Head, H.M.S. 117, 196
RETHYMNIS & KULUKUNDIS 127
REX SHIPPING CO. LTD. 131
RICHARDSON, Lorne 165
Richmond Park 84, 150, 196

Rideau Park 83, 131, 192
Riverdale Park 83, 133, 188
Riverside 123
Riverview Park 83, 123, 188
Robert Dollar 160
Rockcliffe Park 87, 188
Rockland Park 87, 190
Rockside 123
Rockwood Park 87, 133, 191
Rocky Mountains Park 83, 123, 189
Rondeau Park 83, 128, 192
ROPNER, Sir Robert, & Co. Ltd. 172
Rosedale Park 62, 83, 128, 192
Royston Grange 130
Runnymede Park 83, 192
ROYAL MAIL GROUP 129, 130
Royal William 132
Rupert Park 86, 150, 193

SAGUENAY TERMINALS LTD. 133
ST. JOHN D.D. CO. LTD. 191, 199
ST. LAWRENCE METAL & MARINE 190
  WORKS INC.
Saint Malo 133
Salt Lake Park 84, 147, 197
Salvage Queen 95
Samnanger 12, 187
Sapperton Park 130, 193
SAUNDERS, Peter Paul 199
Scottish Monarch 59
SD14, S15 and S26 types 127
Seaboard Enterprise 149
SEABOARD LUMBER SALES LTD. 149
Seaboard Pioneer 149
Seaboard Queen 149, 157
Seaboard Ranger 149, 157
SEABOARD SHIPPING LTD. 149, 166
Seaboard Star 149
Seaboard Trader 149
SEAGULL S.S. CO. OF CANADA LTD. 133
Seaside 123
SECHELT, B.C. 219
Selkirk Park 86, 149, 196
Selsey Bill, H.M.S. 117, 147, 193
Seven Oaks Park 86, 123, 197
Shakespeare Park 87, 131, 191
Shelburne County 123
Sibley Park 83, 134, 192
SILVER LINE LTD. 149
Silver Star Park 85, 198
SIMARD interests 24
Simcoe Park 86, 133, 196
SINCENNES McNAUGHTON LINE 125
SKIBS A/S THULE 43
SONG, V.K. 43
SOUTHERN SALVAGE COMPANY 191
Springbank Park 87, 125, 187
Sprucebranch 124
Spurn Point, H.M.S. 117, 194
Stanley Park 83, 123, 128, 189

STRAITS TOWING LTD. 125
Strathcona Park 85, 129, 193
Streatham Hill 128
Sudbury Hill 128, 150
Sunalta Park 86, 132, 192
Sundale 133
Sundial 133
Sunjarv 133
Sunjewel 133, 144
Sunkirk 133, 143
Sunmont 133
Sunnyside Park 85, 147, 198
Sunprince 133
Sunrell 133, 143
Sunset Park 87
Sunvalley 133
Sunwhit 133
Surfside 123
Sutherland Park 87, 125
Sycamore Hill 128
Sylvia Victoria 43, 47, 48

Taber Park 87, 92, 188
Table Bay 150
Tahsis 149, 158
TAHSIS COMPANY LTD. 148
Tantara 149
Tarbat Ness, H.M.S. 117
Taronga Park 87, 130, 191
Tarsian 127
Tatnuck, U.S.S. 95
Tatuk 149
Tecumseh Park 85, 124, 198
TEEKAY SHIPPING INC. 216
Temagami Park 85, 150, 196
Tento 12, 190
THREE RIVERS S.B. CO. 191
TIDEWATER SHIPBUILDERS LTD. 191
Tipperary Park 85, 150, 193
Tobiatic Park 85, 149, 193
TODD-BATH IRON S.B. CORPN 64
TODD-CALIFORNIA S.B. CORPN 64
TODD SHIPYARDS CORPORATION 64
TORGERSEN, T.B. 43
TORONTO D.D. & S.B. COMPANY 191
Traverse, tug 104
Triberg 133
Tricape 133, 145
Tridale 133, 145
Triland 134
Trimont 134, 144
Triport 134
TRITON S.S. Co. LTD. 133
Tulse Hill 128
Turan 117
Tuxedo Park 85, 198
Tweedsmuir Park 83, 124, 189

UNION STEAMSHIP OF B.C. 47
UNITED STATES MARITIME
  COMMSN 59,70

UNITED SHIPYARDS LTD. 191
U.S. NEUTRALITY ACT 37

V944, U.S.S. 95
VANCOUVER D.D. CO. 192
Vancouver, H.M.C.S. 95
Vancouver County 107, 123
VANCOUVER INTERNATIONAL
  BANKING 216
VANCOUVER ORIENTAL LINE
  LTD. 27,150
VANCOUVER SHIPYARDS LTD. 46
VANCOUVER S.S. CO. LTD. 39
Venkoh, Ven-koh 43
VERSATILE DAVIE INC. 199
VERSATILE PACIFIC SHIPYARDS LTD. 199
VERSATILE VICKERS LTD. 199
Victoria 178
VICTORIA MACHINERY DEPOT LTD. 194
Victoria Park 86, 149, 188
Victoria County 123
Vinland 131

Wabana 129, 139
Waihemo 147, 151
Waikawa 147, 151
Wairuna 147, 152
Waitomo 147, 152
Waitemata 120, 147
WALLACE SHIPBUILDING &
  DRYDOCK CO 192
WALLACE SHIPYARDS LTD. 192
Walton 128
Walvis Bay 150
War Algoma 12, 190
War Atlin 13, 195
War Babine 13, 16, 188
War Badger 12, 186
War Bee 12, 190
War Camchin 13, 188
War Camp 12, 194
War Cariboo 13, 195
War Casco 13, 199
War Cavalry 11, 12, 19, 194
War Cayuse 13, 195
War Charger 12, 194
War Chariot 12, 194
War Chief 12, 194
War Chilcat 13, 199
War Column 12, 194
War Comox 13, 195
War Company 12, 194
War Convoy 12, 194
War Dance 12, 190
War Dog 12, 16, 17, 192
War Duchess 12, 187
War Earl 12, 187
War Edensaw 13, 195
War Erie 13, 189
War Ewen 13, 195
War Faith 12, 187

233

War Fiend 12, 190
War Fish 12, 190
War Fundy 13, 189
War Fury 12, 190
War Gaspe 13, 190
War Haida 13, 194
War Halifax 13, 191
War Halton 12, 190
War Hamilton 12, 190
War Hatbor 12, 190
War Horus 12, 190
War Huron 13, 189
War Hydra 12, 190
War Isis 12, 190
War Joy 12, 187
War Karma 12, 190
War Kitimat 13, 195
War Leveret 12, 190
War Magic 12, 186
War Massat 13, 188
War Matane 13, 190
War Mingan 13, 189
War Mohawk 13, 190
War Moncton 13, 189
War Nanoose 13, 188
War Niagara 13, 189
War Nicola 13, 195
War Nipigon 13, 189
War Noble 12, 194
War Nootka 13, 199
War Ontario 13, 192
War Osiris 12, 190
War Ottawa 13, 189
War Power 12, 192
War Puget 13, 195
War Quebec 13, 190
War Raccoon 12, 186
War Radnor 13, 191
War Selkirk 13, 199
War Shamrock 10
War Seneca 13, 190
War Sioux 13, 190
War Skeena 13, 194
War Songhee 13, 188
War Sorel 13, 190
War Stikine 13, 194
War Storm 12, 20, 192
War Sumas 13, 196
War Suquash 13, 195
War Tanoo 13, 199
War Tatla 13, 199
War Taurus 12, 190
War Timiskaming 12, 190
War Toronto 13, 190
War Tyee 13, 196
War Vixen 12, 186
War Wallaby 12, 186
War Wasp 12, 190
War Weasel 12, 186
War Witch 12, 187
War Wizard 12, 187

War Wombat 12, 186
War Yukon 11, 13, 194
Wascana Park 85, 129, 193
WAVERLEY OVERSEAS
   FREIGHTERS LTD. 134
Waverley Park 86, 128, 198
Wellington Park 86, 133, 192
Wembley Hill 128, 134
Wentworth Park 87, 133, 188
West Hill 128
Westbank Park 85, 92, 196
WEST COAST SHIPBUILDERS
   LTD. 36,183,198
Westdale Park 87, 126, 190
Westend Park 85, 133, 193
WESTERN CANADA SHIPYARD 199
WESTERN CANADA STEAMSHIPS
   LTD. 150
Westminster County 123
Westmount Park 83, 129, 192
Weston Park 85, 150, 198
Westview Park 85, 149, 197
Westwood Park 83, 85
Whiterock Park 149, 196
Whiteshell Park 83, 128, 192
Wildewood Park 85, 125, 198
WILLIAMSON, A.H, 166
Willow Park 87, 188
Willowdale Park 85, 198
WILSON, Capt. James E. 42
Windermere Park 85, 150, 198
WINDSOR OVERSEAS
   FREIGHTERS LTD. 124
Winnepegosis Park 85, 123, 197
Winona Park 67, 86, 150, 198
Winter Hill 128
Withrow Park 83, 123, 192
Woldingham Hill 128
WOOD GUNDY LTD, 166
Woodland Park 87, 188
Worldtrotter 132
Wynchwood Hill 128

Yale County 123
Yamaska Park 83, 189
Yarmouth County 123
YARROWS LTD. 183
Yoho Park 83, 85, 150, 196, 197
YORK-ANTWERP RULES 50

Zinnia 117

OTHER BOOKS AVAILABLE FROM CORDILLERA

**FULL LINE, FULL AWAY: A Towboat Master's Story -
by J.E. "Ted" Wilson with S.C. Heal.**
    Captain Wilson's story is told with clarity, humour, and always in a full historical perspective. The author went to sea in 1933 as a deckboy rising to quartermaster in Scandinavian and Canadian trampships sailing out of Vancouver. Injuries put an end to his deep sea career and from there he was to spend the rest of his working life in the British Columbia towboat industry, becoming a fully certificated master by his late twenties. After service with Vancouver Barge Transportation, Vancouver Tug Boat Company, Dola Towing, and Island Tug & Barge he became port captain for Seaspan International retiring in the early eighties. This has become something of a classic as it is the first time that a B.C. towboat master has told his story in book form. - 167 pp, 65 photos, milar paper-back.

ISBN 1-895590-00-0   Canadian list price $16.95

**THE MAPLE LEAF AFLOAT (Vol 1): West Coast Maritime Memories-
by S.C. Heal.**
    Seventeen salty sea stories, items of history, corporate biographies, plus a wonderful photo album depicting forgotten British shipping lines who were once regular callers in B.C. ports. The creation of Seaspan International, a giant in the towboat industry, and Georgia Shipping a small but interesting coastal transportation company are told in detail. Log barges and the giant Japanese woodchip carriers, visiting Polish fishing vessels, a ship which disappeared, the Greek tramship which was sold under the hammer by the Federal marshal at Vancouver, and other stories are dealt with in detail. - 180 pp, 165 photos, milar paper-back.

ISBN 1-895590-02-7   Canadian list price $17.95

i

New Cordillera books scheduled for 1993

THE MAPLE LEAF AFLOAT (Vol 2): More Maritime Memories - S.C. Heal
Release date March/April 1993.

The second volume in this popular series. Factual history, long-forgotten events, disasters and episodes from coastal and deepsea shipping. Features will include a detailed look at the Evolution of the Lumber Carrier, Far Eastern Shipping Company (FESCO) of Vladivostok, Norwegian liners at Vancouver and a photo album of Norwegian trampships of yesteryear. Like Volume 1, this book will be heavily illustrated and will have wide appeal to shiplovers everywhere. Approx 180 pages and 165 photos.

ACROSS FAR DISTANT HORIZONS: The Life and Times of a Canadian Master Mariner - S.C. Heal.
Release date mid-1993.

This book is based on the memoirs of the late Captain Trevor W. Bridges, and is a co-operative project with the Vancouver Maritime Museum. Captain Bridges, a farm boy from Shanty Bay near Barrie, Ontario went to sea as an apprentice in a tight-fisted Scottish barque in 1902. Rising through the officer ranks he sailed in tramps and ocean liners until gaining command of the Vancouver-owned MARGARET COUGHLAN in 1919. He visited all five continents and had many side adventures and experiences, which took him to Northern India, across Siberia and into large and small seaports around the world. He ended his active career as master aboard Vancouver based war-built freighters. 300 projected pages and profusely illustrated.

SOUTH OF 49 NORTH (Vol 1) - by S.C. Heal
Projected as an American equivelent of "The Maple Leaf Afloat" series, and now in the planning stage. To feature American coastal shipping, tugs and barges and deep sea vessels with particular emphasis on the Pacific Coast and North Pacific. Factual histories and an extensive supporting photo collection.